MISSISSIPPI STEAMBOATIN'

MISSISSIPPI STEAMBOATIN'

A HISTORY OF STEAMBOATING ON THE MISSISSIPPI AND ITS TRIBUTARIES

BY

HERBERT QUICK

AND

EDWARD QUICK

NEW YORK

HENRY HOLT AND COMPANY

ACKNOWLEDGMENT

The authors of "Mississippi Steamboatin' " wish to thank the authors and publishers of the books and articles listed in the Bibliography for the help afforded by their works in the preparation of this volume. Thanks are due also to the librarians, newspaper men, steamboatmen, gamblers, dock loafers, and others who have, consciously or unconsciously, assisted in the writing of this book.

EDWARD C. QUICK.

FOREWORD

THE SPIRIT OF THE PIONEERS

THE river steamboat, American as the sprawling, rushing waters which bore it over winding ways through the heart of this continent, comes down to us as one of our most valuable heritages, gleaming with the sheen of romance. The once homely old stern wheeler, slapping along the wide Ohio between rough, uncultivated banks towards the wider Mississippi is a vivid symbol of great days that are now beyond recall, those days of swift and reckless progress when men strove valiantly towards the unsighted rim of the western world, lured by their adventurous urgings to the farthest reaches of the earth, taking big risks in hope of big rewards.

We smile, sometimes, at the florid eloquence of the men who tell us of those old but gaudy days. To their remembrance all steamers were palatial, traveling with the speed of the wind, churning the muddy waters into foam. Excitement, drama and melodrama they narrate in flamboyant language. And we of to-day? Well, some one has said that in these modern times we spend only the copper from our purse of speech. Can it be that the gold, because of prodigality, has depreciated in value? At any rate the old river men are not afraid to use it; and we, secretly perhaps, prefer the sound of the mellow clink to the tuneless clatter of the copper.

For the exuberant spirit of those pioneers is with us yet. However we deny it, it is in our flesh, our blood and bone. Easier living, the desire for conformity and security, has not killed it; but into how many different channels have we managed to divert its force! No more can we plunge into new lands, so we plunge into anything else that is, or appears to be, new. Only a few of us, a lucky handful who put as little store by fetters as did our forefathers, can leave the treadmills of routine behind and follow the blue-peter. But all of us, sometimes, wish that we might be free to go.

Stand for a while on the wharf at the foot of Canal Street, in New Orleans. Just below us is the ferry landing, packed to a standstill with vehicles and passengers; and beyond is the old steamboat landing that years ago swarmed with the trade of the whole Mississippi Valley. But now there are dingy little market boats clinging to the sloping docks, market boats from the bayous, some of them steamers, some of them driven by consumptive-sounding gasoline engines. Look at them! A sorry jumble they are. But in their midst, like a grey old swan among dirty ducklings, there lies a cotton boat from the Ouachita, with her texas, pilot house and tall chimneys looming grandly above the squat bayou boats, last survivor of a once proud fleet.

Above us a ship rubs the odorous coffee wharf, her paint burned by the tropic sun. And beyond her, a big white liner is making ready to sail. It is noon, and the stevedores have found shady corners to rest in while they eat their lunch. Across the deserted dock we can see the last-minute preparations at the white ship's side. Now the dock is cleared; the gangway raised; the mooring lines are hauled aboard.

A puffing little tug drags the big ship clear of the wharf. The water yawns as the tug boat heads her down-river. Abreast of Canal Street the tow-lines are cast off. The tug kicks up, backing against the stream.

The flat crack of the ship's gun startles the brown river; mail flag and blue-peter drop limply from the fore, the houseflag slithers from the main. Steam obscures the big ship's funnel, her whistle booms; and in that hoarse and magic blast, sounding over widening waters, we hear the whisper of palm fronds and the laughter of dark-eyed women; to our bewitched vision come mountains scorched in the sun's glare, still lagoons in shimmering moonlight; we feel the burning heat of the deserts, the vaporous breath of jungles, the caress of soft hands underneath the white stars.

The tug responds; water boils yellow-white under the graceful stern of the ship, and we seem to hear the clang of the telegraph ringing the engines up. Again, at Pilottown, that bell will sound in the depths of the engine-well, and once again as night is falling, when the pilot is dropped outside the bar. Her whistle will say good-bye to the pilot boat, her bows will ride the rollers of the Gulf; and she is gone, southward, to strange lands of ease, hardships, dangers and delights.

Now the masts of the big ship vanish behind the smoke and roof-tops of Algiers. The brown river seems strangely empty before the Canal Street wharf.

To most of us our country is familiar. Without much trouble we can locate New York, New Orleans, San Francisco, Seattle and Saint Paul. We have a general idea of the land that lies between these places; we know that people like ourselves live there, and we know that some one, somewhere, knows all about every square mile of it. It is now all our country, and for the glamour of foreign lands we must go elsewhere, to Alaska, South America or beyond the seas.

But this was not always so. In the beginning the United States of America comprised only that which lay between the eastern mountains and the Atlantic. Westward stretched thousands of miles of wilderness. Into this wilderness of unpathed forests flowed the Ohio, swirling through its rocky gorges and spreading widely as it continued westward where, finally, it joined an even greater river, the Mississippi. And way down by the mouth of this tremendous river, beyond the forests and the prairies and the cane-brakes, lay New Orleans, the little Paris of the south.

This New Orleans, to the early Americans, was just as foreign as Paris is to-day to their descendants, and very much more difficult to reach.

New Orleans, as early as 1745, was the port to which were shipped the products of the even then growing trade on the Mississippi and its tributary rivers. All the goods from Louisiana, which at that time extended clear to the mouth of the Ohio, were sent down to New Orleans in keelboats and barges, and thence reshipped to France and the West Indies. Loads of pork, hides, tallow, bear oil, lumber and flour came down from the new country and were relayed to the old. And from lower Louisiana the keelboats and barges brought back sugar, cotton, rice, indigo and fabrics from the looms of Europe. But, though the northern and southern extremes of Louisiana managed to supply each other with necessities and some comforts, the greater part of the traffic was down river and from New Orleans to Europe.

For the trip upstream was slow and hazardous. Ships from France came so lightly loaded they were obliged to carry cobblestones as ballast. These stones, however, were not wasted. They went into the pavements of New Orleans. And those same stones, over which chevaliers and hidalgos rode and roistering boatmen tramped, have of late years borne lumbering motor trucks with trailers filled with cotton.

This center of the growing river trade, in spite of

its being called "little Paris," was a good deal like the country of which it was a part; rough and lawless, it was not at all like France, according to a gallant Frenchman who spent some time in Louisiana at the end of the eighteenth century. The country was wild and swampy, the people too uncouth in their ways to suit his fastidious nature. But when we remember that some of the early French in Louisiana were brought over against their will to further the land boom of John Law, and that they were picked up from French jails or in police raids, it is easy to understand that the rough element was more than moderately rough. This Frenchman, however, was better impressed by the Creole women. And, lest the term Creole mislead northerners, it may be noted in passing that a Creole is a person of pure French or Spanish ancestry living in America. It is in these words that he speaks of them: "The women of this country are peculiarly the favorites of nature. Their skin, without being a ravishing white, is fair; their features, though irregular, are agreeable; their lips are of a blushing red; their bosoms are heaving snows; their eyes blue and voluptuous, and their fair hair is often long enough to fall almost to their feet . . . They have been taught by the example of a few female Parisians to sacrifice to the graces in the choice of their clothes and manner of adjustment. Their gowns suit their shapes; they have thrown away their stays, and the gauze shades, but does not conceal, their beauties."

But perhaps our French gentleman had a rather limited eye for beauty and saw it mainly in women. For there is another account of the lower Louisiana country that is much more favorable, one that would give good reasons for the bargeman to loiter about the vicinity of New Orleans after his long and dangerous trip. It is in "The Navigator," written by Zadoc Cramer for the use of flatboatmen before the first steamboat trailed her smoky plume down the Ohio to the Mississippi. Cramer speaks thus of the lower country, "After you enter the Mississippi you begin to wind considerably to the southward, and sometimes east of that point. The climate becomes mild and warm, and the winter gives but a trifling check to the growth of vegetation. The banks of the river, especially below Natchez, are lined with groves of orange trees, whose delightful fragrance, and the beautiful appearance of their flowers, added to the prospect of getting the fruit plentifully, has a charming effect on the feelings, and seems to form a temporary compensation to the wearied navigator for the many inconveniences he experiences, and the toils and hardships he may have undergone since his embarkation."

It is not hard to imagine this pioneer of American trade seated in the roughly built cabin of his barge or keelboat, laboriously writing down by candlelight the bends, reaches and landmarks of the river that he has noted during the day. The boat pulls gently at her moorings in some quiet backwater of the lower Mississippi; the evening breeze, bearing the fragrant scent of green leaves and orange blossoms, rustles the papers on the table in the cabin where the writer is struggling heroically to translate the spell of the southland in words that the boys of the cool green hills up north may read and comprehend.

Cramer's book was written in 1807, when the lands of the upper Ohio and its tributaries had been settled by the men in coonskins, the advance guard of the hardy, adventurous forest pioneers. Can we wonder that these men stowed their crops in flatboats and drifted south with the high water of spring? There was profit in the undertaking; big profits at big risks. And there was the lure of soft air, exotic fruits, and fair women. It was enough to set any young man afloat on strange rivers, to drift between forested banks which secluded hostile Indians and, what were worse, white robbers beyond the law, and to tie up at last before a city of romance. And in those days the whole nation was young; and man's desire, whether for land or lucre or power, for a jewel to hang at a woman's throat or an empire to lay at her feet, or just the implacable lust for knowing the unknown, would not be denied.

CONTENTS

ILLUSTRATIONS

MISSISSIPPI STEAMBOATIN'

CHAPTER I

BEFORE THE STEAMBOAT

"Way down the Ohio
We wander alone;
We're drunk as the devil;
Oh, let us alone."

THE UNITED STATES AT THE BEGINNING OF THE NINETEENTH CEN-
TURY—TRANSPORTATION—POLITICS—GEORGE WASHINGTON'S
ATTITUDE TOWARD THE WEST—TRANSPORTATION ACROSS THE
MOUNTAINS MEETS RIVER TRANSPORTATION ON THE UPPER
OHIO AND ITS TRIBUTARIES—THE FUR TRADE—THE CANOE,
KEEL-BOAT, AND FLATBOAT—RIVERMEN—MIKE FINK—BLEN-
NERHASSETT'S ISLAND—TRADE BETWEEN THE OHIO VALLEY
AND NEW ORLEANS.

MID-AMERICA, in those early days before the steamboats, lay asleep to civilization, its fecund soil, great timbers and convenient but turbulent waterways waiting for the pioneers who would come and wrestle for their possession. That men would some day have to waken it was unavoidable, but few people along the eastern seaboard thought constructively along those lines.

Perhaps the first American to realize that this wealth of land, so well marked by the roads that move, had great possibilities for natural trans-continental travel-ways was George Washington. After the Revolution the various states had extended their boundaries westward along more or less definite lines, and for very indefinite distances. Nobody knew

3

much about the sweep of country beyond the mountains, and the state boundaries were supposed to extend westward as far as anybody would ever wish to go.

But Washington was aware that a state without people is no man's land; and because of this he favored improvement of the Potomac River, a project which later developed into the Chesapeake and Ohio Canal. This was a means by which people could more easily penetrate into the Monongahela country, that rich region surrounding the headwaters of the Ohio. From there the population could spread over areas of virgin land that were practically boundless, in those days of slow travel at least. And where the people go their flag goes with them.

Washington had witnessed the results of the race between the European powers—England, France and Spain—for domination of American land and American trade. The old feuds of Europe, transplanted to the United States, had bred wars between colonists and had enlisted the Indians on the side that made the biggest promises. Nobody thought much of the rights of the Indians in those days, and the red men themselves failed to realize that, whichever side won, they were losers. The old world quarrels had made the Mississippi a perilous and little traveled river, so little known and so little appreciated as a potential artery of trade that the comparatively small Hudson seemed far more important for navigation. But Washington, statesman and economist, saw that the way to settle the turmoil once and for all was to make the west a part of the United States, by filling it with United States citizens.

In 1770 Washington explored the Ohio as far as the mouth of the Great Kanawha, and patented a large area of land, which some accounts place as high as forty thousand acres. It is said that, as he was returning up the river after seeing the possibilities of the country, he was very anxious to continue his surveys without imparting the land fever to his fellow travelers. So, when he saw a bear on an island that looked promising he set ashore to get bear meat. He satisfied his curiosity with regard to the island, but, according to the story, he did not get the bear.

Washington was so favorably impressed with the Ohio country that he wrote to his agent, Colonel Crawford, and instructed him to take out a number of small patents for tracts of land in case it was illegal for one man to patent so great an area. This apparent evasion of the laws loses its reprehensible appearance when we realize that in patenting this territory Washington was not taking it from anybody, not even from the Indians. There was much more land than the people could use, and it didn't matter much who owned it. Moreover, it is doubtful if this tract was ever a source of profit to Washington; for the founding of an agrarian estate in a new country is almost always a losing business, from the very fact that land is cheap. No man will work for another if he can work for himself; and, if he can secure land easily, he can work for himself and earn as much as an employer can afford to pay him.

The character of Washington had been the subject of endless discussion and dispute. Some hero-worshippers would set him up as a bloodless image of virtue. Others object to this, implying that he was no better than a national hero should be. It is true that Washington drank liquor, owned slaves and swore on occasion. It is also true that almost all gentlemen of his time drank liquor in moderation, as he did; that most farmers who could afford slaves owned them; and that Washington was so deeply religious as to regret his outbursts of temper. In sifting the details of Washington's private life we are prone to lose sight of Washington the earnest statesman, the far-seeing economist, who served his fellows devotedly and well. And he had more than a little to do with the opening of the great inland waterways and preparing a path for the pioneers.

Transportation in America started very modestly. The first pioneers settled along the coastline, and as their trade was that of shipping overseas, they needed no inland carrier routes. As the population increased and farms, situated in from the seaboard, were being cleared transportation was begun at its crudest. Men carried what they had to carry on their backs, then by packhorse over wooded trails too narrow for the passage of wagons. And it was only when the increased volume of trade made the wagon imperative that these trails were widened into roads. Means of trade and travel were decided by momentous necessity, without plan and without provision for the future.

It is in this manner that our entire transportation system has been evolved. That is, with few exceptions. Only in the present century has any concerted attempt been made to foresee and provide for the future needs in transportation for the country.

How different from to-day it was when, after the Revolution, the tide of emigration began to swell through Cumberland Gap and down the Ohio. These people, whose promised land lay always to the west, came with their household goods, implements and livestock, sometimes with the lumber for their houses, floating down the river to find a home where the land seemed as if it could be easily tilled. They went until their boats failed, or until they were tired of floating.

The Ohio was the natural course of these seeking travelers, for of all the large eastern rivers, it is the only one that slopes west. Down it went the men and women who settled Kentucky, much of Indiana, Illinois, Missouri, and the river lands of Iowa, Nebraska and Kansas. As late as 1791 the land north of the Ohio was claimed by the Indians; in that year they defeated Governor Saint Clair as they and the French had whipped Braddock. But Mad Anthony Wayne was not so easy; moving warily through northwestern Ohio along the Maumee river he engaged Little Turtle, head of half a dozen tribes, and broke him completely, thus freeing the land for the pioneer.

But long before the first settlers made their clearings along the river banks, the great streams had been the highways of fur traders: French, English and Colonials. These merchants of the wilds used the primitive canoes of the Indians, for the canoe served their purpose and, besides, was the only vessel they had. Some of these canoes were made of bark, but most of them were hewn from the trunks of trees, made small for light traveling, much larger for goods and furs. The bigger ones were divided into compartments, four to six feet long, by bulkheads cut in the solid trunk. Cedar or stout walnut were the choices most favored everywhere except on the Missouri and other western streams, where cottonwood was used. And no simple job at that: it took four men with good hard muscles, swinging their adzes four days, to make a medium sized canoe, one about twenty feet long. The largest came to about thirty feet, with a three and a half foot beam, and carried a mast amidship holding a square sail that relieved tired backs when there was a following wind.

A log canoe with a square stern was called a pirogue, which name was often applied to two such boats when lashed together, with poles to hold them steady, the poles themselves floored over. Rowed by oarsmen at the bow, this pirogue was steered by an oar at the stern. It was rigged with a mast and square sail which was effective with a quartering wind; probably the canoe on the leeward side was pressed down by the leverage of the wind on the sail, and served as a lee-board. An example of this boat was Dube's ferry, on the Mississippi at St. Louis, one of the earliest ferries on the western rivers.

Even after larger boats had come into use for freighting the canoe was used for the local business of the fur trading posts. They were cheap, convenient and relatively swift. Because of this they remained the favorites for messengers and express service. But their use was not confined to short trips or to speedy trips. From the Missouri river country quantities of bears' oil were shipped to St. Louis. Hogs were scarce and lard was high and the fat of the bear was a cheap and excellent substitute.

But there were no barrels to ship the bear oil in, and no stave mills and no coopers to make them in sufficient quantity. The oil could not be put in skins, because it oozed away through the hide; so the hunter-merchants found the simple solution to their difficulty by filling the middle of their three-compartment canoes with the oil and stretching a skin tightly over it! Very little oil was lost in transit. Wild honey was shipped in the same way. Which was probably the first instance in America of the use of a craft itself as the receptacle of unpacked merchandise. What a far cry from the dugout canoe of the Missouri and Mississippi to the huge hold of a Great Lakes' ore boat; but the principle is the same.

Feeling the need of craft larger than canoes, the fur traders of the Missouri and its branches adopted the type of boat known as the Mackinaw. It was made of planks that had to be hewn by hand, an inch and a half thick. These were usually fastened snugly with wooden pins, nails being scarce on the upper rivers. It was flat bottomed and pointed at both ends, five feet deep at stem and stern and shallower in the middle. Some of the larger boats of this type were fifty feet long with a twelve foot beam; the middle part being partitioned off and made water-tight, it was filled with freight over which skins were tightly fastened. There were usually three or four oarsmen in the bow as the boat swept down to St. Louis where it was sold for four or five dollars. Running from fifteen to eighteen hours a day these Mackinaw boats could average between seventy-five and a hundred and fifty miles, carrying a normal load of fifteen tons, and costing about two dollars a day to operate.

An even more picturesque craft was used by the fur traders on the Platte, Niobrara, Cheyenne and some other shallow rivers. It was called a bull-boat, a queer adaptation of the bowl-like boat used by some of the river Indians. The name came from the material of which they were made, nothing less than the hide of a bull bison. Over a willow framework this wet rawhide was stretched, lashed and sewn in place with sinew; then the seams were sealed with a mixture of buffalo fat and ashes. These weird affairs were usually thirty feet long, twelve feet wide and only twenty inches deep. Loaded, they drew from four to eight inches of water, even with a three ton cargo of furs, all done up in bales and lying on poles in the bottom of the boat.

Two men only manned a bull-boat, and their voyage down a shallow river was not without its difficulties. They propelled the boat entirely with poles. There was no sense in using anything else when the river bed was always within easy reach. Every night the voyagers unloaded the boat, piled the cargo on the bank and turned over the bull-boat so that it made a shelter for their furs and for themselves. During the night the wind dried the hide, which was good because the boat drew less water when dry. And in the morning the crew re-pitched the seams with mixed tallow and ashes. If they were lucky they then got the boat back in the water, reloaded it, and floated off again.

But sometimes in the morning there was no water at hand. And that was a trick they had to look out for. In those shallow rivers the wind blows most of the water to one bank or the other; and many a bull-boatman has landed with plenty of water, slept drily and peacefully in the shelter of his odorous boat, and awakened to find only mud where the river had been when he last saw it. And that left him nothing to do but to try to twiddle one thumb one way and the other thumb the other way until the wind changed and blew the water back again.

For boat and cargo could not be carried across the mud and quicksand of the river bed.

The early explorers, as well as the traders, from the eastern colonies, first used canoes in descending the Allegheny, Monongahela and Ohio. When the necessity of larger carrying craft arose, they turned naturally to the one type of boat with which they were familiar; the ship's boat. The sail was useless in the winding rivers; oars were about all that could be used, except in the shallow streams, where poles were handier. Under these conditions it was easy to go down river, but when the voyagers turned upstream it was another and more precarious matter. For the inland rivers were not deep and slow-moving like the Hudson and other tidewater streams. Depths varied, currents were racing. Necessity compelled the use of the cordelle, which combined, as circumstances dictated, the functions of the kedge and the tow-rope. Thus the keel-boat was developed.

Keel-boats carried the travel and the commerce of the inland rivers until the Kentucky frontiersmen developed boats better suited to their needs. And even after the Kentucky flatboats were carrying the bulk of downstream traffic, keel-boats were the only craft making the upstream trip. Keel-boats and their crew were characteristic products of early American transportation.

But a development even earlier than the keel-boat was the galley, a large vessel built somewhat on the lines of a ship's boat, though used for military purposes and not equipped for carrying freight. It was decked over, propelled by oars, and often armed with husky young cannon. Such a galley armed as a gunboat, under the command of General George Rodgers Clark, patrolled the Ohio during the Revolution. And in 1778 the first settlement at Marietta, Ohio, was made by a party of New Englanders, led by General Rufus Putnam, who came in a galley called the "Adventure," a well-built craft forty-seven feet long and twelve feet wide, with a curved, raking bow and clean lines of a swift, coasting boat. Such vessels as this are beautiful, and a joy to the builder's eye. However, beauty must fit in with usefulness. The graceful shape of a schooner's bow is not made for beauty, but for sea-worthiness and speed; they are out of place in a burden-carrying craft on the rivers. The latter flatboats and barges that carried a population on its westward journey were beautiful in a different way, beautiful in their ability to fulfill their function, in their promise of a nation that was to be.

With the growth of trade the keel-boat was improved until it became the best possible craft for upstream work prior to the advent of steam. Most of the river keel-boats were built at Pittsburgh. Sixty to seventy feet long, fifteen to eighteen feet in the beam, with three or four feet depth of hold, they cost from two to three thousand dollars. Designs varied, of course, bearing different names and being adopted to various purposes. The batteau was a large, high-built boat which was rounded at both ends, and could be used for carrying big loads up as well as down the stream. Sometimes one of these vessels carried as much as eighty tons of military stores, Indian supplies, or furs. The handling of such a boat required one man for each ton of freight aboard. Sails of all kinds were used; if the owners neglected to provide sufficient sails, the crew used blankets as makeshifts, and even board screens when the wind was favorable. For the work of propulsion was arduous and the crew welcomed any help from the elements, which were so frequently against them. If a real sailor chanced to be aboard, he probably felt contemptuous of those board or blanket sails, but no doubt he was glad of the chance to rest a while from his rowing or poling and to tell the landlubbers in deep-sea language what he thought of them and their contraptions.

Another variation of the keel-boat was the barge, a large boat generally fitted up a little more elaborately than the batteau. But all the boats were similar, and as the rivers were long and travel slow, there were often several terms for the same type. A boat might be called a large keel in one place, a batteau in another, and a barge somewhere else. But those were the distinctive types of boat in those early days of navigation on the inland rivers; the pirogue, the keel-boat, bull-boat, barge, Mackinaw, batteau, galley and flatboat.

Among all the adventurous crews which poled or

BOUND DOWN THE RIVER

From an old Currier & Ives print in the collection of Karl Schmidt, Esq.

rowed or floated down those muddy waters, the keel-boatmen formed a class unique in American history. Most of them were of French extraction, many with an Indian strain. The traders who employed them considered the St. Louis Creole boatmen better than the French Canadians, as the Creoles were less excitable, less likely to grumble at hard work and poor fare, less likely to have ideas of their own. Creoles or Canadians, they were all a happy-go-lucky crowd, their lives alternating between periods of terrifically hard labor and complete idleness. Aboard, they toiled for long hours with the poles, the oars and the cordelle. Their food was salt pork, lyed corn, navy beans, and wild game. They were not hunters, but on long trips wandering frontiersmen were hired to travel with the boats and keep the crew supplied with meat. These hunters, masters of powder and ball, rarely helped in navigating the boat; they could earn their living with the rifle, which the Creoles couldn't shoot with much success.

Going downstream the keel-boat floated, sometimes helped along by a sail which they could use with a following wind. But these sails, averaging only about a hundred square feet, were small as compared to the size of the boats. But in upstream work sheer muscle power was all the rivermen had to aid in combating the current, and it was then that they bent their backs. Deep water called for oars; but as the greater part of the journey could be made over shallow water, setting poles were the usual instruments of propulsion. Fifteen inch walks ran along the gunwales on either side of the central roofed compartment, or cargo-box; and the boatmen, poles against their shoulders and firmly bedded in the bottom, would double themselves forward and tramp from bow to stern on these footways, laboriously pushing the craft ahead. They worked in continuous lines; as one man reached the after end of the footway, he pulled his pole from the mud, ran forward, and again took his place at the head of the sweating crew.

In swift water, and when it was possible to walk easily on the river bank, the cordelle was used. This was a line, often a thousand feet long, which was made fast to the mast, tied high enough to clear snags in the river, and held at the bow by a bridle; a rope running from the bow to the cordelle, to keep the boat from yawing. All hands jumped ashore, took up the cordelle and, splashing through mud and forcing their way through willows, bucked the boat against the current. Twenty to forty men were needed to cordelle a boat. But even then in very swift water, or in case the boat went aground, the cordelle had to be made fast to a tree or snag on the bank and reeled in with a windlass.

Used as we are to power-driven transportation, it is difficult for us to realize the amount of human energy that was expended in one of those upstream voyages, or to sense the dangers that often went with them. There was one place in particular that was the bane of the keel-boatmen. It stood midway between St. Louis and the mouth of the Ohio where the course of the Mississippi is crossed by a limestone ridge. After running for some distance along this ridge the river cuts through it. And standing in this notch which the current had made in the limestone is a pillar of harder stone, so hard that it has withstood the age-long scouring of the river sand and the battering of huge, floating chunks of ice. It is a column, roughly rounded, about fifty feet high and of like diameter. Vegetation covers its top. To this column the early boatmen gave the name of Grand Tower. And Grand Tower was the scene of many a disaster. On the downtrip there was the danger that the boat would be carried on the rocks and smashed by the swift current; while the trip upstream was marked by the slow and painfully exacting business of cordelling past the Tower. And in case of damage or delay, cargo and crew were very likely to be set upon by the Indians or by the bandits who waited in ambush on the forest-clad banks for the crippled boats with their rich stores and tired boatmen with silver in their pockets.

Ashore, the keel-boatmen played as hard and as roughly as they worked. When a boat's crew landed for the evening in one of the smaller river towns of those days, it was a part of discretion for the town authorities to lock up their offices and have business out of sight. For if they attempted to keep the peace it was very likely they would recover their wits in their own little jail, with the door bolted and the boat-men in possession of the town. But by being con-veniently absent, these officers maintained their dig-nity and avoided physical injuries from the ribald boatmen carousing.

Wearing light cloth breeches and a cap in summer, buckskin breeches and a blanket in winter, the boat-men showed their hardiness in more ways than one. If there was no one else to fight with, no officers of the peace to scare, they would often enliven their hour of recreation by a fight among themselves to settle any argument that had come up during the day. For the boatmen were quick to collect their debts of honor. It was a rough-and-tumble code that pre-vailed, and before a voyage was many days old, the best fighter aboard was wearing a red feather in his cap as a symbol of supremacy with his fists.

And then, when the combat was over, they would take out their fiddles or horns and sing such songs as wayfaring men have always sung: songs of home, of adventure, of sadness and ribaldry.

Like other men who led their lives on the fron-tiers of the world, the keel-boatmen were democratic in theory and practice, acknowledging no authority save that of their commander. An old keel-boat captain, Thomas Carter, illustrates this in his account of the time he carried as passengers Louis Philippe and his two royal brothers on their way from Pitts-burgh to New Orleans and South America. The water was low during the trip and the boat grounded much too frequently to please the hardworked crew. When she stuck fast and the cordelle was taken ashore to pull her off the mud, some barechested and shaggy boatmen would shout into the cabin: "You kings down there! Show yourselves, and do a man's work, and help us three-spots pull off this bar!" And, according to Captain Carter, the Kings gladly lent their royal muscles to the task, happy to hurry the long voyage by their earnest, if unskillful, efforts.

Unlike the keel-boat, the flatboat was developed for the single purpose of carrying goods down the river, and they served a motley company of emigrants, adventurers and traders. Bound for the free lands of the west, the emigrants traveled overland to the headquarters of the Ohio where they bought or built flatboats, loaded aboard their implements, livestock and household goods and floated them down to their new homes. Others, who had tired of their rocky hill farms along the upper streams, fashioned flatboats and moved westward. Traders, many of whom were farmers marketing their own and their neighbors' crops, drifted in flatboats down the Ohio to the Mississippi and southern markets. Some piling their wares in boats without decks, peddled from town to town and from farm to farm until both cargo and boat were sold. Others built larger craft, loaded them compactly and took them through to New Orleans, where they sold the cargo, often for export, and the boat for the lumber in it. In the early days the town of Algiers, across the river from New

Orleans, was built almost entirely of flatboat lumber.

The average Ohio river flatboat was about forty feet long, twelve feet wide and eight feet deep in the hold; but many of the ones that went through to New Orleans were larger. Some were well-built, with planked decks, while others were put together in a slipshod manner, with only a covering of boards, unplaned, over the cargo. In making a boat a shipper weighed the expense of building against the chances he was willing to take of loss or damage to cargo; and some idea of the chances that shippers often took may be gained from one of the old flatboatmen's pilot books, in which the writer warns navigators against mooring their boats in very shallow water or near sloping banks. For, he explains, if the river should fall in the night, an end or a corner of the boat would be fast on the bottom and the consequent strain would cause the vessel to leak or even sink.

The flatboats which the farmers and settlers of Kentucky built in the woods along the river banks, or a little way up some creek, did not represent the best in workmanship and material, and enjoyed an unenviable reputation. And in 1802 a boat loaded with dry goods which belonged to a Mr. Winchester ran on a rock below Pittsburgh, stove in like so much cardboard, and sank. The goods, of course, were a total loss. Winchester sued the commander of the boat for the full value of goods and craft, claiming that at the time of the wreck the commander was in a part of the river where he had no business to be, and through this negligence ran on the rock.

But the commander, who could afford to lose neither the money nor his reputation, returned to the wreck and, with several men as witnesses, carried off the plank that had broken and caused the damage. At the trial, when everything was looking its blackest for him, he introduced the plank as evidence, asserting that it was cross-grained, knotty, rotten and made of the worst Kentucky red oak which nobody but a backwoods farmer would ever dream of using.

"Let's see that there plank," said the presiding Justice, a Dr. Richardson, leaning forward. He examined it with interest. Turning to Mr. Winchester he asked if his boat had been built in Kentucky. Mr. Winchester admitted that it had, but insisted that it was an exceptionally good boat nevertheless.

Justice Richardson, taking up the broken plank, addressed plaintiff and defendant in these words: "Anybody can see that this plank never was fit to use in building a boat. It is of that worthless red oak, just as the defendant says. It is knotty, cross-grained and rotten, and so full of worm holes that it's a wonder the boat ever floated at all. Why, I could stick my finger through it! You can't fool me on those damned Kentucky boats! I was in command of one of the things once, and lost it by striking a yellow-bellied catfish! It must have been a catfish that I hit, because there wasn't anything else near, not a rock or a snag or a floating piece of wood; not even the cork out of a jug. Therefore, I made up my mind that a catfish had flipped his tail up through the bottom. Now, Mr. Winchester, any man who will risk his goods in a Kentucky-built boat deserves to lose them. And this court finds for the defendant."

But all flatboats were not Kentucky built. There were some constructed of massive timbers, well fastened, and equipped for the comfort of passengers and crew. Cargo was stowed solidly except for an aisle through the middle. The cabin was astern and was fitted with bunks, a table, and a brick fireplace which served for cooking and furnished heat on cold days. The boat was steered from the stern by a long oar or sweep that was from forty to fifty feet long. In swift water a smaller oar, called the gouger, was used at the bow. Other sweeps were carried at the sides, near the bow, to aid in steering and to give the boat headway when needed. As a flatboat floated with the current and had no steerage way, it had to be hauled about by hand.

A common generic name for these craft was "broadhorns." The term probably originated in Kentucky, but as to its meaning we are in doubt. Some historians attribute it to the fact that the boatmen used tin horns for signaling at night and to attract buyers by day. But this does not explain why the horns were called broad. Others believe that the custom of decorating the bow of the boat with a particularly large pair of cattle horns started the name. But still, why "broad"? Cattle with big horns were called long-horns. Probably the most satisfactory explanation of the term is in its reference to the long sweeps sticking out sideways from the bow. They might very easily suggest to farmer-boatmen the idea of horns, and in running close to the bank or to another boat their breadth would be fully, and perhaps unpleasantly, apparent.

The first through trip by flatboat from the upper Ohio to New Orleans was made in 1782; but trade increased rapidly, and during the first half of 1801 exports from the United States to New Orleans, then a Spanish port, were carried in one brig, two schooners, seven pirogues, twenty-six keel-boats and four hundred and fifty flatboats. It is easy to understand why upriver trade was proportionately very small: none of the flatboats came back.

After a flatboatman had sold his goods and his vessel in New Orleans he faced the hard problem of getting back home with his money. First of all he had to avoid the human parasites whose specialty was lightening the monetary loads of north-bound boatmen; but if he behaved with a fair degree of discretion he started north with full pockets, a blanket, and as many sidearms as he could carry. It was customary, and often better, for the homeward boatmen to make the trip in parties for the sake of safety.

The first leg of the journey carried them up the

river to Natchez by keel-boat or canoe. And sometimes a large party would buy or hire a keel-boat for the entire journey. In 1807 an attempt was made to start an upriver service for these men with a horse-driven boat; and the New Orleans *Gazette* of July 23 of that year, carried the following advertisement:

FOR LOUISVILLE, KENTUCKY

The Horse Boat, John Brookhart, Master.

She is completely fitted for the voyage. For freight of a few tons only, (having the greater part of her cargo engaged,) apply to the master on board or to

SANDERSON & WHITE

But before this boat reached Natchez several horses were used up on the treadmill and the voyage was abandoned at that settlement. It was at Natchez that most of the returning boatmen left the river to complete their journey overland, on horseback or afoot. Along the forest trails they were quite likely to meet bandits who were not only ready to rob them, but willing to cover the crime with murder as well. It was a lucky boatman who traveled in dependable and resourceful company.

Fortunate indeed the trader who reached his home again! He had plenty of adventures to relate to the young, the old, the timorous who listened by the pot-bellied stove in the village store. He had braved the dangers of wreck on rock and snag and had safely eluded the robbers and tricksters who had made so many boatmen-traders their prey. And not least, he had navigated his craft down the lower reaches of the great river, poling furiously away from the traps formed by bayous flowing out of the stream, swift sluices ready to seize his boat and carry it to rest in marshy backwaters from which it was nearly impossible to get it out. He had sold his goods and brought his profits back with him through the endless canebrakes, swamps and forests. He had been somewhere! He had seen something.

Abraham Lincoln in his youth was one of those frontiersmen who felt the call of far-off places and the distant city of New Orleans. It was while he was down at the delta as a member of a flatboat crew that, so some historians assert, he saw a sight which aroused in him a great pity, one that was to stay with him throughout his life and have wide consequences. It was the slave market. But whether that is so, it is certain that the journey gave the lonely frontier boy an inspiring view of the great world which lay beyond his own small community.

In 1788, when Cincinnati, which was then called Losantiville, was founded, the rush of emigrants down the rivers assumed huge proportions. The old Ohio was dotted with every sort of craft that boatbuilder's art or farmer's ingenuity could devise. Downstream the endless procession floated, carrying the adventurous population of a new world. Occasionally a small boat might be seen, desperately pushing against the current, but these were few and far between. Down, down they went, week after week and month after month, flatboats of every size and description. Here was an ark bearing a family, its goods and all its livestock; here was an unskinned timber raft, with cabins at one end for persons and pens at the other for cattle and horses. Some of the boats were wedge-shaped, some square-cornered; but almost all were built of heavy timber which could be used later in the construction of houses, barns and rude furniture.

From this incessant hive of seekers after land there developed a type of man who proudly called himself half-horse and half-alligator, the traditional flatboat-man. The emigrants who came streaming from the east to the nearly unknown west needed advice and assistance in the momentous undertaking of the river voyage, so they followed the practice of hiring fron-tiersmen, men who knew the rivers, to oversee the building of their boats and to pilot them to their sometimes indefinite destinations. And these fron-tiersmen, vain of their own knowledge of the streams, sure of their own endurance and capabilities in all danger, these self-styled half-horse-half-alligators, delighted in impressing the easterners with their tough and explosive characters.

It is quite probable that the boatmen found it entertaining to exaggerate their own toughness, but it is a well-documented fact that they were hard-boiled citizens. They had to be. No man who loved not adventure and excitement for its own sake remained a flatboatman for very long; for the business was one unbroken succession of dangers, and after a man became accustomed to them, quietude made him nervous. The boatman was always looking for something to happen; and when it did happen, whether it was a snag to be dodged, an Indian to be shot, or a friendly bout of fisticuffs and spiked boots, he met the situation with energy and promptness.

As indicated earlier, a frontier fight was no ring affair. There was no expert referee to call the rounds. In fact there were no rounds. The battle ended when the victorious contestant fell off his victim from sheer fatigue. There were no rules, though; and sometimes both had to be carried away. No natural weapon was barred: fists flew at faces, feet kicked wherever they could find a target; knees bucked at unprotected crotches; teeth sank wherever there was flesh; fingers clutched at throats and thumbs seemed made to gouge out eyes from their sockets. An early traveler in Kentucky remarked that he could tell the character of a hotel by looking at the proprietor. If that functionary had both ears where they ought to be, a traveler could expect a quiet night; but if one or both of the landlord's ears had been bitten off, his love of violence was plain, and it was a warning to lodgers to keep their pistols handy and not be surprised at any roars that might come from the barroom during the night.

It must be remembered, however, that this age preceding the steamboat on our inland rivers was a rough one, and that the rivermen were not the only fighters. A traveling preacher, in 1797, told of witnessing the evening pastime of a gang of roadbuilders, a pastime that he thought very extraordinary. It seemed that the gang chose sides and fought with firebrands. The one rule governing this play, so far as the preacher could discover, was that no man should throw a stick that was not aflame.

But the boatman was equal to all emergencies in rough and tumble at that. Consider the character of Mike Fink, half-historical, half-legendary figure whose exploits have been preserved, and perhaps exaggerated, in countless stories. Mike, who began life as a scout, turned boatman because scouting as a profession was too much of a routine job. Obeying orders cramped Mike's style, and he longed for a field where there was a chance to show real originality.

Before Mike's scouting days were over and he had become a half-horse-half-alligator, he proved his quickness of wit in the following incident which has come down to us: Mike being hungry was stalking a deer at the river's edge. He crept within range, and, finger on trigger to muffle the click, pulled back the hammer. Then he saw a sight that dried up his watering mouth and made him fear for his own scalp. An Indian was trailing the same deer, and by the way he exposed himself it was evident to Mike that he had not seen him. The situation was somewhat delicate and puzzling. If Mike shot the Indian the deer would scamper to safety; if he should shoot the deer, he would be killed by the Indian, and Mike had no desire to become a bald-headed corpse. Mike loved life and he loved deer meat. There was only one thing to do. Quietly, he swung his gun muzzle and waited.

The Indian, a brown, glistening shadow in the green foliage, crouched and aimed at the deer. Mike, equally shadowy, aimed at the Indian. The Indian fired; so did Mike. Then Mike stepped forth to take the choicest cut of venison and add another scalp to his belt.

In the Ohio valley after Mike had become a boatman he was known as The Snapping Turtle, while on the Mississippi he was expressively called The Snag. He was reputed a freebooter, but so far as is known he never made a business of outlawry. Mike was simply an extreme case of rowdy; a tough bird and proud of it. One of his boasts was his excellent marksmanship, and often he chose original ways of displaying it. It is told that one time while going down the Ohio on his boat Mike saw on the bank a negro with exceptionally long heels. He raised his rifle and when he lowered it one of the negro's heels had been shot away. That was going a little bit far, and a boatman asked, "Now what in thunderation did you want to do a cruel thing like that for?" Mike answered, "That nigger had sich long heels he couldn't git on a pair of boots. I fixed him so he can wear one; and if he'll come along the bank next time I'm agoin' by I'll fix him so's he can wear the pair."

Mike wasn't foolish enough to buy provisions for himself and his crew; not when there were plenty of supplies to be stolen at every farm. As a rule he stole as directly and straightforwardly as possible, but occasionally he was not averse from amusing his crew with playful little tricks, if they were profitable. Once, finding his cargo short of meat and liquor, Mike took one of his crew and rowed ashore, landing near a farm where he had sighted a flock of sheep. In his pocket was a package of Scotch snuff. Out of sight of the farm house he caught several sheep, rubbed the snuff on their faces and in their noses, then released them. Whereupon he sent his man for the owner of the sheep.

The owner arrived to find the sheep thus treated to snuff rubbing their noses in the dirt, tearing up the grass, bleating pitifully. Mike looked at the owner sadly and remarked, "Looks like there was somethin' the matter with yore sheep."

The owner, also growing sad, thought likewise, but hadn't any idea what the trouble could be. "What!" said Mike, astounded. "Don't you know what ails them sheep?"

"No," admitted the owner. "What do you reckon it can be?"

"I don't reckon," said Mike, "I know. It's the black murrain. I wouldn't be in yore shoes for all them sheep is worth!"

"Is it as bad as that?" asked the owner, still more sad. "What can you do for it? I ain't never seen it before."

"There ain't nothing to do for it," said Mike briefly, "except to kill the ones as has got it and hide their carcasses. If yore neighbors find out yore sheep's got it they'll be afraid to come to yore place, or let you come nigh theirs."

"Oh, my Lord!" exclaimed the frightened owner. "If I grab them sheep to kill 'em, I'll git the disease on my hands and give it to the others. And I ain't got my gun!"

Mike spat thoughtfully. "Tell you what I'll do. I ain't in any hurry, an' if you'll give me a keg of brandy, I'll kill them sheep for you an' sink 'em in the river where nobody'll ever find 'em. I hate to touch 'em, but I'm willin' to help you out, an' I do need some brandy all-fired bad, so if you got it—"

"I sure have got it," was the earnest response of the relieved owner. "I'll go right up to the house and get it now. And I'll sure be much obliged to you."

"That's all right," answered Mike magnanimously, "you get the brandy an' I'll kill 'em while yo're gone. You can tell yore neighbors you don't know what happened to 'em, an' it won't be no lie, neither."

The owner hurried off for the brandy and Mike killed the sheep, hiding the carcasses under some old sacks in his skiff. Later he went on his way with the brandy, the mutton and the thanks of the deluded shepherd.

Mike Fink was a bully and a boaster who kept his ears intact by living up to his boast. His favorite challenge was, "I kin outrun, outhop, outjump, throw down, knock down, drag out, and lick any man in the country. I'm a Salt River roarer! I love the wimmen and I'm chock-full of fight!"

There were, of course, plenty of peace officers willing to arrest Mike if they could; but Mike himself was a bad man to mix with and he was always accompanied by some member of his crew or others of his hangers-on. Arresting him was like starting a small war, and the officers knew that a man killed in a little war is just as dead as one killed in a bigger war. Thus, only once was Mike arrested, and then when he had his whole crew with him and both he and the arresting officer knew the whole affair was a bluff. Feeling playful, Mike consented to arrest on condition that he come to court in his own way. To this the officer agreed. It was healthier to agree with Mike.

The spring rains were in progress and the streets of the little town where Mike was to submit to arrest and trial were bogs of mud. Mike commandeered a wagon and a team of oxen and on the wagon he set his yawl. With his crew he sailed behind the oxen to the courthouse, yelling, shooting and singing a boatman's song, a stanza of which went as follows:

Hard upon the beech oar!
She moves too slow!
All the way to Shawneetown
Long time ago.

There wasn't much of a trial. With the court-room full of armed boatmen acquittal was the best policy. But thereafter that town enjoyed the unique distinction of having brought Mike Fink into court.

But even a legendary hero's life is not without its troubles, and Mike's domestic affairs were not altogether tranquil. It is reported that once, feeling the need of corrective measures so as to insure the sanctity of his home, he took his wife ashore in the forest and made her build a huge pile of dry leaves. "Now," said Mike sternly, "you lay down in the middle of them leaves." Cocking his rifle with a loud click he made the gentler one who bore his name recline on the leaves to which he at once set fire.

Mrs. Fink kept her increasingly uncomfortable position until the fear of Mike's rifle was no greater than the imminent possibility of being burned to cinders. Then, hair and clothes ablaze, she leaped and plunged for the river. She dove from the bank, and when she came up, gasping, smarting, dripping and plastered with mud, Mike lowered his gun-hammer and growled, "Thar! Maybe that'll learn you not to fool with other men when I ain't around."

People didn't talk much about the single standard of morals in those days, and Mike least of all. But Mike wooed to his earthly cost; if he hadn't loved women so well he might have lived for his liquor longer. The object of Mike's fatal fancy was a lady who had an inextinguishable desire for boatmen. But she was always at first a little coy and Mike flamed for her for some time without results. Then, just as he thought he was about to be admitted into the circle of her amorous arms, another and more desirable boatman arrived. The lady couldn't love two at once, and her choice, to Mike's rage and chagrin, was his rival. There was but one thing to do: he must kill the favorite.

The opportunity soon came. Mike and the successful rival were in a crowd of boatmen gathered for a good time before a saloon. After a good number of drinks of raw liquor they all commenced the agreeable pastime of shooting the tin cup. This was sport for marksmen only. A man would fill a tin cup with corn whiskey and set it on his head. Another would shoot a hole through the cup with his rifle, spilling the liquor over the face of his comrade. The crowd always enjoyed the sight. Then the marksmen, to the tune of cheers and handclapping, would refill the cup, set it on his own head and in turn receive the alcoholic shower bath.

Now the accepted lover of Mike's desire, full of booze and bravado, set a dripping cup on his own head and called on Mike to shoot. And Mike was not too drunk to see his chance, and he shot—three inches low.

But the man who had sprawled there on the

ground, with just enough life left in him to twitch in ever less frequent spasms, had a brother in the convivial crowd, and this brother knew Mike Fink, knew him well enough to be certain that he had not scored that miss by accident. The brother's gun was primed; Mike's was not even loaded. As Mike still stood there, surrounded by the sobered drinkers, a bullet took some skull and hair into his brain through the hole it had made. And two men lay on the ground, dead for the sake of a woman.

The halo of romantic and daring adventure glows about the head of Mike Fink, just as it shines to-day about the heads of criminals who are known by the publicity they get. Doubtless there was some good in Mike, but he was no hero to the men he robbed, and the world was scarcely benefited by his pictur-esque presence.

Now turning from the half-legendary to the strictly historical we come upon a figure of those days who stood at the opposite pole from Mike Fink. In all the intense, and intensely human, drama of the flat-boat era, an age of a population of a country on the move, of adventure by river and forest, of duels and brawls and shipwreck, there is no incident more pathetic to us than that which centered around Har-man Blennerhassett and his island in the Ohio. It is an idyll of the river, a comedy of errors, and a tragedy of foolishness.

Harman Blennerhassett, youngest son of a cul-tured, well-to-do Irish family, came to America in

1796. Then at the age of 32, he had already been admitted to the Irish bar. But he found the prospect of a legal life unsatisfactory, his main interest lying in problems of science. Selling his estates for about $100,000, he collected a large research library and bought apparatus for scientific experimentation; and thus equipped he came to America, bringing with him his wife, daughter of the lieutenant governor of the Isle of Man.

The Blennerhassetts, almost bride and groom, were received in New York society, as Blennerhassett himself expressed it, "in a paternal and brotherly way." After a short stay among these welcoming people they started for the west, reaching Pittsburgh in 1797. From Pittsburgh they traveled by boat as far as Marietta, where they spent the winter. At Marietta they thought of building an estate on what is now called Harmar Hill, but the place was a little too difficult to reach for comfort.

That spring Blennerhassett bought land at the upper end of an island twelve miles down the graceful, leafy banks of the Ohio from Marietta, a tract of one hundred and seventy acres for which he paid the exorbitant sum of $4500. The owner, a Yankee named Backus, had purchased the entire island, nearly three hundred acres, for $900 six years earlier. Not a bad sale, even for a Yankee in the real estate business.

This island was less accessible than Harmar Hill. Blennerhassett may have been prompted to buy it and settle there because he was more in sympathy with the Virginians than with the Yankees of Ohio, and the island was under the jurisdiction of Virginia. Thus he made himself a Virginian but he paid a Yankee well for the privilege.

The Blennerhassetts moved into a blockhouse cabin on their new estate, and there, in 1799, their first son, Dominic, was born. Meanwhile a house was being built, a great mansion with curving colonnades running from a library and laboratory at one end to the servants' quarters at the other. It was a dwelling absurdly out of harmony with life on the frontier, built by a dreamer who expected his money to take care of him in a country where land was cheap and no man worked for another for less than he could make for himself. But Blennerhassett did not understand this. Brought up in a society where land was dear and men were cheap, he looked with pride on his fertile acres, while the shrewd Ohio contractors fleeced him of his money.

For six years the Blennerhassetts lived happily in their island home. He was absorbed in his studies and experiments, and when the annual balance sheet of his estate leaned to the losing side, he hoped for a better season next year and let it go at that. She enjoyed the management of her household, and delighted in the free life of the open air. From her careful and intelligent care of her own children the neighboring settlements benefited: for she was first to introduce into the west vaccination against smallpox, initially in her own children and later among those of the poorer frontiersmen. In only one thing did she fall short of being a perfect helpmeet to her husband. It was that she left the entire management of the estate in his incompetent hands. And he, the visionary, the incurable optimist, feeling carefree for life upon his gloriously wooded island, allowed his fortune to drain steadily away, helping it disappear by backing any adventurous scheme that was presented him.

The year was 1805. Into this situation stepped the urbane Aaron Burr, soldier, politician, discredited in the east and idolized in the west; a soldier of fortune out of luck, ambitious, persuasive, with expensive tastes and little money.

Burr was promoting a colonization scheme on the Ouachita River and in his mind was the dream of empire. He planned that if the United States went to war with Spain, which was probable, he and his well-armed colonists would capture and hold Spanish land for their own. If war did not come, they would buy the land, as set forth in their publicity, and at the opportune moment secede from the United States. But Burr chose to lay his schemes along the potential path of war.

This war was slow in coming. So Burr plotted with Major-General James Wilkinson, United States Army, to provoke hostilities, or at least to make no effort to avert them. If war failed to come he could buy the land.

And thus thinking, as he floated down the Ohio on a flatboat, the big house on the island caught his interested eye. He landed, was presented to Mrs. Blennerhassett who invited him to dinner. Her husband was not at home. And the mistress of the house, perhaps a little lonely there in the wilderness, was glad to spend a pleasant hour listening to this educated adventurer.

Burr went on south where he promoted his colonization scheme. Returning, he again visited the island, but Blennerhassett was not there that time either. So Burr wrote him in December, asking him for a meeting, offering Blennerhassett a chance of wealth and grandeur between the lines. And what more was necessary to offer an impractical dreamer with a dwindling fortune? Before meeting Burr Blennerhassett had thought of leaving the island. Burr must have known this and have seen that Blennerhassett would be easy to persuade. When they met they did not talk of secession; that could come later, when retreat was impossible.

War with Spain as a possibility kept receding, and Burr preferred not to secede. He tried to get an appointment from President Jefferson—and had he got it he might have dropped the Ouachita dream—but the appointment did not come. Only one course was left to him. He bought the Ouachita land in the summer of 1806 for $40,000, one tenth of which he paid in cash. And the next month, in August, started west, looking for adherents to his plan of secession.

He thought he had found one in Colonel Morgan, but instead Morgan, from his home in Canonsburg, Pennsylvania, wrote a letter to President Jefferson in which he told of Burr's suspicious activities.

Unaware that his apple cart was about to be kicked over, Burr continued westward, conferring with Blennerhassett on his island, talking of secession, to which his host agreed, and passed on down the river. The expedition was to come to the Ouachita land in three groups: Comfort Tyler, of New York, to lead most of the emigrants in flatboats; at the island Tyler would be joined by Blennerhassett with fifteen boats, and still farther down the party would meet Burr with six boats.

But preparations for departure were delayed. And meanwhile Jefferson sent an agent named Graham into the Ohio country to investigate. He posed as an ardent champion of Burr and as such gathered plenty of evidence, enough to take to Chillicothe, then Ohio's capital. General Wilkinson turned state's evidence, and on November 27, Jefferson issued a proclamation calling upon all officers, civil and military, to suppress unlawful enterprises in the west.

The gallant militia boys were called out at Marietta, and glad of a chance for violence and plunder, seized Blennerhassett's boats and stores which were being loaded at the wharf by the town. Blennerhassett and Tyler managed to steal a boat and escape down the river before the militia reached the island.

Mrs. Blennerhassett was in Marietta trying to get a flatboat. The militiamen swept through the big mansion, stealing everything they could steal, drinking all they could hold, and smashing everything they could not take with them. Nothing in the house was left unbroken; they even fired their muskets into the walls and ceilings just to see the plaster fly.

Two boys passing the island heard the drunken shouts (for Blennerhassett had a good cellar) and landed to discover the cause of it. They were arrested, but later escaped from the reeling crowd. Returning to Marietta they told Mrs. Blennerhassett of the ruin of her home. She waited no longer, but with her family, slipped down the river in the cold December night.

Blennerhassett escaped detectives posted at Gallipolis and Point Pleasant, and passed the falls of the Ohio at Louisville on December 16. Six days later Aaron Burr came down the Cumberland with two boats and led the party of one hundred men in eleven boats toward the colony of which they had hoped to make an empire.

Later, Burr was tried at Richmond for treason, but acquitted. Blennerhassett's island was sold for its owner's debts and for those which he had contracted in Burr's scheme. The improvident Irishman went to Mississippi where he began to raise cotton; but his plantation failed in the war of 1812 and he never won back his fortune. His dreams and his money gone, Blennerhassett died in the Isle of Guernsey,

February 1, 1831. Mrs. Blennerhassett, after a few years of poverty, died in New York.

Burr's project caused little more than a ripple of popular feeling on the great river of trade and travel which flowed down the valleys of the Ohio and the Mississippi. Dreamers might envisage empires, island castles rise and fall, but the stream of squat, deep-laden flatboats kept on going down the rivers, and the little keel-boats and clumsy barges crept back northward, carrying the goods and fortunes of the people who built a nation by their unremitting toil. The flour, pork, cider, brandy, iron, and salt of the north must find markets in the south; and the sugar, hides and lead of the south, the coffee of the tropics, must be bought for sale to the north.

Trade was booming. The nation was coming to life. In the first ten years of the nineteenth century, Pittsburgh and the Ohio River towns began producing quantities of manufactured goods for home use, with a surplus for export. And what these towns would grow into was forecast by Zadoc Cramer. Writing on navigation of the Ohio and Mississippi in 1808, Cramer says, "It is highly probable that Pittsburgh will become, from the many advantages which nature has placed within the grasp of its inhabitants, added to those which may arise from the addition of art, one of the most considerable inland manufacturing towns in the United States." Pittsburgh was very small when the above was written. If Cramer could see the city to-day he might take a pardonable pride in his gift of prophecy, a pride which would be increased by a view of Cincinnati. Of this town he said: "Cincinnati is handsomely situated on the first and second banks of the Ohio, opposite Licking River. It is a flourishing town. . . . It contains about four hundred dwellings, an elegant courthouse, jail, three market houses, a land office for the sale of Congress lands, two printing offices issuing weekly gazettes, thirty mercantile stores, and the various branches of mechanism are carried on with spirit . . . Cincinnati is likely to become a considerable manufacturing place."

Louisville, third most important of the upper river towns, grew because of its position at the entrance of the Blue Grass region, and from the Falls of the Ohio, a series of rapids around which, at all times excepting high-water mark, it was necessary to haul cargoes, while the boats went over lightly or completely empty. This gave jobs to a colony of laborers and teamsters, and made the two a division point for long voyages. But as early as 1795 Louisville held tobacco warehouses under government supervision and it was about ready to enter into the distilling business on a large scale.

Though Pittsburgh, Cincinnati and Louisville became the principal manufacturing and shipping towns of the upper rivers, the bulk of trade continued to come from the little shippers; from the farms and the hamlets near the waterways, where flatboats were built, loaded with local produce and started for the markets that lay southward.

But in the meantime Europe was playing its games of world dominion without regard to the commercial necessities of the western United States. In 1762 Louisiana was transferred by secret treaty from France to Spain, a fact that was discovered and resented by the French of Louisiana who, far from submitting to a new ruler, drove out Antonio de Ulloa when he tried to take possession of it in the name of Spain in 1766. The colonists were planning independence and did not want a Spanish governor. It was not until three years later that Alejandro O'Reilly, backed up by 3600 Spanish troops, re-established Spanish rule and effected the formal transfer of Louisiana from France.

Hampered by Spanish regulation of the port of New Orleans, the traders of the upper rivers began to realize the absolute importance of the river as an artery of commerce. New Orleans was declared an open port by the Spanish in 1794, citizens of the United States being granted the right of free navigation of the river as well as the right to deposit goods at the city's wharves and to export them thence without paying any charges other than warehouse rent.

But at the end of three years these priviliges were revoked, contrary to the treaty, and there was talk in the west of secession from the east, invasion of Louisiana and the setting up of a western republic.

But such a thing takes time, and the difficulties were destined to be removed before the people were ready to make the break.

While New Orleans was a free port some shippers along the Muskingum and Monongahela regions thought of building sea-going vessels on the upper rivers and sending them direct to foreign markets with western produce. Ships, brigs, and schooners were built at Pittsburgh and Ohio points and sent down the rivers with their cargoes to reach the sea at the Mississippi's mouth and never return to their home ports. But ship-owners and crews had many difficulties; navigating a deep-bellied ocean-going boat through river sandbars and snags required uncannily great accomplishment, more than there was, and delays and losses followed. Increasing after the Louisiana purchase, shipbuilding was killed soon after by the embargo of 1807. Pittsburgh, Marietta, Cincinnati and Louisville were seaports for a short time only.

In the days of Spanish rule in Louisiana, western Americans were not alone in seeing the importance of river trade. A Frenchman, Du Lac, urged the retaking of Louisiana by his country, predicting that New Orleans would become the chief supply depot and commercial city for western American trade. He suggested also that through the upper tributaries of the Mississippi or the Missouri, the fur trade of Lake Owinipike (Winnipeg) could be taken from the British in Canada.

But the King of Spain, having a royally kind heart and wishing to get rid of a colony that was not well-paying, himself ceded Louisiana as a free gift, back to France. And in 1803 the Louisiana Purchase transferred to the United States this territory which had for so long been the plaything of kings and schemers. Its time of absentee landlordism was past. Americans were on the ground and could make something of it.

The flatboat and keel-boat, carriers of a continent of people and their goods, bringers of supplies most needed by those same people in their wrestle with nature, did not disappear at once when steam navigation, in 1811, at last appeared on the inland rivers. As late as 1834 keel-boats to the number of fifty-five arrived at St. Louis. Flatboats were in current use in 1850, and flatboatmen continued to steer their hulking craft downstream, deriding with lurid language the vessel that substituted fire and fearsome machinery for the old, reliable power of human brawn. But gradually the boatman learned that risking his life on one of those churning monsters as she labored, creaking and groaning and snorting her way upstream was easier than pushing a pole and pulling a cordelle. Only a few years then and the old, picturesque flatboatman was gone. He had become an even more picturesque steamboatman, swearing just as colorfully, fighting just as hardily, and carrying on his job of filling up the great continent with its inhabitants and the things they had to have.

CHAPTER II

BANDITS OF THE RIVERS

*"Come aroun' to-morrow night
Ca'se we're gonna have a fight
And de razahs will be flyin' in de air."*

EARLY BANDITS WHO PREYED ON THE FLATBOAT TRADE—ARMED PASSENGER BOATS—COLONEL PLUG—THE CROW'S NEST AT STACK ISLAND—CAVE-IN-ROCK—RIVER BANDITS DISPERSED BY THE COMING OF STEAM—THE HARPES—JOHN A. MURRELL AND HIS ORGANIZED GANGS OF "SPECULATORS"—MURRELL'S PLOT FOR A NEGRO UPRISING—DETECTION OF MURRELL AND THE FAILURE OF HIS SCHEMES.

BANDITRY and river piracy grew into recognized professions during the early flatboat and keel-boat days. Movement of men and goods was slow, the land was wild and cities were far apart. For a gang to ambush and murder a boat's crew, sell the ship and cargo and spend the proceeds in the dives and gambling houses was an easy matter. Many of the flatboatmen were farmers taking their own and their neighbors' goods to market; unused to the lairs of criminals they often joined convivial company in some river tavern and were looted and murdered by the men who had drunk with them an hour earlier.

Some of these river pirates even went out boldly in small boats and boarded their victims' vessels. This was so much in practice in 1788 that the Governor of Louisiana ordered all boats to sail in flotillas for protection. But the boatmen were resolute. They armed themselves to fight pitched battles. Thus in 1794 a packet company operating between Pittsburgh and Cincinnati, advertised the advantages of its boats as follows: "A large crew, skillful in the use of arms, a plentiful supply of muskets and ammunition, an equipment on each boat of six one-pound cannon, and a loop-hole, rifle-proof cabin for passengers."

Not only on the rivers but on the overland routes as well the bandits lay in wait for flatboatman. They worked along the forest road, the Natchez Trace, which led northward, often posing as travelers to the unsuspecting flatboatman with his pocket full of money from the goods he had sold. When their chance came they calmly murdered their victim and stripped him clean, often diverting suspicion to some innocent man. A case in point happened to Dr. John P. Sanderson, a Natchez planter traveling north to buy slaves. On the way he met John Hamilton, a drover who was going home after selling his cattle. Sanderson fell sick on the way and Hamilton carried him to the home of his father where Sanderson recuperated. Afterwards Hamilton guided him for some distance north, then returned to his home.

A few days afterward, Sanderson's body was discovered beneath a heap of brush near the spot where Hamilton had left him. The murdered man's hat was found in a hollow stump and had inside the band a list containing the numbers of thirty-five Mississippi banknotes of one hundred dollar denominations. His brass horse pistol lay near the body, the hammer broken off and embedded in the dead man's skull. Hamilton was arrested. The Mississippi notes were in his possession at the time, but pleading not guilty he claimed that he could account for the money by the fact that he had given Sanderson Kentucky bills for his Mississippi notes.

Long after Hamilton was convicted and hanged, the real murderer, before the gallows in Mississippi where he had been convicted of another crime, confessed that he and a companion had killed Sanderson and that Hamilton had died innocent.

Bandits more crafty than murderous found the banks of the Ohio from Louisville to the Mississippi eminently suited to their designs. There, few settlements existed through the sweep of wild country, and law was a thing each man took pretty much in his own hands; it was quick in the villages—though sometimes faulty as in the case of the innocent Hamilton—but in the scantily inhabited portions it scarcely existed. On this stretch of river bank there sprung up the boat-wreckers, criminals who waited in taverns for flatboatmen to land, induced them into games and drinking and then, while thus occupied, their accomplices went aboard the vacant boats and scraped out the calking or cut holes in the bottom.

"Hey!" one of the accomplices would call, rushing into the tavern where the boatmen were drinking with the outlaws, "your boat's asinkin'." And the befuddled boatmen would go to the door and see his craft and cargo lowering in the water.

"Come on, boys, we'll help him save the cargo,"
the boat-wreckers would call, and running down to
the boat they would save it—for themselves, getting
away with the goods which they unloaded. Some,
a little bolder, simply murdered the whole flatboat
crews, manned the boats themselves and took the
cargo south to market.

Most notorious of these boat-wreckers was Colonel
Fluger, a native of New Hampshire. The Colonel
lived at the mouth of Cash creek, just above the site
of Cairo; commonly known as Colonel Plug, his house
offered many entertainments to weary boatmen:
meals, liquor, gambling, and the society of the host's
wife, a lady known as Pluggy and very generous
with her charms.

Now it was part of Pluggy's business to decoy
her husband's guests, to give them pleasant hours
during which her husband could go aboard their
boats and do his little job of wrecking. But one time
Pluggy, perhaps for the sake of practice, languished
lovingly around Nine-eyes, the colonel's lieutenant,
and this the colonel felt to be a betrayal of his honor.

"Nine-eyes," he said, "we'll have to shoot this
out." Nine-eyes agreed and Plug's own son stepped
off the distance, placing a bottle of whiskey fairly
between the antagonists, a bottle which the survivor
was to drink. Both already drunk, the two men
braced themselves upon the heaving landscape and
let go.

Each had a slight flesh wound. But honor had

been satisfied, and both men downed their share of the bottle amid oaths of friendship.

Colonel Plug did a booming business in boat-wrecking. He had so many victims that he couldn't be expected to remember their faces. At one time a flatboat captain, who had been decoyed by Pluggy and looted by Plug a year before, came back to the outlaw's shanty to see if he wouldn't have better luck this time. Before entering, however, he put most of his crew ashore, arming them with rifles and clubs. Then, while he sat in a card game with some of Plug's men and knew that Plug had gone aboard, he listened for the first crack of a rifle which would inform him that his own crew had encountered Plug. He hadn't long to wait. From the outside darkness came yells, the thump of clubs and the thunder of exploding gunpowder. The captain set in. He overturned the table and swinging a menacing chair broke half a dozen heads on his way to the scene of the big fight. When he got outside Plug had been taken captive, three of his gang thrown in the river and the rest were leaping like jackrabbits to get out of the way. The boatmen took Plug into the forest, stripped and tied him to a tree which one historian says "was just about the size of Pluggy" and laid the cowhide on his back.

After the boatmen had gone he was rescued by Pluggy who, locating her lord and master by his wails, and releasing him from his exposed and em-barrassing position, incidentally saved him for a worse fate.

The end of the predatory career of Colonel Plug is a delightful example of poetic justice. It took place on "a dark and stormy night." A flatboat had tied up in front of Plug's house and the unsuspecting boatmen were losing their money to Plug's sharpers. Meanwhile Plug went aboard and knocked out a plank in the bottom of the boatmen's craft, secure in the knowledge that the noise of the wind, sweeping down the banks and howling over the river, would drown the noise he made. The plank loose, the water rushed up into the boat. And at that moment the hawser parted under the terrific strain of wind coupled with current. Out into the deep black water drifted the scuttled boat, carrying the wrecker, who never came up above the tall waves.

Colonel Plug did not make murder a part of his business. But others of the boat-wreckers were less squeamish, or else less clever. At the "Crow's Nest," on Stack Island, at the head of Nine Mile beach and one hundred and seventy miles above Natchez, was the hangout of a gang of river pirates who robbed flatboats, keel-boats and settlers' houses, murdering all who might bear witness against them.

Very little is known about this gang, not even how they died; but that they did die, and violently, is certain. It was in 1809 and several keel-boats were lying at the head of Nine Mile reach, awaiting a favorable wind. The crews drew together and talked. Most of them knew of the bloody gangsters. They talked of them, of the boatmen they had known, the boatmen who had disappeared with ship and cargo somewhere about the Crow's Nest. There were almost a hundred keel-boatmen gathered there, waiting for that favorable wind.

These boatmen knew the pirates had their headquarters on Stack Island, not far away. It was a good chance—so many men, so little to do—why not? So in the darkness of the night they oared quietly down to the pirates' landing. Each man looked to the priming of his gun. Cautiously they drew a cordon around the huddled shacks where the murderers slept.

The fight was short, sharp and decisive. Only two of the boatmen had been wounded; but the bandit score was too big to count and too much trouble to bury. At dawn they herded nineteen, all that survived, of the bandits into a ring.

Two women and a boy came out of the shacks, imploring for the lives of the nineteen who cowered in the ring of black muzzles. The women and the youth were sent away. The others were never seen again. "Their fate," says the records, "was never known." Is it hard to imagine?

Here are the captives, bandits and murderers all; men who, if released, will return to more crimes, jesting at their escape from death. What to do with them? Keel-boats are not built for the transportation of prisoners.

Here are the boatmen, all hard, uncompromising men. The pay for their labor, their very lives, are constantly menaced by the existence of these island- ers. They remember their comrades who have steered their keels as far as this place and been seen no more.

Powder and lead are precious. Rope? Who thought to bring any rope! But here is an ax, and in the hand of a bull-necked boatman who preferred it to a musket; for an ax is always loaded, never misses fire. And here is a bare tree trunk, cast up by the river that swirls over the wrecks and bodies these pirates have sunk.

One by one the nineteen are led forth in the chill, grey dawn. A defiant curse, a scuffle, the sudden thud of an ax in flesh and bone. Silence, save for the rustle of the great river that flows on as if nothing had happened. Black against the morning light the buzzards are gathering, wheeling down with the swish of ragged black wings—lower, lower—let's get away from here!

Even the Crow's Nest itself is no more. The floods and the earthquake of 1811 overwhelmed the island and sunk it deep in the bed of the river, wiping out the grisly tokens of crime and crime's reward.

Farther north, on the Illinois shore of the Ohio, was another murderer's resort. It was in a cave, cut by the centuries of water upon limestone, with a main cavern of two hundred feet in length, eighty feet in width and twenty feet in height. Above it

An old wood-cut from "The Life and Adventures of John Murrell"

THE FLIGHT OF MURRELL

is a smaller cavern, reached by a chimney-like passage of about fourteen feet. It is called Cave-in-Rock, or sometimes Rock-in-Cave, and made an ideal spot for river marauders.

Early in the eighteen-hundreds a renegade named Wilson established himself and his family in this cave and put up a sign above it announcing, "Wilson's Liquor Vault and House of Entertainment." Outlaws flocked to this kindred soul of theirs and made an encampment on Hurricane Island which was near by. Wilson's plan was to get boatmen into his cave for drink and ribald entertainment and while they were enjoying themselves his men would murder them, man their boats and sell the cargoes down the river.

News traveled slowly in those days. If a boat's crew did not return as soon as the shipper expected the delay was laid to poor market conditions or to robbery on the return trip overland. Wilson continued his business until finally the people of the neighboring country attacked his stronghold and routed his bandits, most of whom escaped into Kentucky, Tennessee, Arkansas and Mississippi, where they continued their string of crimes. Wilson himself was killed by one of his own gang for the price that was put upon his head.

Once, it is interesting to note, Cave-in-Rock had an entirely different kind of tenants. Some time after Wilson's gang was cleaned out some boatmen stopped there and found it occupied by a party of women and children from Kentucky. They had come with their men, bringing their household goods, and the men had left them there while they went back after their livestock. This was the first stage of their migration to new homes farther west.

The boatmen were surprised to find women engaged in housekeeping in a robber's cave with no men about. Perhaps they didn't know that these women were the sisters, wives and daughters of the men who fought over the Dark and Bloody Ground, and that any of them was skillful enough with a musket to knock the eye out of a turkey as it sat on her back fence.

Some of the river outlaws followed the boatman's trade, taking up thievery and banditry only as occasion presented itself. Of such was James Girty, a Pennsylvanian, whose boast was that he had never been whipped, and who was never punished for any of his frequent misdeeds. He was a nephew of the notorious Major Simon Girty, of Girty's Island fame in the Maumee River near Fallen Timber; another uncle of his was George Girty, also a bad character of the frontier. All the Girty's lived with the Indians and as Indians and were supposed to have instigated many an Indian atrocity. One of the many mistresses of James Girty gives him credit for having a body less impervious to bullets and bears than most men have. Instead of ribs, she said, he had solid plates of bone protecting his breast and back against steel or claw. And who is so impolite as to doubt a lady's word!

When Cave-in-Rock was attacked by law-abiding neighbors there were flushed from its stronghold two of the most heartless river pirates known in gory history: Micajah and Wiley Harpe, brothers known respectively as Big and Little Harpe. This pair, after Wilson's defeat, are supposed to have gone into the southeast. Little is known of them from the time they left Cave-in-Rock until they came into Kentucky from North Carolina where they had committed many robberies and murders. When they reached Kentucky Big Harpe had two women with him; Little Harpe lived more modestly, with one woman and a child. The child, however, was killed one day by Big Harpe because, he said, it made too much noise and disturbed him.

Big and Little Harpe posing as itinerant preachers, and the three women as gospel singers, the party came through the woods of Kentucky and stopped at the house of Moses Stigall. Hospitality was wide and deep over the land at that time and Stigall took them in. Their presence was very pleasing to Mrs. Stigall: they held family prayers, said grace lengthily at table and sang from the treasured hymn book of the Stigall home. They arrived the day before Stigall was going on a journey. And though Stigall said they could stay on until he came back, they also went away, devoutly telling him that there were many souls to be saved and their time was short. Before going Big Harpe, out of the goodness of his heart, gave Stigall a supply of gunpowder from his own horn, as Stigall was short of it.

Then the Harpes said a sanctimonious goodbye to Stigall, his wife and child and to a young man named Love who was at the house. Stigall rode one way, the Harpes another. But that night the Harpes doubled back, murdered Mrs. Stigall, her child and young Love, and stole everything they could carry from the house.

The crime was discovered the next morning. Neighbors went riding for Stigall. He told them of the Harpes' visit as he turned sadly back with them and on reaching the settlement a posse was formed which later tracked the pseudo-preachers to their camp. The posse arrived just as the murderers were leaving. A few shots were fired at the galloping rumps of their horses. Spurring on through the wooded trail the posse came upon the women, who had been abandoned. Little Harpe, they said, had left Big Harpe, cutting southward.

Big Harpe was concentrated upon by the posse. Riding after him they gradually strung out in a line, the position of each depending upon the speed and strength of his mount. A man named Leeper was in front, riding a fine Kentucky mount. And Leeper was gaining on the man in front of him, Big Harpe himself. He saw him ahead in the forest, but could not shoot because he didn't dare take his attention from the bridle in the devious forest path. But when Harpe dashed into an open glade Leeper let go the reins and raised his musket, a big-bore gun loaded with ball and buckshot. Harpe aimed over his shoulder; his gun snapped. Leeper fired and the bellow of his weapon was heard clear to the end of the following line. Moses Stigall heard the shot and prayed Harpe might live until he could reach him.

Harpe reeled under the buckshot, but did not fall. Dropping his gun, he lay along the neck of his horse and plunged away through the forest, Leeper after him. Now Harpe was clinging on with both hands; and his mare, no longer feeling the spur, slowed down. Leeper rode alongside the wounded Harpe and threw him to the ground.

As Leeper stood over him Harpe begged for his life. "Just give me a trial! A jury! A jury! That's all I ask. I'm innocent! Don't kill me," screamed Harpe.

And Leeper, standing over him, seeing the blood on Harpe's chest where the bullets had come out, said, "No need to ask for mercy. It can't reach you any longer. You're about dead now."

But still Harpe pleaded. He was still begging when Stigall rode up and slid from his horse. Stigall muttered, "By God, I prayed you'd live," and took his eyes from Harpe's distorted face long enough to examine the priming of his musket. It was good. And slowly and deliberately Stigall swung the muzzle before Harpe's face, pulling back the hammer.

Harpe's head flopped from side to side like a decapitated chicken before it expires. He screamed, whined and bawled for mercy—he who had shown mercy to neither man, woman nor child—but all Stigall answered was to jab the muzzle into the outlaw's chest and speed his journey with another bullet.

Even then Stigall in his frenzy was not satisfied. But with his hunting knife he cut the head from the riddled body, and climbing a small tree by the side of the woodland trail, he cut off the top and neatly trimmed the stub to a point. And on this point he set the staring, slack-lipped head to grin down upon all who passed as a warning of a Kentuckian's vengeance. That skull was there for many years, whitening in the wind and sun; it stayed there until an old woman of those Kentucky hills, needing powdered skull in a medicine she was concocting, climbed the tree and stole it. But the gruesome reminder still remains in the name of the nearby village: Harpe's Head, Kentucky.

The three women traveling with the Harpes were jailed near the scene of the Stigall murder, but were later released and sent to their homes, the sheriff believing they deserved more pity than harshness.

The Harpes were criminals of the ordinary sort, working alone or with small gangs that had no particular organization. In all times and places, such men have run their predatory courses and died by violence or drugs or disease. But the unusual social conditions of the early nineteenth century produced one criminal who led all the rest; a man who, but for his early training and the vicious twist of his mind, might have risen high in politics or finance. Except for a few betraying faults, which all criminals possess to their cost, he might have made himself dictator over an empire of crime. This man was John A. Murrell, America's greatest bandit, whose ambitious program makes Jesse James like a penny-ante player at Monte Carlo.

Mr. Murrell was known to his contemporaries as "the Great Land Pirate," but he was really the super river pirate, for he robbed boats along the river as well as the returning boatmen, who chose the overland route from New Orleans.

And it was the advent of the steamboat which made Murrell forsake his picturesque form of robbery at the point of the pistol and dream of a well organized criminal association that was just about one hundred years too soon.

It is at this time impossible to separate fact and fiction in the life of John Murrell; however, there is no doubt that he existed. Nor is there any doubt that he was fearless, merciless and infinitely cunning. He was from eastern Tennessee, tall, handsome and muscular, a splendid specimen of the half-horse, half-alligator type of man.

Beginning as a petty thief along the Mississippi he soon showed qualities that made him a leader of men, and women too, if he happened to be at leisure.

The river pirates of that period found that the

most practical way to dispose of their victims was to disembowel them and consign the remains to the river. Murrell boasted to his followers that no man he robbed ever floated up to testify. And they never did. Murrell, however, was shrewd enough to see what would happen to river robbers when steam navigation became better established. Accordingly he made a trip up the river from New Orleans as far as Cincinnati. On this trip he posed as an itinerant preacher and he was careful to keep away from any violent crimes. He found, however, that between prayer-meetings he could visit the lowly sinners, who infested all river towns. And these he organized into a dues-paying secret society having grips, passwords, etc., and what was more important and modern, they retained lawyers from a common war chest to defend unfortunate brothers who might be persecuted by the law.

This Mystic Clan, as Murrell called it, had two circles—the inner one had some very prominent names on its roster and the society grew to be a very prosperous organization. This clan, which was in no way related to the later Ku Klux organization, was used to steal and resell negroes and horses. And had Murrell been content to direct their board meetings and furnish the business go, he might have died rich and respected; but long hours in the saddle, together with a flaming ambition made routine business impossible. He dreamed of a slave rebellion, directed by his society, which might make him Ruler of a black Empire, or which would at least furnish an opportunity for the clansmen to rob the banks while the slaves fought their masters.

To further this ambitious scheme, he travelled as far as Mexico. In the land of the don the broad-minded Murrell was a Catholic, but he soon returned saying that the Mexicans had no stomach for a fight and that he would depend on the negroes.

Murrell's weakness seems to have been boastfulness. To impress a young recruit he recited his plans and embroidered his past. The recruit proved to be a spy and Murrell was convicted of negro stealing and sentenced to prison. It was only after Murrell was safely in prison that Virgil Stewart, the pseudo recruit, dared to expose the plan for a slave uprising.

At once there was a storm of denial, and abuse was heaped upon Stewart; while Murrell began to appear as a victim of persecution. Impatient members of the clan, though, tried to release their leader by starting the rebellion prematurely. Their plans were detected and along the Mississippi there flamed a series of savage lynchings, together with merciless flogging of negroes and whites of doubtful character. River piracy was dead and the greatest river pirate coughed away his life in 1847, a victim of prison sickness. Murrell was only forty-three years old when he died, but it must be conceded that he had seen quite a little of life—and that he must have had some manly qualities to have held the loyalty of the 2500 rough and tumble characters whom he commanded.

Murrell died a savage jungle cat, crushed by the dawning age of steam, to which he could not reconcile himself. He was a colorful figure, though, who undoubtedly had qualities that in another environment would have carried him far—captain of industry—political boss—perhaps even a champion prizefighter. Alive, he had passed at various times as a lawyer, a doctor, and a preacher. Dead, he marked the end of an epoch.

Ever increasing numbers of steamboats were now mingling with the flotillas of clumsy flatboats that floated down the river—the dense cane-brakes and forests no longer erupted either white or red savages, but the men who were learning the steamboat business were made of a metal that had been tempered by such characters as Colonel Fluger, Wilson of Cave-in-Rock, James Girty of the Crow's Nest—and Murrell, America's greatest man-on-horseback.

Roistering fighting men of the Mike Fink brand formed the crews of the early steamboats, destined to face no more perils—except those of snags, sandbars, floating ice, bursting boilers and other minor accidents of navigation.

CHAPTER III

THE "NEW ORLEANS"

*"Gangway, catfish, cross dat bar.
We'se a-comin' on de Guidin' Star."*

FULTON MAKES STEAM NAVIGATION COMMERCIALLY PRACTICAL—
THE FULTON-LIVINGSTON MONOPOLY—NICHOLAS J. ROOSE-
VELT PATENTS THE SIDE PADDLE-WHEEL—INVESTIGATION BY
ROOSEVELT OF THE PRACTICABILITY OF STEAM NAVIGATION
ON WESTERN RIVERS—THE "NEW ORLEANS" BUILT AT PITTS-
BURGH—THE STEAMBOAT RUNS UP-STREAM IN THE OHIO—
THE TRIP DOWN THE RIVER—THE NEW MADRID EARTHQUAKE
—THE "NEW ORLEANS" ARRIVES AT NATCHEZ.

WHILE the frontiersmen of the midwest took long
and dangerous ways along the rivers with their cargoes in makeshift vessels—flatboats, keel-boats,
barges, and so forth, the steamboat, which was to
change all this, quicken the scene, enliven trade and
bring greater prosperity, by an arduous process of
trial and error was being developed in the east.

For it can hardly be said that the steamboat was
invented by anybody, and the picture of that craft
being born in the mammoth brain of Robert Fulton
is a myth. On the contrary, it was the fruit of the
efforts of many men. It had its beginning in the
late years of the eighteenth century with Watt's
steam engine, whose appearance was bringing to a
close the age of man-power and animal-power. And
it was inevitable that this power of steam should be

applied to such an obvious purpose as that of driving a boat.

But the method of application of steam to boat was far from obvious; the mechanical difficulties encountered by men who first tried to turn steam power to useful work can hardly be imagined in these days of drop forgings, turret lathes and multiple boring jigs.

How great the difference between our steamships of to-day, cutting the waves with only the white wake to show the power of their engines, their whirling screw under water, every movement perfect, and the early boat of Rumsey, who drew water into his boat and pumped it out the stern for propulsion! And the experiment of Fitch, using paddles which he drove by cumbrous steam-turned cranks! Though his models were often equipped with paddle wheels, many of the mechanical contrivances of Fitch and others were so crude they excited nothing but wonder that they could even go through the motions of machinery, much less draw a boat. For a steam cylinder he used a barrel; for a boiler he had a copper kettle with a wooden cover! It is not surprising that Fitch once wrote during his troublesome experiments: "I know of nothing so perplexing and vexatious to a man of feelings as a turbulent wife and steamboat building."

Accuracy was impossible in those days of early steamboat building. An early American founder and machinist once thought he had made a big steam cylinder. Big for its day, it was only twenty-four inches. And when he delivered it he complimented himself on his excellent work, declaring that at no point was the bore more than a quarter of an inch out of round!

Steam pressure then had a force of from seven to ten pounds to the square inch. But the first engines used only a pound or two, and some none at all, depending for their power on the pull of steam condensing in the exhaust end of the cylinder. Fulton's engines employed both pressure and vacuum, but with such low pressure and such inefficient condensing the cylinder had to be so large and the piston movement so slow that not much headway was made. After the low and leak-weakened steam pressure and the uncertain vacuum had pushed and dragged a rag-packed piston through an uneven cylinder, spun a top-heavy fly-wheel, rocked a cumbersome lever beam and turned a paddle wheel shaft that was in bearings thrown out of line by a sagging hull there was not much power left for the paddle blades.

Starting at the beginning on steamboats, Fulton's first model was a small skiff, driven in spurts by a single oar over the stern, which oar was jerked by the straightening of a hickory bow, turned and brought back for another stroke, and the bow redrawn by Fulton himself. From here he progressed step by step most painfully, trying various methods of applying power to water, adapting and improving the primitive engines of his time until at last he had a boat that would not only run but keep on running.

To perfect this boat Fulton used no important principle or device that had not been used before. He simply took what lay at hand and, by experiment, made it work. He had countless discouragements and his greatness lies in the fact that he rode over them, lifting steam navigation from the field of conjecture and planting it solidly as a servant of mankind.

The famous "Clermont," Fulton's first successful boat, was scarcely more than a land engine set in a hull, a crude affair if ever there was one. The ponderous engine and boiler embedded in masonry and the condenser standing in a well of water, made a weight that was nearly as great as the boat could carry. And the first rudder was so small that it was almost impossible to steer the craft by it. But during the winter Fulton practically rebuilt the "Clermont," correcting the faults in machinery, improving passenger accommodations, covering the paddle wheels with solid timbers.

He made a good boat in spite of the disbelieving world and the attacks of the sailboat captains who, hoping to delay the improvement of the steamboat as long as possible and thus avert the doom of their own business, rammed Fulton's paddle-wheels every chance they got. But every boat that Fulton built was an improvement on its predecessor, and he made the steamboat a business enterprise.

Owned principally by himself and Chancellor Liv-

The "Baton Rouge"—an old Anchor Line sidewheeler loading at New Orleans

ingston, Fulton's company was in a peculiar position. Since it had to carry the inevitable load of debt for long and expensive experimentation, it was entitled to government protection by patent; but there was very little on the boat that could be patented! So Fulton tried to protect his company by state monopolies, acquiring one in New York, and more in other states. But they did not last long.

The queerness of the state of patent rights regarding steamboats is illustrated by the case of Nicholas J. Roosevelt who took out a patent on side paddle-wheels. He may have been first to operate a model side-wheeler in this country, but the side-wheel had been used centuries before in other countries, especially in China where the wheels were made to go by man or animal power. Roosevelt, once connected with Fulton and Livingston, did not try to enforce his patent against them, but did manage to make independent steamboatmen who wanted to build side-wheelers pay him royalty.

Before patent rights and state monopolies on steamboat building broke down Fulton and his associates were planning to extend them to western waters. They were to build a boat at Pittsburgh and float her down for the much needed service between Natchez and New Orleans. But knowing that western rivers were far different in their demands from the Hudson, Nicholas Roosevelt was sent to explore the Ohio and Mississippi and make a report.

It was to be a honeymoon trip as well as one of

business, and the flatboat which Roosevelt built at Pittsburgh in May, 1809, for the journey to New Orleans was fitted up accordingly. In the after part were a bedroom, dining room and pantry. Forward was a bunkroom for the crew and a brick fireplace where the cooking was done. The deck was flat, with seats and the luxury of an awning. For use in gauging depths and currents a large rowboat was on board.

Thus equipped, with a pilot, three deck hands and a cook for crew, the Roosevelts started out in midsummer down the green, delicately curving banks of the Ohio where, already, the sturdily built houses and log barns of the frontiersmen were rising from the fields which their axes had cleared.

They reached Louisville and stayed three weeks while Roosevelt talked with rivermen and inland capitalists, from neither of whom did he receive any encouragement so far as steamboats on the big rivers were concerned. The old boatmen liked and admired his nerve, but thought steamboats would be useless on the rushing, treacherous waters of the Ohio and Mississippi. The water was often too shallow for so big a boat thus driven, they pointed out.

But Roosevelt went ahead, getting trade statistics, estimating the prospective business of steamboats. For he knew they were coming. And when he found coal on the banks of the Ohio he bought and arranged for the opening of mines to supply fuel for boats not yet built. He did this even before he had investigated the lower rivers, when he yet had to convince capitalists that steamboats inland would pay. Yes, he gambled,—on a wild chance most people thought.

They went into the land of armed Indians, many of whom were hostile, of river pirates and thieves. One night the honeymoon couple, in their cabin where they lay sleeping, the boat being always tied up for the night, were awakened by the sound of moccasins padding in the adjoining room. Roosevelt jumped up, taking both pistols. But though the visitors were Indians they only wanted whiskey; and with this Roosevelt good-humoredly supplied them.

It was late summer when the Roosevelts came into the stagnant heat of Natchez. There they left the flatboat on which they had spent the first part of their honeymoon, and went on south in a rowboat, spending four nights in the cramped quarters of the new craft, three on the bank under the stars and twice had the pleasure of sleeping in the high-ceilinged rooms of southern colonial houses where planters entertained them,—all in all a variety during their nine days' voyage to New Orleans.

With his report of the favorable conditions for steamboating on the western rivers, Nicholas Roosevelt and his wife took the first ship leaving New Orleans for New York. It was not an easy trip under any situation, but theirs was made worse by the outbreak of yellow fever, and they were glad to see land again at Old Point Comfort. Thence by stage, they reached New York the next January, 1810, after a nine months' absence.

After Roosevelt returned to New York Fulton and Livingston were convinced that steam navigation in the west was practicable, and in the next December they incorporated the Ohio Steamboat Navigation Company, the names of Daniel D. Tompkins, Robert D. Livingston, DeWitt Clinton, Robert Fulton and Nicholas Roosevelt appearing on the papers. Roosevelt had already gone to superintend the building of the first boat at Pittsburgh, on the Allegheny side of the city at the foot of Boyd's Hill. She was a hundred and sixteen feet long with a twenty foot beam, round bellied and sitting deep in the water. Like Fulton's earlier boats, she carried two masts and sails, but whether she had side wheels, like the "Clermont," or one or two wheels at the stern is not known. But as Fulton had patented side wheels it is probable they were used on this boat.

Roosevelt brought shipwrights and machinists with him from New York to do the work, the boatbuilders of Pittsburgh being inexperienced with mechanics and knowing only flatboats and barges. The timber came from the surrounding forests and was dragged to the Monongahela and rafted to the shipyard. High water flooded the scene of building more than once, nearly causing an abortive launching, and a loss of $38,000, which was the cost of building, but the calamity was averted, and on Saint Patrick's Day, 1811, the "New Orleans," so named for her port of destination, was rolled into the water.

Six months later, during a short experimental trip on the Monongahela, she handled easily and the machinery worked well. Roosevelt decided it was time to start. Mrs. Roosevelt agreed, saying, "Yes, it's time we were going." Whereupon her friends in Pittsburgh were struck with horror. "My dear lady, you will be risking your very life! This steamboat is all very well, but what if it should blow up? Or fail to work? Then you would be left stranded, Heaven only knows where, with the child you're expecting! My husband," these friends told her, "says you may strike a rock or a snag and be sunk! Those rivers are dangerous!" And both sexes went to Nicholas Roosevelt, seeing no impression could be made on his wife, and exclaimed again at the foolhardiness of taking her.

But she went with her husband just as all those pioneer women had gone, taking pride in their share of the work and the risks and the hopes of pioneer life. She too was a pioneer and as she had taken part in her husband's days of uncertainty and preparation, so would she share his triumph or defeat.

The first night out of Pittsburgh the Roosevelts remained on deck until the stars were pale under the coming light of morning, then they retired to the after cabin which, though built for the use of women, they used as the only passengers. With the capable crew of captain, pilot, engineer, and six hands the boat plowed steadily through the silent forests that night, and Nicholas listened anxiously to the sound of her machinery, checking her speed by the landmarks that were passed. Going with the current, she made about nine miles an hour; but that was pretty good.

They anchored the second night at Cincinnati and took on fuel before a wide, deep audience of townspeople bursting with curiosity and predictions. Afterwards the wise ones told each other, "She came *down* all right, but I bet we never see her again, cause she'll never come *up* the river, not any contraption like that!"

Three days later, at midnight on the first of October, the "New Orleans" rounded against the stream and dropped anchor before Louisville. This accomplished, the engineer released the safety valve so as to take off pressure from the boiler; there was a frightful blast of escaping steam and the citizens of Louisville tumbled out of bed and, rushing to the river bank, prepared to see Gabriel himself, or, at the very least, the comet of 1811 setting the world on fire. The sight before them was nearly as interesting: a long, slate-blue boat lying calmly under her billowing plume of steam.

The historic visit was marked by a public dinner given the Roosevelts by congratulating but skeptical townspeople. Roosevelt gave a return dinner of his own a few days later in the main cabin. And at the proper time, while his guests sat about with their liquor, machinery began to clank and the ship began to sway and swing. Immediately the dinner table was deserted; the guests rushed on deck in high excitement, fearing the boat had broken loose and was headed for the dangerous falls of the Ohio just below. But Louisville was not upstream; it was downstream, and getting farther downstream every minute as the "New Orleans" made headway against the current. The steam pressure rose, the speed increased and the safety valve roared. And no longer could the diners be doubtful; they had seen the marvel with their own eyes. Trust a Roosevelt to do a job up brown.

The Roosevelt baby was born at Louisville. Meanwhile Roosevelt ran the "New Orleans" up the river to Cincinnati and back to show that a steamboat could be counted on to navigate the river either way. When he returned the water had risen and he decided he would try to negotiate the difficult Falls of the Ohio downstream. It was a rocky stretch of turbulent water, and something of a test. Mrs. Roosevelt and her baby were on board. For she chose the thrill of running the rapids to the safe but uncomfortable journey by wagon to the lower anchorage.

Everything was ready and Roosevelt engaged a Falls pilot. People lined the bank, waiting to hear the news of catastrophe as the boat shoved off from Louisville towards the Falls. The pilot gave the order for full speed ahead, and the vessel trembled under the mounting pressure of the boilers. It was a long and hazardous stretch over those sharp rocks and there were only five inches of water between them and the keel of the swiftly moving boat. But she made it, and came out upon the broader, smoother water beside Sand Island.

The crew of the "New Orleans" relaxed: they had shown their craft to be no floating sawmill, which was what she had been mistaken for; and they had shot the rapids at the Falls of the Ohio. The rest of the trip seemed simple and easy. But it was to be neither the one nor the other. Even as the ship lay anchored below the Falls, crew and passengers on deck saw the water jump up into waves and the river bluffs suddenly crumble and cave in, and grew physically sick at the sight.

It was the first shock of the New Madrid earthquake, the most violent and extensive which the country has known. That year was unusual and calamitous for the west in many ways. Heavy spring floods had brought contagious disease; the muggy weather of summer had continued through the fall. Hunters noted apprehensively that the squirrels were migrating in herds from north to south, always a portentous movement. The comet had disappeared; people worrying about where it had gone, wondered what next would befall them. But the earthquake, with its central point somewhere near New Madrid, Missouri, drove all other fears from their minds. It is terrible to feel that the very earth beneath us is unstable, likely to burst out at any minute, but this disagreeable fact was brought to the minds of people all through the Ohio and Mississippi valleys, into the Carolinas, Tennessee, Georgia, Virginia, Maryland, Pennsylvania and even in Massachusetts.

With the first shock the "New Orleans," jerked at her anchor and shuddered as if she had suddenly been run aground. It was a fearful moment. But though the tremors continued throughout the voyage they had less force, and while the ship was under way the vibration from the machinery counteracted them so far as their effect on the passengers was concerned. However, the Roosevelts knew that rumbling was still going on beneath the surface of the earth, for Tiger, the big Newfoundland, cringed against his master's legs and whined.

Farther down the river, at the mouth of the Ohio, the bottom lands were flooded, lying under water deep enough to cover the tops of small trees. And there the Roosevelts saw Indians paddling about between the branches, Indians who looked in amazement at the strange craft that smoked so furiously and slashed the waters. Some fled at her approach, believing it a thing belched up from the earth; others paddled towards it for a closer look. And one long pirogue, with a dozen paddlers, shot abreast of the steamboat and tried to outstrip her. For a time steam and man power ran an even race, then arms began to fail and the Indian bark fell behind.

To add to the perils there was a fire on board that

night, the cook having stacked some green wood too close to the stove in the forward cabin. A blaze charred some of the woodwork and, though the crew quenched it, the feelings of crew and the passengers were heightened.

Also, the coal which had been taken aboard at Roosevelt's mines and stored in the small bunkers, gave out. And from then on, except for some coal they found at Yellow Banks by the opening of a mine, their fuel was wood. And the boat was tied up till nearly evening while the crew went ashore to cut it. They tried to get Indians along the shore to help with the axes, but the red men were superstitious of the sight of the "penelore," thinking it might have something to do with the comet they had seen streaking across the sky, or be the cause of the earth's mysterious upheaval, certain it was not for their good. And in this last they were right: it was the steamboat which brought the hordes of settlers to drive the Indian from his home.

Shaken by repeated shocks, her company nervous, sleepless and morose, the "New Orleans" still continued her voyage in spite of the inauspicious signs. It was a strange river they were on now, even to Andrew Jack, the lynx-eyed pilot. Familiar trees and bluffs that once had served to guide him had now toppled over and disappeared under the wide, yellow sheet of water. Islands lay hidden or with shapes unrecognizable. The current which he had once traveled was now obstructed by treacherous reefs and bars. There was nobody to tell him how the channel lay. Under this strain the boatman lost his bluff breeziness. Only by luck and the most vigilant eye did he take the boat down that uncharted path into the heart of the earthquake.

Mid-westerners of to-day dread the tornado, but think an earthquake is something that happens in California. How many know that, only a little more than a century ago, the ground between Cairo and the mouths of the White and Arkansas Rivers rose and sank in great undulations, turning uplands into lake beds, and heaving up swamps and river-beds to dry and whiten in the sun? Reelfoot Lake, in Tennessee, is one of the largest of the earthquake-made lakes. Forests and cane-breaks sank to form this lake, and for many years the trees and cane could be seen through the clear water, standing on the bottom, tenanted by tortoises and fish instead of squirrels and birds.

A man who was riding through the woods near New Madrid at the time of the most severe shocks describes the earth convulsions as a series of great waves in the ground, like waves in the sea. As the waves advanced, the trees bent forward and whipped crashing back, often interlocking their branches in tangled masses. Even the leaves lying on the ground were shaken and whirled about by the motion of the earth. Great fissures opened in the ground, and through some of them spouted torrents of muddy water, carrying sand and fragments of shale.

Like the dry land, the river bed heaved and sank, throwing up blackened tree-trunks that had lain for years in the mud of the bottom, and sucking down islands and banks so that not a leaf remained to show where they had been. An elevation of the whole river-bed at one point caused the current of the Mississippi to recoil upon itself and flow tumultuously backward for several hours. Then the bed sank, or the river cut through the elevation, and the water resumed its course. A flatboatman tells of seeing the whole Mississippi flowing into a fissure in its bed, and feeling his boat pulled irresistibly toward the jaws of the double cataract. But the chasm filled or closed; the watery walls met in huge up-flung spouts and billows that tore his boat to pieces and left him clinging to a bit of wreckage in the swirling current.

Another boatman, making an unlucky start from the mouth of the Ohio on Friday, December thirteenth, tied up two days later after a run of a hundred and sixteen miles. At two o'clock the next morning the first shock jarred him wide awake. There was no wind, but the treetops were whipped as if by a tempest. The steep banks began tumbling into the current, carrying down tall trees that, in falling, lashed the water like great whips. Along that bank was no place for a boat; he cut it adrift, choosing the open river rather than the unstable earth.

Dawn showed the river red with mud, broken by

thunderous spoutings where gas and bituminous shale and rotten wood were forced up through the bottom and to the surface. The boatman tried to land on a small island, but the ground sank under the weight of a man, and the gas-filled earth of the whole island shook under his step. Finally his partner landed on a larger island. Here the earth was cracked and covered with fragments of woody matter in all stages of change from wood to coal. On the beach were funnel-shaped holes where jets of water had thrown this matter out of the earth. The boatmen measured one of these craters. It was sixty-three feet in diameter and sixteen feet deep at the center. Around this hole was a great quantity of coal or near-coal. Some lumps weighing as much as twenty pounds had been thrown a hundred and sixty paces from the crater.

Throughout the region of this earthquake there was no volcanic action; probably it was the greatest earthquake that has occurred in a non-volcanic region since history began. The up-thrown coal and shale came from comparatively shallow depths, and the gases probably were products of vegetable decomposition. Although the earth did not disgorge its elemental fires, the people who experienced the earthquake were in no way disappointed by the lack of pyrotechnics. It was a thoroughly adequate earthquake.

Down through this region of wreck and terror

came the "New Orleans," feeling her uncertain way through mud-red water, her blue sides stained with yellow clotted spume. By day the sun glared like a hot copper disc through a haze of purplish red. The boat wallowed through the earthquake waves that threatened to cast her on bank or bar, dodging as best she might the blackened snags suddenly up-flung in her path. By night her crew moored her at some island in midstream, fearing the fate of the boats they had seen thrown up on the banks or crushed by falling trees and earth. Continually they heard the crash of falling banks and snapping trees, and the hiss and bellow of geysers of gas and mud. One night darkness overtook them before they found a place to tie up. By the light of a flaring torch, they made the mooring-line fast to a tree that stood out of the water at the lower end of a dimly-seen island. During the night the boat was shaken by repeated shocks; great waves drenched her deck, and her hull trembled with the impact of floating logs and driftwood. In the red dawn the voyagers looked about them in amazement, for there was no island; from bank to bank ran the tumbling waste of water carrying floating trees and wreckage. At first they thought they had broken loose and were drifting, but watching the bank showed that they were not moving, and the mooring-line still strained over the bow, down into the muddy river. They could not pull it loose; it was fast to the tree that had been engulfed with the island. They cut the cable, gave the engine steam, and plowed on down the river, away from that place of peril.

The Roosevelts found the village of New Madrid a place of consternation and terror. Some of the people had fled for their lives from the banks of the river; others begged to be taken aboard the steamboat and carried away from this place of earth-chasms and destructive waters. This the boat's company could not do; they had no more food on board than they needed for themselves, and there were no supplies in the town. Many of the stores and houses were gone, fallen into the fissures that had opened in the earth. These cracks all ran in the same general direction, southeast to northwest. Seeing this, the people felled trees across the direction of cleavage, and sat or lay on the fallen trunks to save themselves from being buried alive. The churchyard in the town had fallen, with its dead, into the stream, and been swept away. In some places, the opened earth exposed the huge bones of the mastodon, to lie in view after centuries of burial.

Leaving New Madrid, the "New Orleans" steamed on south, following the changed and changing river in its course through a chaotic wilderness. From New Madrid to Vick's Plantation, now Vicksburg, there was not the semblance of a town. A trading station at Chickasaw Bluffs and another at the mouth of the White River were the only habitations of white men that they passed. But gradually the earthquake shocks diminished and ceased. The river-banks no longer showed the raw scars of slides and cave-ins. The boat had come through intact, her people were safe, and at Natchez, just ahead, they would meet civilization again.

At last the buildings of Natchez drew in sight; the voyagers looked at the town, and looked at each other; a haggard, ragged crew, strained and spent, but triumphant. They knew a hearty welcome awaited them in the town, and it may well be imagined that all who could be spared from the work of navigation made a rush to overhaul and don their shore-going clothes which, in the perilous days of the earthquake, they had wondered if they would ever wear again. The engineer, Baker, knowing they were due for a stop of several days, banked the fire under the boiler. He, like the rest, wanted to get out of that boat as soon as possible and feel firm ground under his feet.

Abreast of the town, where the people stood waiting on the bank, the boat turned and rounded against the stream. To her builder and her crew, this was the hour of fulfillment. Past were the brooding forests of the Ohio, the sombre reaches of the Mississippi, disturbed for the first time by the hiss of steam and the thresh of paddle wheels. The earthquake waves, the toppling bluffs, the tumult of the earth itself in travail; days of red twilight and nights of black terror, all seemed like a nightmare that had gone by.

Suddenly, passengers, pilot, and engineer—especially the engineer—realized that all was not well. The fire had been banked too soon, and the steam pressure was failing. The wheels turned slowly and more slowly. The boat lost headway—drifted, stern first, with the current.

On the bank the people wondered. Doubtless there was a general murmur of "I told you so."

But on the boat there was action. All hands manned the axes, split wood into splinters, and crammed it into the furnace door. The steam was shut off; the dying fire leaped up, belching smoke and burning chips from the stack. The mounting steam hissed as it pressed against the weight of the safety-valve.

Baker pulled open the throttle, the paddles bit into the water, and, trailing smoke and steam, the boat ramped up to her place before the crowd. As the anchor splashed over the bow, a negro on the bank threw up his hat and yelled, "Old Mississipp done got her master now!"

CHAPTER IV

DEVELOPMENT OF STEAMBOATS AND STEAMBOATING

"Who's on de way, blood, who's on de way?
Oh, we'se on de way, blood, we'se on de way."

FIRST SHIPMENT OF GOODS BY STEAMBOAT ON WESTERN RIVERS—
SERVICE AND LOSS OF THE "NEW ORLEANS"—THE 1911
REPLICA—BOATS FOLLOWING THE "NEW ORLEANS"—CAPTAIN
SHREVE'S "WASHINGTON"—END OF THE FULTON-LIVINGSTON
MONOPOLY—SHREVE'S SNAG-BOAT—EVOLUTION OF THE STEAM-
BOAT—OTHER BOATS—THE PERENNIAL "NATCHEZ"—THE
FINAL TYPE OF RIVER PACKET—THE "J. M. WHITE"—STEAM-
BOATS AS A FACTOR IN TRADE AND MIGRATION—THE
"WESTERN ENGINEER."

IN the minds of Americans, adventure in the wild
west is linked with the name of Theodore Roosevelt.
But that of Nicholas J. Roosevelt, who was a brother
of the Colonel's grandfather, is almost forgotten.
Yet the illustrious Theodore in this respect was only
living up to family tradition; for grand-uncle Nicholas went west when the west was really wild. And
he went not for his health but for a livelihood for
himself and his family. And his service to this
country in bringing steam to the west is one in which
his descendants and their fellow countrymen may
well take pride.

When Roosevelt's ship, the "New Orleans," put
out from Natchez on the last leg of her eventful trip
to her namesake city, she carried a shipment of cotton

which the owner, against the advice of his friends, had entrusted to this strange and dangerous-looking craft.

That was its first piece of freight. But landing at New Orleans safely on January 12, 1812, it began making weekly trips up the river to Natchez and back, going at once into trade. For this, on that part of the river, she was fairly fitted: her route was deep enough for successful navigation; her average up-current speed was three miles an hour; cabin fare was profitable on the uptrip at twenty-five dollars, and to New Orleans for eighteen, and her repairs were not large.

Her fate, that of the first steamboat on the rivers, foretold the fate of many of the others that were to follow. On July 14, 1814, some time after carrying General Coffee and Don Carol from Natchez to New Orleans with troops to aid Old Hickory in his defence of the Crescent City, she was caught by a fall of the river while tied up at Baton Rouge, and the receding water left her impaled on a stump. The crew with other boatmen worked furiously to get her off—and ripped a deeper hole. Slowly she filled and went down, crumpling her hull like paper.

Roosevelt had been of great service to river navigation. But he was not of the river himself. Though his craft had made the first steamboat trip down the Ohio and Mississippi, Roosevelt remained an easterner, just as Livingston and the rest of that company were easterners. To make the steamboat traffic hum, build boats that would ably carry the many emigrants into the new land, take care of their produce and bring them necessary goods, a river man was needed, a man who knew the demands of the rivers, who could steer a craft in a pitch black night through snags and rocks and come out with not a timber scratched.

That man was Captain Henry M. Shreve, who first comes into the picture as commander of the "Enterprise," the second boat made by Daniel French and Daniel D. Smith. French was a maker of engines, one of which made steam for the "Enterprise," a stern-wheeler eighty feet long with a twenty-nine foot beam. She was launched at Bridgeport on the Monongahela in the spring of 1814, and that winter was taken by Shreve to New Orleans, where General Jackson demanded her services. But war or no war the Fulton-Livingston monopolists had her seized, and she is of importance chiefly because it was over her that Shreve fought his first skirmish against the easterners who said they had to be paid for every steamboat built on the western rivers.

In 1815, while Shreve's case was going to the United States Supreme Court after he had won in inferior court, the "Enterprise" made her first trip from New Orleans to Louisville under steam; going on flood water, it was not regarded as a conclusive test, but Shreve was not worrying about conclusive tests and the "Enterprise"; he had gone on up the river with a big job in mind.

This job was the "Washington." It was built that year at Wheeling by George White under Shreve's exacting direction. Shreve, as a river captain, had seen the foolishness of building a river boat to look like a sea-going vessel. They were pretty enough, but prettiness wasn't all that was required for the work they were called upon to do. Shreve had seen steamboats run aground in water over which flatboats floated with ease. He wanted a boat that was thoroughly navigable, not a boat like the "Vesuvius" or the "Aetna" or the "Buffalo," which the Fulton-Livingston company had put into service down river. The "Vesuvius," for example, had grounded on her first run from New Orleans to Louisville and lay helplessly on her side for five months. No, Shreve didn't want a boat like that. He wanted a flatboat. Let all the other builders make deep, round hulls and set their machinery down in them! Shreve wasn't going to do it! He would fashion a flat, shallow hull and put up his boilers and engines on the main deck, damned if he wouldn't. And he'd put a second deck over the main deck. Yes, sir!

And so Captain Henry M. Shreve built the first double-decker on the rivers, the first of those boats that were so ugly they were good-looking, that were to bring the settlers on into the west, and that were, incidentally, to cast a glow of romance over the whole frontier scene.

But it was not only in its outward appearance that Captain Shreve changed the steamboat. He also revolutionized the engines which were to make the steam. Those of the Fulton boats were heavy, low pressure condensing machines with stationary vertical cylinders; and French's engines were much the same, except that the cylinders oscillated. When Shreve came to design he used stationary horizontal cylinders with oscillating pitmans, the type that nearly all the boatbuilders were to follow. The cut-off valve, which utilized the expansive force of the steam and made a saving of one-third in fuel, was Shreve's. And he also developed steam pressure high enough to obviate the pull of condensing exhaust steam, to accomplish which he put flues in his boilers, dispensing with the heavy, bulky condenser which had kept the Fulton boats low in the water and limited their freight capacity. Why use the same water over and over again when there is plenty in the river and a little added pressure will more than make up for the relegation of the condenser-vacuum to the junk pile? Shreve answered this question for himself, and all the river engineers that came after him profited by his decision.

Shreve's "Washington" was 148 feet long with engines, built by French closely after Shreve's plan, having a 24 inch bore and a 6 foot stroke. Going down to New Orleans in September, 1816, he demonstrated over every mile of water the superiority of the flat-hulled, high-pressure boat to all others. And in the next spring, March 12, 1817, he began a round trip from the Falls of the Ohio to New Orleans, which took him just 41 days, the upstream journey being made in 25 days. The water was at normal, but the boat rode high over the rocks in the Falls. And back in Louisville once more the townspeople gave Shreve a public dinner.

"Gentlemen," said the master of ceremonies after a complimentary speech to Captain Shreve, "we have seen how Captain Shreve, by the wondahs of his new craft, has brought us so much closer to the seaboa'd at N'Awlins. But, gentlemen," the speaker went on, his voice impressively hushed, "some of us will live to see the day when the trip from New Orleans to Louisville will be made in ten days, I am confident." If the speaker lived for 34 years more he saw that trip made not in ten days but in four days, nine hours and thirty-one minutes!

And the time was to come, in just twenty years from the date of the dinner, when river boats of the type of Shreve's "Washington" outweighed in tonnage all ships of the Atlantic seaboard and the Great Lakes combined. But that was a long way off, and much trouble lay in store for the boatman meanwhile. For Chancellor Livingston and his company would not give up their fourteen-year monopoly without a fight. And Shreve was willing to fight them. On his first trip down with the "Washington" Shreve was met by Livingston, who inspected his boat and admitted her many advantages over his own. "But," said Livingston, "I tell you, young man—you deserve well of your country, but we shall be compelled to beat you in the courts."

And with the case of the "Enterprise" still undecided, Shreve steamed into New Orleans with the "Washington." It was seized and held by the law. But Shreve got a court order which held the Fulton-Livingston company responsible for any damages he might suffer while his vessel was detained. Livingston saw that he was in for a long fight and privately offered Shreve an equal share in the Fulton rights if he would arrange to lose his case. But Shreve was not the man to do that. No, sir! He'd fight it out.

That legal battle for the right of the westerners to build their own boats in disregard of the Fulton-Livingston company lasted three years and cost Captain Shreve a fortune. But at length he won, and on every point. And thus he opened the Mississippi to free navigation for all times to come.

But even before the case was decided the "Washington" was no more. Shreve had built well, but he had made one mistake: weak boilers. On June 9, 1817, while the "Washington" was going full speed ahead there was an explosion on the main deck and a simultaneous outrush of steam that enveloped the vessel as if it were in a cloud. The boiler had broken, tearing the timbers with it, and the "Washington" went down in deep water. Shreve escaped, and lived to do more good service to the rivermen by building and operating a boat to take the snags—those Nemeses of so many craft—out of the river. It was made by fastening two steamboats together by timbers, with a sort of cow-catcher in front. These beams were run against the discovered snags, raising them out of the water and bucking them into small, harmless bits. This snag-boat was first made by Shreve in 1834, and the Government gave him a job of clearing the rivers of these menaces to navigation—the steamboat business had advanced that far.

Though the "Washington" was sunk, she lived in replica. For Shreve had established the type, a craft distinct from those of all other rivers, and the demand for these boats lasted for more than half a century, with finer boats being made every year. And they were nearly all built along the rivers, in Cincinnati, where in 1819 the "General Pike" was commissioned as the first mail steamboat to run between there and Louisville and St. Louis, and in many other towns along the Ohio. In 1820 the east tried to enter the field with a few boats built at Philadelphia and New York and sent to New Orleans under their own steam, but they were of little avail among the fleeter, more suitable craft from up the river.

Boat by boat and year by year these inland vessels improved in speed, carrying capacity and passenger accommodation. First they looked like flat canal boats with paddle wheels at either side. Their cabins were narrow aisles between curtained bunks, leading to small eating rooms in front and rear, the one ahead

FROM AN OLD PRINT OF "THE MESSENGER"

Charles Dickens Saw the Ohio From This Steamer

for the men, the other for the women. Between 1830 and 1840 they broke out in a rash of gaudy ornamentation, gingerbread woodwork and heaven only knows what not. But all carried their machinery on the main deck, the boilers forward and the engines in the waist between the paddle-wheels. However, their actual build varied. Some had their cabins astern on the main deck, and carried deck passengers forward, or up above the boilers on the boiler deck. Others had two cabins aft, one atop the other. The cabins of still others were on the boiler deck, with the impecunious or super-thrifty passengers being carried on the main deck astern. This type proved its superiority over the others and became standard for steamboats.

The hold of the average steamboat carried freight; the main deck held the boilers, engines, kitchens, accommodations for deck passengers and room for as much more freight as could be piled aboard; the boiler deck contained the cabins, consisting of the boat's office and the barroom, staterooms in the waist and the women's cabin aft,—all this reached by stairs leading up from the forward part of the main deck called the forecastle; a promenade ran round the boat between the staterooms and the rail; the roof of the cabin was called the hurricane deck and held another row of cabins, for the officers, called the Texas. Staterooms were so called because, originally, each room was given the name of a state, and the Texas was the Texas because it was an addition to the cabin capacity of the boat, just as the Lone Star state was an addition to the Union. Over and above all this was the pilot house.

A river pilot's position, symbolically and actually, was on top of everything, with nothing above him but the tips of the two black smokestacks, which sometimes had white lead rings around them. These came up through the hurricane deck at the sides of the boat and left him an unobstructed view forward, backward and at either side, so that in shoal water he could see the shallows, the bars and snags better than any man aboard. A ship's pilot sometimes sends a man up in the crow's nest to warn him of the shoals; if the ship's pilot could climb up the mast to the crow's nest himself and take the wheel with him, his situation would be the same as that of the river steamboat pilot.

Thus steamboat design settled firmly along the lines of utility, comfort and safety; and beyond that each captain was allowed to go as far as he liked. And go it he usually did. Each captain wanted something to set off his boat from all others. Sometimes it was a bright painting on the paddle boxes; sometimes a picture on the pilot house. Almost every boat carried some characteristic ornament between the chimneys. On the "Natchez" boats (of which there were many) it was a bale of cotton; others had single stars, stars in rings and in intricate design; anchors, gilded globes—one boat, whose captain always wore a queer top-piece, flaunted a big white hat between her chimneys.

Seven of these "Natchez" boats were owned by Captain Thomas Leathers. Two of them were ripped through by snags and a falling river; one was captured by Federal soldiers during the War of the Rebellion, and four were burned. But this dauntless old riverman went on building, and each boat was a little finer in appearance than the last. His fifth boat to be named "Natchez" was said by rivermen to be a wonder. She cost, complete, $200,000. Her carpets alone represented $5,000, and the chandeliers were of sparkling cut glass.

Hand in hand with luxurious fittings and improved lines went speed. And of the swift boats there was none that ever outraced the "J. M. White." Built to excel at the time the boat-maker's craft was mature, the "J. M. White" was put together at Elizabeth, Pennsylvania, in the upper yard owned and operated by Samuel Walker the elder, according to the careful design of William King. And she made Billy King the leading boat designer of his time and brought much money to J. M. Converse, her builder, and Robert Chouteau, her financier, both of Saint Louis.

King's departure from the ordinary was simple. He placed the wheels of the "J. M. White" twenty feet farther aft than was usual in a boat of that size. He had watched boats under way and noted that they made two swells in the water: one forward and one aft. Why not make his wheels so they would bite into the after swell and thus gain speed! And so he submitted this plan to Converse, the builder. But Converse shook his head. "It won't go, Billy."

"Then I'm damned if I make the boat," said King, and walked away.

Converse, not wanting to lose King as designer, asked Walker what he should do about it. "Dunno," said Walker. "Maybe it's better and maybe it's not. But I'll tell you this much: when Billy King gets his head set on a thing the devil himself couldn't make him change it." So Converse asked Chouteau, the backer, about it, and Chouteau replied, "You let Billy King go ahead if he wants to build her that way. He knows his business."

The "J. M. White" was launched, went down stream. Coming back from New Orleans to St. Louis she broke all records into as many pieces as the snags were broken into after Captain Shreve's snag-boat got after them: three days, 23 hours and 9 minutes! It remained a record for all time in steamboat travel, for it is extremely doubtful if even the famous "Robert E. Lee," in 1870, made any better speed than the "J. M. White," as the river at the time of the latter's great run was some miles shorter. Old steamboatmen hold that the "J. M. White" could never be beaten.

The "J. M. White" was also excellently built, her passenger accommodations being the ultimate in river travel luxury. Each stateroom was fitted with a double bed instead of bunks, and that was far from all. She had a certain grace, an economy and neatness. And when builders saw her and noted her record run, Billy King had a dozen requests to make a boat that would beat her. Make a boat that would beat the pride of his heart! Billy King glowered. "If there's ever a boat built that'll walk away from the "White" I'll make another to beat *her*, but not until then!" He never was required to fulfill his promise. The "J. M. White" was his darling, and he was so jealous of her that, fearing somebody might try to copy her design, he sent for the model at Elizabeth, a beautiful thing of white pine and black walnut, and broke it into fragments.

It was the Captain Shreves and the Billy Kings who made the steamboat supreme in her day. For fourteen years after the "New Orleans" made the first trip, steamboat traffic was slow. At the beginning the Fulton-Livingston monopoly had to be fought and after that the tobacco and hemp growers of Kentucky, Tennessee, Ohio and Indiana had to be shown that it was cheaper to ship by steamboat rather than send their produce to New Orleans in flatboats, have the crew sell the boats and take deck passage or walk home. And steamboats had to become practical enough commercially so that the charges for carrying and for passengers could be greatly lowered. For when steamboats began to make the run, cabin fare from New Orleans to Louisville was about $140. Later $100 would buy cabin fare clear to Pittsburgh; still later, in 1833, a man could go from New Orleans to Pittsburg for about $40 in the cabin, and on the deck, where he supplied his own food, he could ride for $10 or $12.

Thus the steamboats grew in value. And between 1810 and 1840 they carried the emigrants into the new land in such numbers that the Indians were completely driven out and it became the white man's country, the land that was bristling with factories and farms along the route of the Ohio and Mississippi boats, the plains and prairies which were being planted. And all of this produce was being hauled by the steamboats.

Much of these goods went down the river to New Orleans, that old-world city where the beautiful Creoles lived. This city reached its highest relative position in American business in 1839, when its trade equalled that of New York. How the wharves swarmed there under the warm blue sky, and the steamboats fumed, and clanged their signal bells as they maneuvered about the docks!—those bells that were later to be replaced by the steam whistle, made compulsory by law, just as the importance of New Orleans was to fade when the Erie Canal was opened up, making a path from the north to New York and underbidding the exorbitant charge on traffic made by the southern city.

Steamboat traffic was by no means limited to the

Ohio and lower Mississippi. The fur trade had grown steadily in importance and captains took their steamboats up the Missouri, linking St. Louis, the center of the trade, with the country between the Kansas and Nebraska rivers, the territory from which a new emigrant trail was to be beaten out, carrying settlers and goods to Oregon and California. St. Louis had long been great in the fur business through the efforts of such old traders as Ashley, Campbell, Sublette, Manuel Lisa, Perkins, Hempstead, William Clark, Labadie, the Chouteaus and Menard, and in 1819 had a population of 4000. But when Missouri was admitted into the union and Mexico became independent, a wagon trade was started between St. Louis and Santa Fe, and this was of great importance to the steamboat traffic. Advancing from 15,000 pounds in 1822, it reached half a million pounds in twenty years.

From that time, 1842, onward until the Civil War river trade was at its best. During this period Ohio, Illinois, Iowa, Missouri and Arkansas were settled and developed; cotton was being grown widely in the southwest; Tennessee, Mississippi and Louisiana, exporting 5,000,000 pounds of cotton in 1811, were then exporting more than 200,000,000 pounds. In the forties the steamboat tonnage of the Mississippi valley, exclusive of New Orleans, was 15,000 tons greater than that of all the Atlantic ports; and, in 1843, New Orleans had twice the tonnage of New

York. Shipyards at St. Louis, New Albany, Cincinnati and Louisville became the biggest and busiest establishments of their kind in the world.

And all this in less than thirty years! Yes, in less time than that. For even in 1819 the steamboats were so undeveloped that they looked like monstrous, ungainly and extremely impermanent toys, and not at all like vessels that were to supply the needs of millions of people in the midwest and open up the new country. There was one of them, for example: the "Western Engineer." In 1819 it came down from Pittsburgh, carrying an exploring expedition under Major Stephen H. Long, to a point five miles below Council Bluffs. It had a bow made after the fashion of a huge serpent with its black, scaly head rising high in the air and a devilishly open mouth through which the steam of the exhaust issued. Her best speed was three miles an hour, except when floating downstream, and the object of her builder had been, evidently, to make her look like anything but a steamboat. He had carefully housed all of her machinery, so that, to the Indians, she looked as if she was moved by some kind of spirit.

The engine was no better than the design. The pistons had frequently to be repacked; there was no blow valve on the boiler, from which mud had to be taken every day while traveling up the Missouri, some unlucky member of the crew having to scoop it out; the valves got worn by mud and sand—maybe the "Western Engineer" impressed the Indians; it certainly was of no advantage to steamboating, unless it was to live as a reminder of how that craft developed.

The conquest of the rivers by steam was accomplished by the same type of men who opened them to the keel-boat and the broadhorn, the alligator-horse boatmen. From this rough but sound beginning, the steamboat business developed many men of the finest type. No weakling could remain long in this exacting occupation. They were pioneers, and Theodore Roosevelt was right when he said of the American pioneers that they "had to be good and strong—especially, strong."

The boatmen who handled their craft on the swift and changing rivers were little different from the other pioneers who traveled with them to new homes and built the West. Between 1830 and 1840 a clergyman who had done some traveling on the rivers of the West wrote a book in which he viewed the lusty young empire through spectacles of the deepest and most puritanic blue. Let all westerners thank the old pessimist for that book. Who knows how many men of his own sort it kept back in witch-burning Salem where they belonged? His description of life aboard an early Mississippi steamboat was written from the heart. No art could improve upon the clergyman's own words, or his own italics, "One of these large boats, filled with passengers, is almost a *world* in miniature. In the cabin you will find ladies and gentlemen of various claims to merit, on the forward part of the boat are the sailors, deck hands, and those *sons of Vulcan*—the firemen—possessing striking traits of character, and full of noise, and song, and too often of *whiskey*, whilst *above*, in the deck cabin, there is everything that may be called *human*—all sorts of men and women, of all trades, from all parts of the world, of all possible manners and habits. There is the half-horse and half-alligator Kentucky boatman, swaggering, and boasting of his prowess, his rifle, his horse, and his wife. One is sawing away on his wretched old fiddle all day long, another is grinding a knife or razor, here is a party *playing cards*, and in yonder corner is a *dance* to the sound of a Jew's harp, whilst a few are trying to demean themselves soberly, by sitting in silence or reading a book. But it is almost impossible—they are telling wondrous tales and horrible Indian stories, the bottle and the jug are freely circulating, and the boisterous and deafening laugh is incessantly raised, sufficient to banish every vestige of seriousness, and thought, and sense. A friend of mine, some time ago, went down from Cincinnati to New Orleans on board the steam-boat ——, which carried fifty cabin passengers, one or two hundred deck passengers, one negro-driver with his gang of negroes, a part of a company of soldiers, a menagerie of wild beasts, a whole circus, and a company of play-actors!"

Horrible! How the old gentleman must have suffered at the sight of other people enjoying themselves!

CHAPTER V

THE OHIO-LOWER MISSISSIPPI TRADE ROUTE

"Oh, rollin' up de river, steamin' at de moon,
Chase de possum up de bank and cook de grizzlum coon."

GEOGRAPHY OF THE RIVERS—INDIAN NAMES OF THE RIVERS—SET-
TLEMENTS AT THE EXTREMITIES OF THE OHIO—LOWER MISSIS-
SIPPI TRADE ROUTE—NEW ORLEANS THE MARKET FOR THE
AMERICAN WEST—CHARACTER OF THE OHIO AND MISSISSIPPI
RIVERS—FAUNA AND FLORA OF THE MISSISSIPPI STRANGE TO
EARLY VOYAGERS—NEW ORLEANS, IN THE EARLY DAYS—
EARLY JOURNEYS OF PIONEERS—STEAMBOATS AS SEEN BY DIS-
TINGUISHED TRAVELERS—STEAMBOAT FARES ON THE OHIO—
MOVEMENT OF POPULATION DOWN THE OHIO AND MISSISSIPPI
—THE RIVER DRIFTERS.

SOME home-boosting geographers have held that
the lower Mississippi and the Missouri rivers should
bear one name and be considered one river, making
it the longest river in the world. Others of the same
sort have said that the Ohio and the lower Mississippi in reality form one stream. However nice
it would be to add length of rivers to our leadership
in railroads, skyscrapers and flivvers parked end to
end, these estimable geographers are mistaken. The
old explorers, perhaps more by chance than by design, saw and named the rivers of the Mississippi
System in a way that later geographical science has
approved.

For the Mississippi rises in the region of Minnesota, a region of myriad lakes in a high land that,
by imperceptible, almost accidental margins, divides

105

the rivers that flow into the warm Gulf from those that flow into the icy Arctic. And in some early epoch of geological history, the mouth of the Mississippi was not very far below Cairo. All the lowlands now lying south of that point were built by the river. As for the Missouri it begins its journey in the Rockies, and flows through plains and prairies to its confluence with the Mississippi. While the Ohio, rising in the Appalachian Mountains, in a region different from the place of origin of either of the others, flows to the Mississippi in its own characteristic way. Each river is distinct in its water, its scenery, and its moods. But together they form a branched system that afforded to the American pioneers their highways of trade and travel when highways were exceedingly scarce.

Early explorers tried to give various names to the river which gradually became know as the Mississippi. De Soto, in 1541, called it the Rio Grande. Before that time, in 1520, Cortez had named it Rio del Spiritu Sancto, and in 1528 Cabeza de Vaca had puzzled his brain for a name without finding one. Other Spaniards called it Palisado and Escondido; and the explorers gave various names, which Indians applied to the river: Chucagua, Ochechiton, Tamalisieu, Tapatu, Malabouchia, and Mico. Probably they mistook various other rivers for the principal one. Some old maps of 1580 or thereabouts give the name variously as Chucaquax, Canaveral, and Rio de Flores.

The original Algonquin name of the river was Mech-e-se-be, meaning great waters, and given it by the Indians whom La Salle and Marquette visited. These Frenchmen, however, entitled it anew. La Salle called it the Colbert, Marquette piously called it St. Louis, and Joliet gave it the name of Buade. In 1661 Peñolosa, governor of Mexico, used the name as Mischipi, in 1672 Marquette gave it as Mitchisipi.

The generally accepted meaning of Mississippi is "great waters" or "father of waters," though some students of the Indian languages translate it as "river of meadows and grass." However this may be, let us be thankful that, of all the names the river has borne, the original Indian name is the one that stuck.

The name of the Ohio is also Indian, probably a contraction of the Delaware tribal word, "Ohio-peekhanne," meaning "very deep and white stream." Apparently they thought of the Ohio as white in-asmuch as the frequent strong wind whipped it into white-caps. If explorers attempted to name the Ohio after their particular kings, saints, or financial backers, the names have been lost. "Ohio" is a very easy name to remember, and never had to be changed with changing ownership.

Though geographically the Ohio and the Mississippi are distinct streams, the two rivers form one trade route. It was so in the beginning of western trade, when the pioneers established their farms, and later their industries, on the headwaters of the Ohio, and shipped their products down the rivers because they could not ship them any other way. And it is so to-day. On or near the upper Ohio are the coal, the iron, and the manufacturing plants, from which New Orleans is ready to export all that comes down for that purpose, just as in the days of flatboats. Along the lower Mississippi is a rich agricultural country that buys manufactured goods and ships cotton. And into New Orleans come the products of the tropics, to be shipped north.

On the Ohio were the Falls, a series of rapids at whose head the city of Louisville grew up, a natural division point in the voyage from the Monogahela Country to New Orleans. Special pilots were required to take boats over the dangerous water. When the river was low, boats had to be sent over empty, or almost empty, while the cargo was carried past the Falls in carts. In later years a canal was built around the obstruction. Few of the big steam packets of the lower rivers went above the Falls.

When this trade route was first used, the shippers were at one end, the market at the other. Between was wilderness, marked by a scattered handful of white settlements. Setting out in his keel-boat or flatboat from the upper Ohio near the Monongahela the frontiersman held his pole in readiness to keep his loaded boat from striking a snag or rock as it swirled down the swiftly moving Ohio. There were countless rock bars between the pale limestone and sandstone cliffs before he reached Louisville, where

The "Ouachita"—a lower Mississippi type

(Stanton's "American Steam Vessels")

he either unloaded his cargo and sent the boat over empty or else took a chance with the rapids there at the Falls and ran the risk of splitting the bottom of his boat. Once past Louisville he was in wider water, floating slowly down between bluffs and craggy precipices such as Battery Rock, Tower Rock and that gaunt, evilly-remembered Cave-in-Rock. And if he went down in the spring he often traveled a veritable yellow sea. For the Ohio drains a humid and mountainous country and floods even more violently than the Missouri or Mississippi. One Ohio flood, that of 1832, brought the water up at Cincinnati 63 feet above low water mark.

His hickory shirt spotted with sweat and his coonskin cap on the rough boards beside him, our early trader-farmer-riverman must have been struck with wonder as his flatboat careened into the Mississippi from the Ohio's mouth. For from then on the scenery changed, was no more like that along the Ohio. There were the low banks of bare clay, mile after mile of drooping willows, acres of cane-brakes and, instead of maples and hickory and walnut trees, along the banks stood the curiously shaped cottonwood.

Of the cottonwood, so familiar to all of the middle west, one early navigator said, "This tree on examination has been found to be the same with the Lombardy poplar." This old observer must have thought that, in the wide, open spaces, the Lombardy poplar had at last a chance to spread out and be itself!

Among the birds of the Mississippi the early merchant-adventurers also found wonders. In a flat-boatman's book on navigation is a footnote: "The pelican is said to have a melancholy countenance, is very torpid, and to a great degree inactive, so much so, that nothing can exceed its indolence but its gluttony. . . . It is asserted that they seem to be fond of music. . . . Their pouches are frequently dried and converted into bags or purses, sometimes embroidered, for the use of the ladies. The pouch of this bird is said to have given rise to the fabulous story among the ancients, that it fed its young with blood from its breast." Careful old teller of wondrous tales! The pelican was too strange to be true, but too good to keep.

The earlier travelers found not only wild animals but birds in places where we do not find them to-day. In 1848 a traveler wrote, "The paroquet is now seldom seen north of Cincinnati. They are abundant below Louisville."

Early navigators had some difficulty with the river water, which was their only available soft drink. It was so muddy that they had to let it stand in jars over night before they could see through it. It acted medicinally, and was supposed to purify the blood, and rivermen preferred it to water from wells or springs. River water was the usual drink throughout the later years of steamboating.

New Orleans itself, end of the long downtrip, in 1806 was vaguely French, but with a strangeness added to it by the low land on which it was built and the ramparts against Indian attacks. Almost a mile long from the gate of France, at the south, to the Gate of Chapitoulas, at the north, it extended for several squares back from the river to the Rampart. And outside the city's northern gate lay a suburb. For a block or two back from the river you could have seen the rows of brick houses, with their tile roofs coloring under the warm sun. But many of the other buildings were of frame and shingle. The Place d'Armes, in the center of the city, with a tall church and the town house facing it on one side, ran along a level parade ground where, of an evening, more strange sights met the eye of the voyager from the upland country. For all kinds of people were to be seen in New Orleans: swarthy Spaniards in their curious dress; bisque-faced Italians, with their sharp, grating speech; laughing negroes, moving slowly, shoulders hulking, strutting, lolling, and their soft, ingratiating voices; tall or pudgy Germans going about their work and play with equal efficiency and perhaps secretly longing for a cold stein of beer, not liking the more fiery drinks; Frenchmen, cocky and debonair, pleasantly sounding their vowels as they made love to whatever maid happened to be at hand; bearded Englishmen with grey, aloof eyes, feeling a gnawing for those Creole girls whose beauty helped make the city famous and not knowing quite how to go about it.

A gay city, a gaudy city, not like any other. In 1832 she was all bustle and business. A writer on navigation says of New Orleans in that year, "There are sometimes from 1000 to 1500 flatboats lying at the wharves at a time; steamboats are arriving and departing every hour; and a forest of the masts of ships is constantly seen, except in the sultry months, along the levee. There are often five or six thousand boatmen from the upper country here at a time. No place in the United States has so much activity crowded into so small a space, as this city in the months of February, March and April."

What a place to visit for the shy, gangling, hickory-muscled youth of the upper country; what a port for the steamboat officers and crews to pull up to after working their arms sore at the engines, the loads of freight, and tussling with sandbars and snags. . . . And only a short while before they would be back on board again, bound for the thinly settled banks upriver.

What a pity that some of the distinguished visitors who came to the land of steamboats in those days didn't visit New Orleans and give their impressions of it along with their accounts of travel farther up the river. If they had, some of the Britishers, like Charles Dickens and Mrs. Trollope, might have been a little more gentle. Edmund Flagg, however, had the proper enthusiasm that fitted and characterized the times. In his book on "The Far West," published in 1836, he thus described the arrival of a steamboat:

"A gay hurrah of music arrested our attention and

looking up, I perceived the packet boat 'Lady Marshall,' dropped from the moorings at the quay, her decks swarming with passengers and under high pressure of steam, holding her bold course against the current, while the merry dashing of wheels, mingling with the clang of martial music, imparted an air almost of romance to the scene. There are few objects more truly grand, I had almost said sublime, than a powerful steamer struggling triumphantly with the rapids of Western Waters."

Another writer, Charles Dickens, was not so favorably impressed. He looked on this highly provincial means of travel with a critical eye. On his American tour he went by steamboat from Pittsburgh to Cincinnati, and wrote it up for the people back in civilization. And possibly this greatest of all reporters was among the first of the foreign writers to know that Americans will read uncomplimentary remarks about their institutions for the pleasure of returning them. He describes the boat: " 'The Messenger' is a high pressure boat, carrying forty passengers, exclusive of poorer persons on the lower deck. There was no mast, cordage, tackle, or rigging, only a long, ugly roof, two towering, iron chimneys, and below on the sides, the doors and windows of the staterooms; the whole supported on beams and pillars, resting on a dirty barge, but a few inches above the water's edge, and in this narrow space between the upper structure and this barge's deck are the furnace fires and machinery, open at the sides.

"Within, there is one long, narrow cabin, the whole length of the boat, from which the staterooms open on both sides, a small portion of it in the stern, partitioned off for the ladies, and the bar at the opposite extreme. There is a long table down the center, and at either end a stove."

Rather crude, but possibly Dickens was not feeling appreciative. A story is told of a happening on this same trip which, if true, illustrates his state of mind. The tale runs that the great writer, on his arrival at a western town, was greeted by the mayor, the city council, and the other principal citizens assembled for the occasion. They proceeded to the hotel, which was operated by the mayor, and that official doffed his civic function and assumed the rôle of host. A reception was planned in the lobby, but Dickens escaped to the bridal chamber which had been reserved for him, followed by the reception committee, the hackmen, the bell-hops, and the citizenry in general. But the mayor-host was not through yet. He had prepared a speech, and when an American has a speech on his chest he must get it off. At the door he pulled down his vest and began an oration of welcome which would make the most impassioned after-dinner speaker of to-day appear like a candle beside a flaming arc. They could make that kind in those days.

Wearily, Dickens held up his hand. "My good

man," he said, "if I want anything I'll ring, you know."

Mrs. Trollope, in 1830, comments on the separation of the sexes on the boats of the American west. She seldom saw the men except during the "short, silent periods" devoted to meals. She remarks that while American men "do not scruple to chew tobacco in the presence of women, they generally prefer drinking and gaming in their absence."

It is true that many of the passengers must have gambled—for wasn't poker born to the world in those days! And that they drank it must also be sadly confessed. That is proved by extant accounts of how steamboats were christened, which was a little different performance from that of christening a sea-going vessel.

When a boat is launched at sea a bottle of wine is spilt over her bow. Steamboatmen, however, seldom spilled wine over any part of their craft. Whatever there was to drink they made use of themselves. And it was usual at the launching of a big boat for the builder to prepare a barrel of egg-nog and set it in a convenient place, with tin cups around it, for the free disposal of the crowd. Instead of pouring a libation into the river, they poured it into themselves where they were sure it would do some good.

Some travelers who were accustomed to the boats and stages of the east complained that western boats seldom started on time. It is true that they were often an hour to a day late in starting. A voyage on the western rivers was a long voyage, a much more momentous business undertaking than one of the short trips of the east. A western captain could ill afford to start with his hold and cabins only half filled, and he generally delayed his departure until he had all the business he could get. This, of course, was not true of the later packets which ran on strict schedules.

Steamboat fares on the Ohio averaged about three cents per mile, for distances of fifty miles or more. This included berth and meals. Stage-coach fares were about six cents per mile, and the passengers paid for their meals and lodged at hotels.

The first settlers along the Ohio came overland, but it was not until the steamboat made the river a two-way route that the mingling of stock which built the population of that section was consummated. First to come were the Irish, Scotch-Irish, and German merchant-adventurers and settlers, occupying the Monongahela Country. Then came the Virginians and Carolinians. And after them the Yankee immigrants, to the vicinity of Cincinnati and Marietta; and a group of New England families that built up part of Kentucky. Finally the Ohio region was neither northern nor southern, but a mingling of the two.

But the settlement of this country was not free of land swindles. Gallipolis began as a land boom in the wilderness. The victims were French colonists who knew little of the country and paid their money for the promises of unscrupulous speculators. They did not find their new homes as they had been led to expect. They suffered sickness and want, and many left the place. A few remained to see the town revived and developed in the natural course of trade and settlement.

Through all the changing human life that plied the rivers since the first pioneers settled the country beyond the Alleghenies, one type of navigator persisted. This was the shanty-boatman. Shanty-boating began back in the flatboat days when some settler with the spring wanderlust built a shack on a raft and embarked with all his possessions for no destination at all. With the coming of steamboats and the peopling of the river banks the shanty-boaters traveled in swarms. Many of them made their floating homes into stores or shops. A business afloat was an easy life. If trade did not go well, the traders could live off the country. Among the itinerant merchants that loafed down the rivers from 1820 until the Civil War were dealers in dry goods, cheap jewelry and catch-penny trinkets, and small peddlers in produce. Artizans of many trades frequented the creeks far from the larger towns and worked their trades where they had no resident competitors. Blacksmiths, tinners, tinkers, sometimes cobblers and tailors exchanged their services for food and supplies and a little money. In the later years of this period photographers mounted their apparatus in shanty-boats, gaily painted with their advertising, and made a livelihood demonstrating the wonder of picture-taking to the farmers and townsmen along the rivers.

Venders of medicines found the shanty-boat life an ideal one. Their only expense was for bottles. In the woods they found roots, barks, and herbs amply sufficient to give their cure-alls the necessary bad taste and sickening appearance. There was plenty of water in the river. The only other ingredient necessary to their success was talk, and they were full of that. Malaria was prevalent along the river, the people's knowledge of medicine was vague, but their credulity solid and tremendous. They paid well for the medicine-man's talk and a bottle that might contain almost anything; the medicine-man went on to new fields. When he came back it was with another make-up and another bag of tricks, and the people were ready to take another chance on another Latest Discovery of Science or Old Indian Root and Herb Remedy.

Gamblers and lottery operators drifted down the rivers, sometimes by themselves and sometimes with traveling saloons or with boats that carried two or three women from the vice districts of the northern cities, also small shows of a more or less shady sort often traveled by shanty-boat; the good shows going in big theatre-boats, with tow-boats in attendance, and giving to the small river towns the only good make-believe drama they ever saw. Of the real kind there was plenty, and most men carried their own court, judge and jury on their hips or in a holster.

Even preachers fitted up shanty-boats for themselves and their families and drifted down the rivers, holding meetings in tents or in the open air. But not every man who tied up his boat before a little town and exhorted the people to repentance was an honest to God divine. All too frequent were the impostors who shouted for temperance, took up collections for putting down the Demon Rum, and in their idle hours did their best to put down the demon direct from the mouth of the jug. They could be preachers, cheap showmen, medicine-men, or gamblers as occasion invited. Mark Twain's inimitable characters, the Late Dauphin and the Duke of Bilgewater, are not of the boatman-writer's imagination; he took them from the life.

In the later years, after trade was well organized in the river towns, the majority of the shanty-boaters were hoboes, drifters; literally, the floating population. Because of the many farms and villages along the upper Ohio, the Ohio-Lower Mississippi route carried more of these than did the other rivers. In the summers they rented and worked small farms, or got jobs doing any kind of work, skilled or unskilled. Some of them were excellent mechanics who might have done better to stay in one place, but when the autumn was in the air the river called them. They embarked in their drifting craft and followed the season south. Men with families took the families along. Often single men found women

who were glad to travel with them on a lazy voyage
to a southern clime, and at the end of the trip another Cincinnati Sal or Marietta May would be
added to the underworld of New Orleans or Vicksburg or Natchez.

The drifters went their lazy way with the current,
fishing, stealing chickens and pigs, occasionally stopping to work when the stealing was poor. They
stayed in the south till spring, then shipped or bought
deck passage on north-bound steamboats, and hunted
other jobs or other little farms along the upper rivers,
to buy or build new boats in the fall and make the
trip again.

Times changed on the rivers. Hulking flatboats
going down and little keel-boats crawling laboriously
up the streams gave way to the "New Orleans" and
the "Washington" and the early boats that followed
them. The proud packets of the sixties came and
passed, but the shanty-boaters drifted on. It is
only in the last few years that their floating homes
have become almost a thing of the past.

There are few shanty-boats now. Have our people stopped drifting and settled down to steady work
as a highly regulated people should? Look in the
tourist camps and you will find them. A second-
or fifth-hand car costs less than a shanty-boat and
goes anywhere. Camped in their old tents beside
their rusty cars are the one-time shanty-boaters,
surrounded by their ill-assorted baggage and their
swarms of dirty children. Times and methods change
fast, but the people are much the same.

CHAPTER VI

THE UPPER MISSISSIPPI

"It rained so hard de day Ah left, de river here was dry,
Ah thought Ah'd sholy freeze to death; Susanna, don't you cry."

BENDING down from the Ohio, embarking at St. Louis, steamboats, barges, flatboats and keelboats dotted the lower Mississippi every day and night of the first few decades of the nineteenth century; but at that same time the upper stretch of the river, say from Cairo northward to the Falls of St. Anthony, was still in comparative wilderness.

Cairo itself had only two buildings: a log cabin and a warehouse for the keel-boatman's stores. Cape Giradeau, Ste. Genevieve and Herculaneum averaged a dozen families each. Alton, Clarksville and the town of Louisiana were represented by the tiniest clusters of dwellings. Where Quincy now stands was then—this was 1823—one rough cabin where John Woods, later Lieutenant-Governor and acting Governor of Illinois, was clearing land for a farm. At Hannibal the only settler was John S. Miller, a

122

blacksmith, who later moved to Galena where there was a smelting furnace surrounded by a dozen log houses and some frame shanties. The whole town of Canton, Illinois, then called Cottonwood Prairie, was a farm owned by Captain White.

Some hundreds of miles up the river towards the Falls of St. Anthony the water was broken by the pirogues, bateaux and various craft of the keel-boat type manned by the fur traders and steered by the French-Indian pilots on the upper Mississippi, the Wisconsin and the Fox.

But the steamboat was already on the way, bringing civilization with it. On May 10, 1823, Captain Crawford in his "Virginia" went up the uncharted channels of the Mississippi between the banks of Illinois and Iowa, of Wisconsin and Minnesota, through stormy and treacherous Lake Pepin (merely a great widening of the river as it goes into the Minnesota country) to the Falls of St. Anthony which his craft was first of all the steamboats to see. Crawford had no one to tell him the course of the channel, where to steer and where not to steer; for though there had been another steamboat to precede him on the upper reaches of the Mississippi, it had not gone nearly so far. This boat was the "Zebulon M. Pike," built at Henderson, Kentucky, made like a keel-boat, with a low-pressure engine, one boiler only, and uncovered side-wheels, and capable of traveling three and a half miles an hour upstream.

Captain Crawford also made slow progress. But

his trip incidentally hurried the coming of other steamboats which were to make better time and open up a new field for the emigrants who were waiting across the Alleghenies or who, already settled in eastern Ohio or Kentucky, found their lands hemmed in by other settlers and wanted to go farther west.

The "Virginia" offered Daniel Smith Harris, then a boy of 15, who had just come to Galena where he was later to make himself a power in the steamboat world, his first sight of a machine-driven vessel. Harris, with his parents and his four brothers, Robert Scribe Harris, Martin Keller Harris, James Meeker Harris and Jackson Harris, had come to Galena on a keel-boat. The steamboat fascinated him and in it he and his brothers saw their life work.

Soon there were other smoke trails floating over the wild country of the upper Mississippi, following the course made first by the "Virginia." The Harris boys went early to work on a steamboat, the machinery for which they picked up in the junk yards of Cincinnati. And it was this well-assembled junk that drove the "Jo Daviess," first of the long line of steamboats the five brothers built at Galena. Other men, people with more money, saw the great value of the new kind of transportation and had boats built along the Ohio for use on the upper Mississippi.

And what a curious array the captains and pilots who manned and steered those steamboats on the upper Mississippi were! Asa B. Green, captain and owner of the "Equator," wrecked on St. Croix Lake in 1858, was a God-fearing, God-talking Methodist minister; Thomas Cushing, before becoming a pilot, was a well-thought of opera singer in New York; Orrin Smith, Sr., president of the Minnesota Packet company, was so devout a churchman that he refused to run his boat between midnight Saturday and midnight Sunday and forced the crew on the idle vessel to hear Sunday services which, no preacher being obtainable, he delivered himself. Captain William H. Laughton was an Englishman who jumped overboard so often to save people from drowning that he nearly made a profession of it. He saved nine in all and was once given a silver cup and a set of resolutions from his passengers for diving after a little girl who had fallen over the rail. Captain John B. Davis, who had command of a vessel at 19, was a steamboatman who would try anything once. While in command of the "Freighter" he attempted to cross the flooded land between Big Stone Lake and the Red River of the North and was grounded on the prairie and wrecked about ten miles from the lake. Another was pilot David Tipton, who began on a keel-boat in 1820, soon went into steamboat piloting which he continued until, at the age of 84, he dropped dead at his wheel.

Titled blood was not uncommon among these boatmen. Count Ageston Haraszthy, a political refugee, owned and commanded the "Rock River" which ran between St. Louis and Mendota, Minnesota. Robert

C. Eden, younger son of an English baronet, bought an 80-ton sidewheeler called the "Enterprise" and, filling her cabin with books, cruised about on the Mississippi, Wisconsin, St. Croix and Fox Rivers. He dressed roughly and was known to the rivermen as Bob, captained his own boat, but had a pilot, deck hand and engineer, the latter being George Byron Merrick who wrote an account of his river life. During the Civil War Eden served as major in the Thirty-seventh Wisconsin Infantry and after the struggle ended returned to England and entered the ministry.

A captain of one of those boats was a devotee of prize fighting, and pulled the "Kate Cassell" into a woodyard near Hastings, Minnesota, to allow his pilot, J. B. McCoy, to fight out a quarrel with a St. Louis freight handler named Parker. Here a ring was roped off, seconds chosen and bottle holders and sponge bearers supplied from the crew and passengers. It was a hot and heavy slugging match and an enjoyable diversion to the passengers. There is no report that any one was shocked; on the contrary there was general regret that the captain, his sense of business getting the better of him, pulled the bell for departure before a knockout.

Commodore Davidson, one of the biggest boat owners on the upper Mississippi, was another of the pious but strong-armed captains. No gambling or dancing or other public diversions unsanctioned by Methodists were permitted on his boats. However,

SCENERY OF THE UPPER MISSISSIPPI

Captain Laughton, commanding the commodore's "Alexander Mitchell," was made of more earthy material and on a certain Sunday he allowed a few of his passengers to engage in the Virginia Reel. They danced until late under the brilliant chandeliers of the cabin, and then went to bed, not feeling any immediate effects of heavenly wrath upon their sin. The boat kept on going down the river. It seemed as if they were to escape punishment.

But they weren't. At three o'clock the next morning a tornado screamed its way over the land and swooped down on the "Alexander Mitchell." Both chimneys were ripped off, the roof of the pilot house sailed upward and onward, followed by part of the hurricane deck on the port side. Trudall, the mate, was standing by the boat's bell when the twister struck. It passed on, taking Trudall with it, blowing him a full quarter of a mile to the shore where it neatly dropped him.

"You see," said the commodore sternly, "that's what comes of dancing."

A strange bunch. And adorning their steamboats just as strangely! Captains painted their paddle boxes with the name of their boat on the background of a brilliant sunburst; with grey eagles, golden eagles, black eagles, war eagles and spread eagles; the "Minnesota's" paddle box carried the state's coat of arms; the "Minnesota Belle" had the picture of a corn-fed maid with a bundle of wheat and a reaping hook; the "Northern Belle" also had a buxom female on the paddle box; the "General Brooke" and "Phil Sheridan" carried enormous portraits of their namesakes, and so forth, list without end. Others had their cabins blazing with lurid paintings, many of which were symbolic warnings to travelers against strong drink.

And their music! Brass bands for the big boats, cornets and orchestras for the smaller ones. Ned Kendall's cornet, it was said, could make any boat popular. Then there were the harmonious-souled negroes. Shipping as waiters, barbers, porters and deck hands they played stringed instruments and sang as only they could play and sing those haunting, joyfully-sad melodies and hymns. The "Excelsior" appeared with a calliope, the first on the upper Mississippi to have one of those—well, a steam calliope has always been a steam calliope. Other boats followed the example of the "Excelsior" but they were never very popular with the grownup travelers, although the children came, as now, from miles around to hear them.

Yes, a curious lot. An editor of the *Prescott Paraclete* wrote severely: "The river (upper Mississippi) is navigated, with but few exceptions, by a class of low-bred, ungentlemanly, and sometimes ruffianly vagabonds, who seldom, if ever, treat a person with as much respect as a well-bred hound deserves. This we know from personal observation on the best boats of the river." And Captain Charles J. Allen, Corps of Engineers, U. S. A., included in a report for a

River Improvement Association the statement that "Most of the river pilots are possessed of but little knowledge beyond that required in turning a wheel."

Poor ignorant pilots! All they knew was every bar and rock and snag in the river, every landmark on the bank, and how to take their boats to their destinations through wind and water and pitch-black night! And they knew perhaps a little of human nature from the many people they had steered through every kind of weather, and a little of the world from the strange places they had seen: cosmopolitan New Orleans, the thronged levees of St. Louis, from the wild-cat money swindlers and the land booms such as the one at Nininger, Minnesota, where one man, the only one in town, printed a fake newspaper with pictures, social notes and news of the supposed town and thus leading the emigrants still in the east to pay large sums for lots on the wild banks of the Mississippi. And they knew the Indians, too, these pilots.

From the time of the first steamboat on the upper river until every Indian in the adjacent states was in the white man's power, steamboats carried troops and supplies for campaigns against the red men, and sometimes took part in the fighting. The engagement that finally drove the Sac Indians from the land east of the Mississippi was the battle of Bad Axe, fought on the Wisconsin bank of the river August 2, 1832.

The Sacs, dissatisfied with the country to the west,

had crossed to the east bank to raise a crop. The fact that they brought their women and baggage with them tends to show that they came peacefully and not as a war-party. But the settlers, and probably the land-grabbers, were alarmed. They appealed to the Government, and three thousand militia were sent to expel the Sacs.

As the troops neared the Indian camp, a scouting party of about fifty men disobeyed orders and went too far from the main column. They encountered six or eight Sacs who were going peaceably about their business and fired on them. One or two of the Indians were killed. The scouting party captured three and chased the others to their camp. Black Hawk, chief of the Indians, was angry at the slaughter of his people. If the white man brought war, war it should be. He sent out a party of warriors that killed twelve of the scouts and sent the others back to their comrades as fast as they could travel.

The Indians broke camp and fled north. The troops overtook them on the bank as they were about to cross—the steamboat "Warrior" was in the service of the army, carrying troops, supplies, and cannon. She steamed into the river before the Sacs as the column drew in behind them. She fired with cannon into the massed crowd of Indian men, women, and children, and followed with musketry. The troops closed in behind. The Indians abandoned all resistance and did their best to escape across the river.

Few escaped the fire of troops and boat. The little remnant of the band that managed to get across the stream was followed and massacred by a party of Sioux. These Sioux had at first refused to help the white men fight the Sacs, but at the last moment they offered their help and it was accepted. They carried a United States flag and their leader wore an army uniform furnished by an army officer.

In this way was a piece of land won for the white man's farms and towns and booms. Seldom have troops and steamboats been used in ways less creditable to the white man's civilization.

More than thirty years later, the white man's lust for land was not yet satisfied. In May, 1863, Winnebago Indians numbering 1,856 were removed from Blue Earth County to their new reservation in Nebraska, westward before the white man's march.

On May 8 eleven hundred of the Winnebagos were camped on the river bank at Mankato. A few days before, their warriors had killed two Sioux, and the scalps of the victims, stretched on hoops and decorated with ribbons, were mounted on poles in the center of the camp. In the afternoon the Indians paraded the streets of the town, carrying these trophies. All that night the tom-toms beat while the warriors danced their last scalp-dance before their long journey.

The next day 405 of the Indians were put aboard the steamboat "Pomeroy" and 355 aboard the "Eolian." On the hurricane deck of the "Pomeroy" they set up their scalp poles. About them stood twenty young warriors, half-naked, painted, their heads bound with green wreaths. Other warriors were grouped around them, all chanting in time to the measured beat of the tom-tom. At two o'clock in the afternoon the boom of the boats' whistle cut through the sound of the chant and the war-drums. The white men's fire canoes beat the water, but over the thresh of the paddles rose the beat of the leather drums and the voices of the warriors. "He-ah! He-ah!" they chanted as the boats turned and headed down-stream on the road over which their unwilling passengers could never return. The Indians were leaving their homes because they could not hold them, but they were leaving defiantly, grouped about the scalps that were not yet dry, singing their parting song to the land they were not to see again.

The next day, May 10, the "Favorite" took away 338 more of the Winnebagos, and on the fourteenth another boat took the last of them.

On April 22 a party of 270 condemned Sioux had been taken from the Mankato prison to Davenport, Iowa. A party of acquitted Indians and some squaws who had been serving as cooks went with them. They took their leave of Mankato in a way far different from the savage good-bye of the Winnebagos, a way perhaps more pleasing to the unreflecting of their white conquerors. During the winter these Sioux had been converted to Christianity by the missionaries Williamson, Riggs, and Pond. As the boat took them away they sang, in the Sioux tongue, hymns to the white man's God. Passing Fort Snelling, where their squaws and children were imprisoned, they sang to the tune of Old Hundred their favorite hymn, "Have Mercy Upon Us, O Jehovah."

Doubtless the Christian religion was good for the souls of the Sioux, and their prayers for mercy were answered by the God whose white children so strangely lacked that quality. But who can help admiring the barbaric departure of the Winnebagos, going out with their war-trophies displayed above them, Indians to the last? He-ah! He-ah! Red men cannot be white. And why should they want to be?

Steamboats on the upper Mississippi did service in the Civil War as well as in wars against the Indians. Early in the spring of 1861 the "Fanny Harris," under Government charter, went up the Minnesota River to Fort Ridgely and brought to St. Paul the Buena Vista Battery of light artillery on its way to become famous as the Sherman Battery and later in the Army of the Potomac as Ayres' Battery. At the time of the trip it was under the command of Brevet Major John C. Pemberton.

From St. Paul to Fort Ridgely is about a hundred and fifty miles in a straight line, but about three hundred by the twisting river. When the trip was made the Minnesota was flooded over her banks; carrying a nineteen foot rise from the especially heavy snows which had melted, she was like a torrent in the channel and like a still lake outside it. And it was through that watery scene that the old stern wheeler was headed, three hundred miles of bucking cross-channel currents that threw her against the trees that lined the stream and held her there until some one set out with a line in the yawl and made it fast on the opposite bank, enabling her to drag free by the power of her capstan.

The Army officer aboard with the order for the battery to move kept urging speed at all costs, and the crew, excited at the prospect of war, did all they could to oblige him. Even as the upperworks of the "Fanny Harris" smashed ahead among the branches of the trees, the officer kept hectically repeating, "Never mind that! Never mind that! The Government of the United States will put a new cabin on your boat. Just keep your wheel turning and your machinery in shape. We've got to have troops in Washington at once or we won't have any more country than a jack-rabbit."

And the old "Fanny Harris" lumbered crashingly ahead from dawn till dark. For, in spite of the demand for speed, they couldn't navigate at night. And these hours while the boat was tied up were used by the crew to mend her battered places. By the light of torches men from the engine room got out on the wheels to mend the broken arms and buckets, clinging desperately to keep their footing above the rushing black current. At dawn she would be ready to repeat her trip of the day before.

But no progress was swift enough for the business at hand. Near Belle Plain it was decided by the heads aboard to cut across the bend, run ten miles over the flooded prairie and thus avoid twenty miles of bad river. Up in the pilot house the signal was given, and down on the main deck the engineers responded. Gathering steam the "Fanny Harris" rammed viciously at the fringe of trees that bordered the channel, lying between her and the open, flooded fields. Too long to be pointed directly at them, she was obliged to make her charge at an angle. There was an awful cracking, a moment of suspense, then she vaulted up, bending over and breaking trees that were six inches thick until the resilient trunks slipped off her guards and closed tightly on her wheel, tearing off a dozen arms and a dozen buckets before the pilots could ring the engineer to shut off the power, and stop the revolving wheel.

It looked as if the "Fanny Harris" was doomed to stay there a while, notwithstanding the need of federal troops in Washington, the Army officer's anguish or the cursing of the crew.

Engineers shouted, "There! I seen it comin'! Why didn't you give the order to close the throttle!" This to the pilot.

And the captain, cracking his big knuckles: "God A'mighty! God A'mighty!"

And the aloof, a little condescending pilot: "Thunderation! Carry the anchor ahead and drop her. We'll pull her out of the trap by the capstan."

All hands went furiously to work. She yielded, slid back, and the wheel was swiftly repaired. She had slipped back into the channel in a way that gave her a chance to buck the trees with a direct spurt.

"Try her ag'in," was sung out. The pilot began jangling his bells, the engineers bent over their engines and just as the "Fanny Harris" slithered up the wet, springy trunks the bell rang again from the pilot house and the wheel was stopped before the trees whipped against it. And now she was pointed across the free, open water that covered the prairie.

Four days after she left St. Paul the "Fanny Harris" ran out her landing stages at Fort Ridgely.

Pony couriers had brought word of the coming of the boat, and the battery was ready to be loaded aboard when she got there. All that day and night the artillerymen rolled their guns and carried their equipment on deck while the boat's crew sweated to get all repairs made in time for an early start.

Next morning they started out with the heavy and important cargo, again bucking the cross-currents, riding over trees, smashing branches while the boilers sizzled. Two days later they came into the Mississippi at the green, open plain of Fort Snelling, the end of the "Fanny Harris" journey. One of her chimneys was broken off ten feet above the deck, and there were only thirteen feet of pipe left on the other. Her upper works were hopelessly wrecked, but the hull was sound in spite of the battering it had received.

That was long ago, when the Minnesota was still navigable. Since then there has been such cultivation of its basin—begun by those people whom the steamboats brought—that the water which formerly flowed into its bed now evaporates. But in 1862 there were 413 boat arrivals in St. Paul from the Minnesota River.

CHAPTER VII

THE MISSOURI

"Oh, when Uncle Henry was a little tiny boy
A-sittin' on his daddy's knee,
Says: 'If I ever grow up to be a man,
A steamboat man I want to be.'"

BIG MUDDY THE LAST TO YIELD TO STEAMBOATS—DIFFICULTIES OF
NAVIGATING THIS RIVER—STEAMBOATS IN THE FUR TRADE—
JOSEPH LA BARGE—EARLY BOOTLEGGERS—SWINDLING THE
INDIANS—INDIAN ATTACKS—MAKING THE FUR FLY—GOLD—
GUERILLAS OF THE CIVIL WAR—THE END OF THE RAINBOW.

FOR years after the Ohio and the lower Mississippi had become a charted and scheduled trade route and the upper Mississippi a frequented stream, the settlements along the lower Missouri, the Big Muddy, were the last outposts of civilization, and the upper Missouri was almost a river of mystery. A few white explorers had seen its banks and given their reports to a world that apparently cared little about a region so remote. Other than these, the only people who knew the river's course were the Indians and the fur traders.

The Missouri is formed at Gallatin City, Montana, by the confluence of the Gallatin, Madison, and Jefferson Forks. The real upper section of the Missouri is the Jefferson Fork, known in its middle course as Beaver Head River and in its upper course as Red Rock Creek. This stream rises near the

138

crest of the Rocky Mountains, eight thousand feet above the sea, 398 miles beyond the forks, at a point on the boundary between Montana and Idaho. The Jefferson Fork, the Missouri, and the lower Mississippi form a channel 4,221 miles long from source to Gulf, the longest continuous channel in the world. The length of the Missouri from the Forks to the mouth, twenty miles above St. Louis, is 2,547 miles.

The first steamboat to ply the Missouri was the "Independence." In 1819 this boat ran from St. Louis to the mouth of the Chariton and back, shortly before the "Western Engineer," beginning the numerous governmental exploring expeditions, went up as far as Council Bluffs.

Steam navigation on the Missouri began, as on the other rivers, with boats of the deep draft type; they were particularly unsuited to the Big Muddy. The typical early Missouri boat had side wheels driven by a single engine with a heavy flywheel; machinery was forward of the wheels, freight and passengers carried aft, while the landing stages were astern. The crew's quarters were in the hold. The early boats were built with keels and drew six feet of water with the same loads that in later boats required only three feet. The first "Yellowstone," built in 1830-31, was 130 feet long, 19 feet in the beam, and 6 feet in depth of hold. She drew 4½ feet light, and 5½ feet when carrying a load of 75 tons. She had one engine, two chimneys, and one rudder. Her wheels were 18 feet in diameter with

6-foot buckets. The main cabin was aft on the main deck, and the ladies' cabin was in the after-hold. Her boiler deck was open.

The later boats on the Missouri were a tremendous improvement. Flat bottomed, about 220 feet long by 35 feet beam, with a carrying capacity of about 500 tons, they drew only about 30 inches light and 50 inches loaded. They were propelled by stern wheels, which were found advantageous in the narrow upper stretches of the river and in navigating at low water when the whole river often flowed in a channel not much wider than the boat. They carried two engines astern, direct connected to the wheel, fed by boilers forward. Multiple balanced rudders gave them the necessary ease of handling. Forecastles were equipped with steam capstans and hoists and the heavy spars used to push the boats off sand bars. In the holds were trams for handling cargo. Passenger accommodations were good, although not so luxurious as those on the smart packets of the lower Mississippi.

The Missouri, carrying its heavy load of mud, was the most changeable of the rivers. Sand bars formed over night. At every trip the channel was new. There were two regular floods, one in April from the melting snow in the river valleys, and a higher but more gradual rise in June when the snow streams ran down from the mountains. Cut-offs were frequent, banks were torn away and built up with astonishing rapidity. Once, in digging a well on river-built land, the diggers found a Bible lettered with the name of a boat wrecked at the spot a few years before. In cutting away its banks the river carried down so many trees that the snags sometimes made the channel almost impassable. About seventy per cent of steamboat wrecks on the Missouri were due to snags. But strangely enough, night navigation on the Missouri was easier than on the Mississippi—the Missouri at night looked clear and whitish and was easy for a pilot to read, while the Mississippi was like tar.

Grounding was frequent in the shallow, changing channels. Sometimes the boats, flat and flexible as they were, wormed their way over bars like eels. Sometimes a pilot whose boat was stuck on a bar would reverse his wheel, not to back off, but to force water under the boat. The moment he felt her lift he turned the wheel ahead and shot the boat forward. When this was unavailing he sparred the boat off. Heavy timbers shod with iron and rigged with pulleys, the spars were swung over the sides by the derricks on the forecastle and set on the bottom; then, by the power of capstan and tackle, they were driven downward and backward much as setting-poles are worked by hand. But in addition to the forward push of hand-worked poles, the spars had lifting power that could raise the boat off the bottom while the wheel forced it ahead. Sometimes in the swift current warping was necessary. A timber a little smaller than a railroad tie, called a "dead man," was carried ahead of the boat and buried on the bank, with stakes to hold it in place. From this timber a line was taken to the capstan of the boat, and she dragged herself over the bottom by winding up the line.

More than in the other rivers, the swift currents and changing banks of the Missouri produce whirlpools, sometimes of monstrous size and power. In 1867 the "Bishop" was swamped by a whirlpool formed by a cut-off. About the same time the "Miner" was nearly wrecked below Sioux City in a whirlpool of such violence that the center of the eddy was twelve feet below the level of the river. The "Miner" was warping when the whirl caught her and swept her into the stream, throwing her almost on her side. Water surged across her deck. Two men were washed overboard and instantly sucked down in the spinning vortex of the pool. Only by herculean efforts did the crew get the boat out of danger.

The first important use of steamboats on the Missouri was in the fur trade, and this business furnished the principal business of steamboats until about 1850. The first regular packet, the "W. D. Duncan," began making regular trips from St. Louis as far as Fort Leavenworth in 1829. But above this point the American Fur Company used keel-boats. With these craft they had endless delays, difficulties, and high costs. A whole summer was required to reach the extreme northern posts, and often the ice

From an old Currier & Ives print in the collection of Karl Schmidt, Esq.

"HIGH WATER" ON THE MISSISSIPPI

closed in before they got there. Large crews were needed for small cargoes, and the men all had to be brought back. Headed by William B. Astor but practically under the control of John Jacob Astor, the fur company was represented at St. Louis by Bernard Pratte & Company. In 1830 they determined upon the use of steamboats.

Their first boat was the "Yellowstone," built at a cost of about seven thousand dollars, with spare parts and a blacksmithing outfit amounting to another thousand. The "Yellowstone" began her first trip in the spring of 1831, but was caught by low water above the mouth of the Niobrara, and the cargo was lightered to get her off. That fall she reached Fort Tecumseh, later Fort Pierre. In the spring of the next year she plodded into Fort Union. Her voyage, though slow and troublesome, was considered successful. Even so she did better than the keel-boats.

The following spring the fur company sent up the "Yellowstone" and the "Assiniboine." The "Assiniboine" ventured above Fort Union and was caught by low water. Winter set in before she could free herself and she remained there until the next spring.

On this trip the "Assiniboine" reached a point near the mouth of Poplar River. In 1853 the "El Paso" went 125 miles farther up, to a point above the mouth of Milk River. On July 17, 1859, the "Chippewa" came within fifteen miles of Fort Benton. This was considered a remarkable voyage at the time. The boat had reached a point 3560 miles from the sea, 2565 feet above sea level, all the way by steam on an unimproved river. In the following year both the "Chippewa" and the "Key West" beat the record by making Fort Benton. The "Chippewa" burned in 1861, a little below the mouth of Milk River, at a place called Disaster Bend. Some deck hands went into the hold to steal whiskey, and set fire to the cargo through carelessness with the candles they carried. No lives were lost. After the passengers were put ashore the burning boat was set adrift, and in a short time some gunpowder in her hold exploded, tearing her to pieces.

Fort Benton remained for all practical purposes the head of Missouri River navigation. On high water in 1866 the "Peter Balen" steamed 31 miles above Fort Benton, to within six miles of the Great Falls. On this same flood the "Tom Stevens" and the "Gallatin" are said to have gone a mile or more farther. Above the Falls the river is navigable to the Three Forks.

That was the navigable course of the Missouri: from St. Louis way up to Fort Benton, through new, unsettled land peopled mostly by the hostile Indians who had been driven by the white man's musket from the land farther east. And of all the steamboatmen who helped tame this last wild stretch none was better known or more highly regarded than Joseph LaBarge, pilot, captain and owner, who spent virtually his whole life on the river.

LaBarge was a man of resource and probity, a jaunty, soft-voiced Frenchman who mingled good sense with his lack of fear,—a representative type of steamboatman of those days. The year of the great flood on the Big Muddy, 1844, found him as pilot of the "Nimrod," one of the American Fur company's boats. Over the bottoms near St. Louis the river was so spread out beyond its bed that the sheet of yellow water was like a sea. The channel was no more; it had been completely filled up, and new courses had been cut by the swift, ever-changing currents. Nevertheless LaBarge picked his way safely back to St. Louis and, undaunted by the disappearance of the wharves, which were under water, ran the "Nimrod" straight up Washington Avenue to Commercial Alley and made her fast through the window of the J. F. Walsh warehouse that stood on the corner.

Returning up the river in that year the "Nimrod" carried a quantity of liquor, which was forbidden in the Indian territory. Sharp watches were kept by the government agents to see that none got through. One of these agents, Joseph Miller, one time Methodist preacher, and now stationed at Bellevue, boasted that no whiskey had ever got past him. And he did his best to carry out his boast. Each ship that came up as far as Bellevue was carefully inspected. Miller rummaged through the passing boats from one end to the other, snooping like a terrier after a rat. He broke open packages of merchandise, overturned piles of freight and probed bales of blankets and clothing with the slender, pointed rod which he had made for that very purpose.

The "Nimrod," pushing up towards Bellevue, had its quantity of liquor stored in flour barrels, innocent looking objects consigned to Peter A. Sarpy, the company's agent at Bellevue. The flour barrels were well forward on the main deck, and the moment the boat landed they were rolled ashore to the company's warehouse.

The last barrel had disappeared into the warehouse when Miller came down to inspect the boat. He searched from stem to stern, from hull to pilot house, but he found no liquor. "H-m-mm!" said Miller and tightened his thin lips. His was a suspicious nature, and the fact that the boat remained tied up at the wharf aroused it. So, posting a man to watch and give him warning if he saw anything that looked like it contained whiskey, he went to his office.

LaBarge waited till after midnight. Then he broke out the deck hands and ordered them to spread thick tarpaulin over the forecastle and gangway. "Now bring those barrels aboard," said LaBarge, and the roustabouts muttered, wondering why the freight had to be reloaded.

"Can't you see!" said one of the brighter deck hands to the others, "All them barrels is marked P. A. S.? That means they got to pass."

The barrels were rolled aboard, their sound deadened by the thick tarpaulin. But there was a noise as the last barrel came over the gangway and the guard posted by Miller, being also of a suspicious nature, blew his whistle for the inspector.

"Get aboard! The line has parted!" called La-Barge sharply to the workers, and cut the mooring line as he said it. The boat began to drift. But not for long. Steam was up in the engine room and a tap from the pilot's bell caused the paddlewheels to turn, and the "Nimrod" swept out into the channel.

Miller arrived on hot feet, but too late. A queer sight! Now he was positive there was liquor aboard the "Nimrod." If the line had parted by accident, as LaBarge had said, why then did the engineer have steam up? It was a piece of trickery, he was sure. And when he looked in the warehouse and by the light of a torch saw that the flour barrels were gone he was more sure. It was a case for the Federal authorities.

For a while there were threats of cancelling the license of the fur company to trade. But the United States attorney would not bring suit on the company's bond without the testimony of LaBarge. And somehow LaBarge could never be found. He stayed away from the sight of the law until the case was finally compromised through the efforts of Thomas H. Benton.

It was on this trip that a storm, striking above Bellevue, lifted the roof of the pilot house from over LaBarge's head and took it sailing over the land. But LaBarge wasn't going to remain without shelter.

He had some of the buffalo hides, which beasts served as meat for crew and passengers of many of the boats of the Missouri, sewn together and stretched over the place where the roof had been. On another occasion LaBarge made cylinders of buffalo hide to replace the chimneys that had not been carried away by a thoughtless tornado.

LaBarge didn't always, however, get the better of the shaggy bison. There was the time at Handy's Point when the men aboard the "Nimrod," hard up for meat, saw four buffalo swimming across the river.

"Get out the yawl," ordered Captain LaBarge, and the yawl went out with himself in the stern and John Durack, the mate, an Englishman who had served in the British Navy, in the bow; Durack had a lasso which he was to throw around the head of one of the beasts as soon as it was shot by the rifleman on deck. The shots were fired and the yellow water grew pink with blood. Durack uncoiled the lariat and swung it out. But instead of falling over the head of the wounded animal it settled about the powerful neck of one that had been untouched. There was a snort. The yawl leaped forward, propelled by an angry bull who swam to a sandbar and then, on firm footing, yanked so hard at the rope that he pulled the stem out of the yawl and thundered over the prairie, trailing the rope and stem with him.

Once an inexperienced but somewhat cocksure traveler was walking the deck with LaBarge as the boat approached a town. "Captain," asked the traveler, "what town is this?"

"This, sir, is Independence," answered the captain. The traveler consulted a map he carried, prepared by more or less reliable geographers for sale to emigrants, and watched with interest the landing of the boat.

Some time later they approached another town. "Captain," asked the traveler, "what town is this we are coming to?"

"This is Westport," answered the captain.

The traveler examined his map. "Captain," he said, "are you sure you are right about these towns? This map says Westport is below Independence, and we are going up. Are you sure that wasn't Westport we passed, and this is Independence?"

"I have navigate' this river a long time," said LaBarge. "Ever since there been towns, that one been Independence and this one Westport." And the captain walked away to attend to the business of landing. But he could not forget the reflection on his knowledge of river geography.

Some days later the boat encountered a great flock of wild geese. The traveler with the map came running to the captain. "Captain," he cried, "what are those big birds?"

The captain glared. "Look at you' damn map," he answered. "Maybe he tell you!"

In 1847 LaBarge took the "Martha," owned by

the American Fur company, up the Missouri with the annuities given the Indians by the government on board beside the regular freight. These annuities, consisting of food, clothing and other trade goods, were a source of profit to the fur company's agents. For those rascals, after scaring the Indian agents by tales of massacre, had them place themselves under their protection and thus got to handle the government business, making the Indians come to the fur company with their furs to get the annuities which belonged to them.

There was naturally trouble, and at Crow Creek, where the fur company had a post in charge of Colin Campbell, the "Martha" encountered a band of Yankton Sioux who were bent on having their annuities at once and from the Indian agent himself.

The government agent aboard was a new man at his job and didn't know what to do. The company agent was an old-timer and knew the usual course, which was to unload the annuities at Fort Pierre and let the Indians go there for them. He told this to the government agent; but as the Indians had a certain warlike countenance the government agent compromised. "If I give them a good lavish meal and part of their annuities they'll be satisfied," he thought, "and then I can take the remainder of the goods on up to Fort Pierre."

This was done. The Indians, who had been cutting wood for the steamboat during the harangue, put down their axes and came aboard to partake of the feast. Food was laid out and they ate it. Then a part of their goods was given them. However, they were not to be tricked. They wanted all of what was coming to them.

"No," said the government agent. "Go to Fort Pierre. Goods at Fort Pierre. No goods here." And he made motions for them to clear out.

The Indians shuffled off the boat, muttering. Meanwhile Etienne Provost, one of the ship's officers, had sent the crew ashore for the wood. The disgruntled Indians met the crew. There were a few words and then sticks began to fly as the Indians belabored the boatmen, forcing them back to their vessel.

Provost, a daring, strapping riverman, stood by the gangplank and laughed as the men scurried for the deck. "You run from Indians!" he scolded them. "Etienne Provost, he not afraid! Come," and stepping jauntily down the plank Provost went ashore, his crew following.

"You not fight wit' Etienne Provost!" said the boatman as if in surprise. "You afraid?" And the Indians backed away, grunting assent.

While Provost stood there, laughing as if he were amused greatly at the ridiculous notion of Indians being able to fight, the crew gathered up the wood and carried it to the boat. When the last stick had been loaded, Provost slowly turned his burly shoulders to the watching Indians and went aboard.

As he stepped on deck a Sioux lifted a rifle, and

a deck hand dropped dead on the forecastle even before the puff of white smoke from the Indian's gun was seen. The sight of the white man wriggling on his back exhilarated the Indians. They rushed the enemy, overrunning the forward part of the steamboat.

Standing beside Campbell as the Indians came over LaBarge asked, "What they want, these Indians?"

Campbell knew well enough. He answered, "They want this boat, and it looks like they're going to try to get it."

"So!" said LaBarge and called to a deckhand. "Breeng up that cannon."

The Indians, after boarding, stood uncertainly, fearing surprise in the unknown parts of the boat. Their pause gave Nathan Grismore, the engineer, time to hoist the cannon into the after end of the cabin. It was loaded with boiler rivets.

As the Indians began a menacing advance LaBarge took his lighted cigar from his mouth and moved it steadily towards the cannon's vent.

It was all that was needed. The Indians wheeled and dashed for the gangplank, stumbling, falling in their hurry to get away from the cannon's mouth.

LaBarge ordered the cannon up on the hurricane deck. And those of the crew who were not in the water, clinging to the boat's paddles, responded. With the threat of the muzzle before them the Indians held off while the engineer got up enough steam to move the boat out into and up the channel.

On a later trip made up the Missouri by LaBarge with annuities for the Indians the same trouble occurred. This time LaBarge had his own boat, the "Shreveport," and another, the "Robert Campbell," which he had chartered, and on which he traveled as commander. The annuities he carried were for the Sioux, Crows, Black Feet and Assiniboines and amounted to about $10,000. Besides these government stores there were freight and a large number of passengers, which included Samuel M. Latta, agent for the Sioux, Crows and Mandans; Henry W. Reed, agent for the Blackfeet; Henry A. Boller, author of "Among the Indians," and Alexander Culbertson with his Blackfoot wife.

The journey, made at low water, was painfully long, and the two ships were constantly moving through a country where the Indians only held off from shooting them because they knew their goods were on the way. At Fort Pierre LaBarge found several bands of Sioux encamped, waiting for the annuities. And near by were the wigwams of the infuriated Two Kettles band which had just seen eight of their number shot down by soldiers near Fort Randall.

The Indians met the boat and there was a parley. It ended in about two-thirds of the Indians' goods being given to them. Discovering the fraud, they appealed to Captain LaBarge, but he could do nothing for them. The parley became a wrangle and when the boat moved off the Indians were thinking of vengeance.

They followed the "Campbell" for six hundred miles, from Fort Pierre to Fort Union, shooting at every chance. Each time the boat stopped alongside a woodpile to load up fuel there were Indians in hiding who jumped out and attacked with spears, arrows and rifles. On the "Campbell" the harried crew and passengers barricaded the sides of the boat by piling up the cargo.

In spite of this continuous danger, Louis Dauphin, whose rifle supplied meat for the two boats, slipped to the bank and went in search of game whenever the supply was low; and each time he was put ashore the crew and passengers doubted he would come back. One day when LaBarge was standing on the forecastle he saw a hat ahead, apparently floating upright on the river. And turning away he said to the mate, "We will be hong-gree to-night. For is not that Louis Dauphin's hat?"

The mate's eyes followed the captain's pointing finger. He looked long and carefully at the headpiece drifting towards them. "Blamed if it ain't," he admitted. "I figured he'd go out once too often."

But even as he looked the headgear came nearer to the boat and beneath the wide, greasy brim was the face of the hunter. And as Dauphin crawled aboard he explained why he had returned thus and empty-handed.

Some Indians, perhaps as many as a thousand or more, were camped near Tobacco Garden. They were gathered to capture the boat. Louis Dauphin had discovered that much—for he had been playing scout—before one of the bands which had been following the "Campbell" saw him and made him take to flight.

As Dauphin gave him this news LeBarge nodded slowly, frowning. He knew the place where the Indians were encamped. Not far off, Tobacco Garden was the bottom land at the outlet of Tobacco Creek, and a bad place for an attack. Tobacco Garden itself was on the north bank of the river, 88 miles below the Yellowstone. But near by on the opposite bank the lowlands were covered with great trees, growing close to the caving bank. There was a narrow beach below, and the channel ran so close to the bank that a boat would have to come within 100 feet of shore—easy firing distance. And sixty yards beyond was a sandbar. Though it would probably mean a fight, there was nothing to do but go on.

The two boats were supplied with meat that night by a band of Grosventre Indians, and went on. But a party of Sioux found out that the Grosventres had sold the meat to the boatmen and furiously attacked their fellow redskins, driving them across the river. The steamboats went on.

It was about noon the day they came into sight of Tobacco Garden, and from a distance they could see a large body of Indians encamped in the bottoms opposite. LaBarge knew there was no way of getting past without stopping, unless he wanted to run the risk of having a good portion of crew and passengers killed by Indian bullets and spears.

The boats slowed down and LaBarge gave the order to moor to the sandbar. The "Robert Campbell" was about a hundred yards ahead of the "Shreveport."

At once the Indians demanded the balance of their annuities. That was all they wanted, they said. Just give them what was theirs and they would go away. Otherwise—well, events would have to come about.

Captain LaBarge told Latta what they were up against. But Latta refused to give them their goods. "You send a yawl over to the bank, captain, and have a couple of the chiefs brought aboard. All we need is a little diplomacy. We'll give the chiefs some presents, that's all they want. Then they'll go back and quiet the rest of the Indians."

LaBarge jerked his shoulders angrily. No, he wouldn't order out the yawl and take the chance of having a part of his crew killed in order that Latta could continue the swindle. But if any of the crew volunteered for service, that was another matter.

A crew did volunteer. At first Latta was to go along, but when he found that the yawl was actually to put out across the water to the bank lined with warriors he went down to his cabin and sent word that he was sick, but that the yawl should go ahead.

Manned by seven boatmen, with Andy Stinger at the steering oar the yawl pushed off towards the bank where a chief and three braves, a little ahead of the others, stood ready to welcome them. One had a rifle, two had spears.

The yawl reached the bank and swung around with the current, exposing its side to the waiting Indians. The two with spears leaped suddenly and lunged out. Stinger jumped out on the river side and began tugging at the yawl. The two men in the bow lay flat on their bellies.

Both spears sank mortally into boatmen; a third went down with an arrow fired from the bank in his throat, before Stinger got the yawl into deep water. The two braves, not daring to follow in the yawl, jumped out. Swimming, Stinger pulled the yawl to the middle of the stream. There, he climbed over the side and with the three others that were unhurt rowed to the sandbar where the steamboat waited, ready to spurt ahead. At the sandbar the three unwounded men jumped out and ran for the boat, leaving Stinger with the three dead. He started to curse as the two howitzers from the hurricane deck of the "Campbell" and the one from the "Shreveport" belched out their lead at the Indians. He kept on cursing as the Indians fled under the shot. He was cursing even after the red men were out of sight.

"Those three—*)('&—%‡"?@¢ hounds" to go

off and leave him to bring in the yawl with the dead men! "The blank-blanked-star-dashed-hyphenated-parenthetical!" He used some boatman's language that would singe the ears.

The howitzer fire had killed 18 and wounded about 50 men besides destroying 20 horses, Pierre Garreau, interpreter at Fort Berthold, informed Captain La-Barge days later when the "Robert Campbell" and the "Shreveport" landed at the fort after burying the three victims to white man's greed opposite the mouth of Little Muddy Creek.

First it was furs, then annuities to Indians, then Mormons (whom the steamboats carried most of the way when that sect was driven into Utah), then the Mexican War which brought the Missouri River traffic and the settling of the far west. Expeditions for the conquest of New Mexico and California set out from Fort Leavenworth, Fort Kearney, St. Joseph and other river points; and troops and supplies came up the river to Westport, now Kansas City, and the forts and traveled overland from there.

Then it was gold in California, gold in Colorado, gold in Montana; war—and at last a peaceful emigration. When the Forty-niners began the rush that changed California from a quiet Spanish colony of herdsmen to a land of gold-mad men from every part of the world, the steamboats brought the gold-seekers from every part of the country. Down the Ohio they came, from the farms and shops of the east; up the Mississippi from New Orleans; down from St.

Paul,—all to St. Louis and up the Missouri to Westport, Leavenworth, Fort Kearney, Omaha and other points, thence to set out on the long journey overland. And by 1854 the California fields swarmed with fortune hunters. The peopling of the far west continuing to spread, trade and travel for the country west of the Rockies continued to flow up the Missouri to the mouth of the Kansas, boats leaving St. Louis daily with emigrants and freight.

Colorado was filling up with men who had come for the precious ore found in Pike's Peak when James and Granville Stuart made discoveries in Deer Lodge Valley and started the rush to the mountain country that was last to be won by the white men.

Before this field was developed, discoveries were made in 1860-61 on the Salmon and Clearwater rivers in Idaho. Emigrants came from the east by the Missouri River and Great Salt Lake, others came from the west coast. Before the stream from the east had gathered full force the discovery of gold in Montana stopped it there, in 1862, close to the headwaters of the Missouri.

The town of Bannock sprang up at White's Bar, on Grasshopper Creek, and in less than a year after the discovery the town had five hundred people. In the north a discovery was made on Big Prickly Pear Creek. This convinced prospectors that the whole region at the headwaters of the Missouri was gold-bearing. Every stream and gulch was a possible bonanza to the hardy optimists who swarmed into the country to pick up their fortunes. In 1863 the Alder Gulch discovery was made. Here Virginia City, first territorial capital of Montana, grew like a mushroom, and in two years had two thousand people. In 1864 gold was found in Last Chance Gulch, thus Helena came into being.

The Missouri River carried all the trade of the Montana gold fields, boats running within a hundred or two hundred miles of the mines. The season of navigation in the north was short and busy, and the winter long and hard. Often parties from the mines, reaching this head of navigation after the last steamboat had departed in the fall, went down the river in Mackinaw boats rather than wait through the winter for the next spring's steamboat. Going through the Indian country they risked their lives and their gold dust, but the cities were gay and the mining towns were dreary, and they took the chance.

The most memorable of the Mackinaw boat trips was made by J. B. Hubbell, of Hawley and Hubbell, in 1866. Hubbell had advertised a steamboat to leave Fort Benton on her second trip about September 15. He promised that if the steamboat did not get as far up as Fort Benton he would take passengers down in a Mackinaw boat until they met her. On October 20 the steamboat had not appeared. About thirty passengers, with their gold dust, embarked in a Mackinaw built especially for the trip. It was 80 feet long, twelve feet wide, housed for 50 feet of its length with bullet-proof walls on both sides. The boat carried two masts with square sails, according to keel-boat practice. She started early in the mornings and ran late at night. The crew moored her to snags during the dark hours, to avoid attacks from shore. When they arrived at Fort Union, they found that the steamboat had come that far and turned back. The crew manned their oars and pushed on at their best speed. On November 22 they arrived at Sioux City. The river was full of ice. Two days later they would have been frozen in. For this trip Hubbell collected $175 per passenger.

The American Fur company tried to monopolize the business of the gold fields, but there were many competing boats, which led to some sharp rivalries and races. In 1862 LaBarge and Harkness & Company ran two opposition boats, each company trying to be the first in the fields. The fur company's "Spread Eagle" left St. Louis three days ahead of the rivals' "Emilie," but the "Emilie" overtook the "Spread Eagle" at Fort Berthold. For two days the boats ran close together each straining every timber to get ahead of the other. Crews of both vessels had entered into the race to win. Up in the pilot house the pilot kept a wary eye and a steady hand; down in the engine room the firemen fed the blaze for all they were worth while the engineers stood tensely at their throttles.

They ran this way for two days, and then at the beginning of the third the "Emilie" inched ahead and bore down upon a sandbar overgrown with willows and called a tow-head. Bailey, pilot of the "Spread Eagle," steered for the regular course at the right. But Captain LaBarge knew the river better, knew there was enough water for him to take the "Emilie" through the shorter channel at the left. He turned into it.

On the "Spread Eagle" the maneuver was discovered, and forcing the fires till the safety valves sang, Bailey too made a dash for the left-hand channel. In the great spurt the "Spread Eagle" drew alongside the "Emilie" and tried to pass, but couldn't. The "Emilie" was creeping maddeningly ahead.

The infuriated Bailey spun his wheel and sent his boat crashing into the "Emilie's" side. At the shock Captain LaBarge stepped out of his pilot house with a pistol in his hand saying "Stop that boat or I kill you," and he meant it. Bailey saw he meant it and dropped back. Captain LaBarge returned to the pilot house and the "Emilie," not much damaged, kept the lead to the end of the trip.

The aftermath also shows a good side to LaBarge. Bailey lost his license for ramming a rival boat. LaBarge asked that he be reinstated, and he was.

Indians had hardly ceased to be an active menace to navigation on the upper Missouri when the Civil War made steamboating on the lower river a hazardous enterprise. Missouri was a slave state, but most of the Missouri River steamboat business was with loyal people, and Confederate sympathizers considered it a legitimate object of confiscation. Guerrilla bands attacked the boats and for a time almost drove them off the lower river. Another difficulty was in getting pilots who favored the Union cause. It is said that at the outbreak of the war all the Missouri River pilots but two favored the Confederacy. General Lyon was obliged to go to the Illinois River for pilots when he wanted to move troops up the river in June, 1861. On the other hand, the demands of the war stimulated business on the upper Missouri. There was a constant movement of troops and stores. In the later years many refugees from both armies passed up the rivers to the gold-bearing regions of Montana. The bad effects of the war on Missouri River trade were practically confined to the river below Kansas City. Here the danger was from the south bank, where the channel ran close to the shore. Boats tied up at the north bank or anchored in midstream to avoid being boarded by the guerrillas whose fire they often received. Shields of boiler iron, much like those used on the upper river to guard against Indian snipers, were placed on the side of the pilot house toward the danger. Occasionally, when much Government freight was on board, the boats carried parties of soldiers for protection as far as Kansas City.

In the latter part of March, 1863, the "Sam Gaty," bound for the gold fields of the upper river, was attacked by guerrillas near Sibley, Missouri. She was heavily loaded, carried a full list of pas-

sengers, some paroled Union soldiers, and forty freed
negroes, called at that time contrabands. While the
boat was running close to the land the guerrillas
caught her under their guns and ordered her officers
to land. Unable to avoid the guerrillas' fire, the
officers obeyed. The guerrillas came aboard, robbed
the safes, took everything of value from the passengers, and threw overboard all freight that might be
of use to the Government. All the negroes and some
of the paroled soldiers were taken ashore and shot.
Then the boat was allowed to proceed.

Later this band, commanded by a man named
Hicks, was overtaken by Kansas troops under Major
Ransom. Many of the guerrillas were killed, their
camp destroyed and their equipment captured, and
the band completely dispersed.

The introduction of steamboats on the Missouri
marked the beginning of the period in which the
white man conquered the country west of the Mississippi. It had required two centuries to take the
country east of the river, a march of one-third the
distance across the continent, winning less than one-
third the territory of the continental United States.
In 1829 some sections east of the Mississippi were
still Indian land. In the next twenty years, as railroads developed in the east and steamboat trade and
travel were extended in the west, Americans settled
the Oregon Territory, took the southwestern territory from Mexico, settled the Pacific Coast, and over-
ran the intervening country of mountains and plains.

This migration, the largest in history to occur in so short a time, covered about two million square miles of land. It completed the age-long journey of the race from east to west—at last the white man had girdled the earth.

CHAPTER VIII

SOME DRY STATISTICS

"Ah stepped across de Richmon',
Ah stepped across de Lee,
Ah stepped across de Natchez
And she flewed fum under me."

STEAMBOATING A UNIQUE BUSINESS—GROWTH OF THE STEAM-
BOAT TRANSPORTATION SYSTEM—FREIGHT RATES, FARES, AND
RUNNING EXPENSES—THE EFFECT OF HIGH WHARF CHARGES
—THE LIQUOR BUSINESS ON STEAMBOATS.

THE steamboat transportation system that grew
up on the Mississippi and its tributaries between
1811 and the Civil War was remarkable in many
ways. Not the least remarkable was the fact that
its units, the steamboats, were in most cases owned
and operated by individuals. In the east the boats
on the Hudson and other rivers were controlled by
companies and operated by salaried officers. In the
west, the owner of a boat as a rule financed his own
project, borrowing the necessary money on his own
responsibility. He built the boat according to his
own ideas of what a steamboat should be. And when
she came from the ways he generally took command
of her himself.

The responsibility of the owner-captain of a western steamboat went far beyond the matter of navigation. He watched the work of his engineer in the
care of the machinery and the purchase of fuel, oil

and other supplies. He checked up his steward in the matters of food, tableware, linen, and all the other things necessary to the operation of a passenger boat. Under his eye the mate attended to the loading, stowage, and unloading of freight. And with the clerk he went over the boat's accounts, decided where he was making money and where he was losing, and regulated his policies accordingly.

On the captain's business acumen and his ability to get and hold the trade of his customers depended the success or failure of his venture. He owned his business, and as an employer his authority was almost absolute. He must meet shippers and passengers, know his customers and their families, and by his own personality maintain his business relations with them. He made rates, fixed schedules, adjusted claims, acted as host to his passengers, and was necessarily an agreeable gentleman. Especially on the lower rivers, his relations with shippers and travelers were more or less permanent. A boat's patrons developed a friendly interest in the boat and her master, and seldom transferred their business to another unless it was to take advantage of a big reduction in rates.

These rate cuts came about when some owner made up his mind to freeze out a competitor. Sometimes passenger fares fell so low that it was cheaper to travel on a boat than to live at home. Sometimes a competing captain who saw his losses mounting transferred his business to some other run. Often, however, both competitors stuck until one reached the end of his financial resources, and his boat was taken and sold by his creditors. Steamboatmen were proud and tenacious. Many a captain, rather than move his business and acknowledge defeat, hung on until the red flag at the door of the New Orleans custom-house announced the sale of his boat. And in a short time, with his finances in order again, he would be walking the deck of another boat, finer than the last.

For several years after the introduction of steam by the "New Orleans," the steamboat business was one of uncertain operation, high costs, and great risks. The boats were crude and the art of navigation undeveloped. It was the uncertainty of any business in its formative stage.

By 1831 there had been 348 boats built for service on the western rivers, almost all of them in the west. Eighty were built in 1832, and about the same number in 1833. At the end of this year about 500 had been built, and a little less than half of them were in service. Compared to the eastern boats, the craft of the western rivers was short lived. The timber of which they were made was of more rapid growth and not so well seasoned as in the east, service on the western rivers was harder, and the risks of navigation greater.

In the following years steamboat building increased rapidly. In 1849 the number of steamboats

The "Charles P. Chouteau,"—a sternwheeler of the seventies carrying a record cargo of cotton

(*Stanton's "American Steam Vessels"*)

on the Mississippi from 1834 was given in an engineers' report:

Year	Number of Steamboats on the Mississippi	Approximate Tonnage
1834	231	39,000
1840	225	49,000
1843	672	134,400
1844	686	144,150
1845	789	157,713
1847	958	200,000
1849	1,000 (probable)	250,000 (probable)

The distribution of American steamboat tonnage in 1842 is a study in the development of the country:

Southwest:

New Orleans	80,993	
St. Louis	14,725	
Cincinnati	12,025	
Pittsburgh	10,107	
Louisville	4,618	
Nashville	3,810	
Total southwest		126,278

Northwest:

Buffalo	8,212	
Detroit	3,296	
Presque Isle	2,315	
Oswego	1,970	
Cuyahoga	1,859	
Total northwest		17,652

Seaboard:

New York	35,260
Baltimore	7,143
Mobile	6,982
Philadelphia	4,578
Charleston	3,289
Newbern	2,854
Perth Amboy	2,606
Apalachicola	1,418
Norfolk	1,395
Boston	1,362
Wilmington	1,212
Georgetown	1,178
Newark	1,120
Miscellaneous	4,767

Total seaboard 76,064

GRAND TOTAL 219,994

this may be compared with the steamship tonnage of Great Britain in 1834:

	Number of Steamships	Tonnage
England	434	43,877
Scotland	105	13,113
Ireland	84	17,674
British Dependencies	49	8,032
TOTAL	672	82,696

In 1842 the steamboat tonnage of the Mississippi valley had grown to exceed the entire tonnage of

Great Britain in 1834 by more than forty thousand tons and had more than half the entire registered tonnage of the United States. In 1842 Pittsburgh had more steamboat tonnage than Philadelphia, Boston and Charleston combined. Pittsburgh and Cincinnati together had a tonnage five thousand greater than all the Great Lakes ports combined.

In 1843 the boat-building industry of Cincinnati employed in the heavier portions of the work 320 hands at the boat yards, 200 joiners, 200 foundrymen and enginemen, and 50 painters, a total of 770. In that year Cincinnati led the towns of the Ohio valley in boat building.

BOATS BUILT IN 1843

Place	Number	Tons
Cincinnati	45	12,035
Louisville, New Albany, and Jeffersonville	35	7,406
Pittsburgh	25	4,347
All other places	15	3,000
TOTAL	120	26,788

In 1832 there were six regular packets running between St. Louis and New Orleans, besides numerous boats that ran on schedules that varied to accommodate business as it developed. In that year the round trip between these points required about twenty-four days. The usual cabin fare was $20 downstream and $25 upstream: deck passengers $5 either way. Freight rates averaged 37½ cents per hundredweight downstream and 62½ cents upstream.

From St. Louis to Louisville there were ten regular boats and a larger number of irregular ones. The round trip required ten or eleven days. Cabin fare either way was $12, deck passage $4, and freight about 25 cents per hundredweight. Some of these boats ran regularly to Cincinnati.

In a memorial prepared for Congress by the citizens of Cincinnati in 1844, it was estimated that in 1834 there were 230 steamboats in operation on the western rivers, with a tonnage of 39,000. On this basis they estimated the cost of river transportation for that year:

For 60 boats of more than 200 tons each, 180 running days at $140 per day....	$1,512,000
For 70 boats of 120 to 200 tons each, 240 running days at $90 per day.........	1,512,000
For 100 boats of less than 120 tons each, 270 running days at $60 per day.........	1,620,000
TOTAL EXPENSE FOR YEAR............	$4,644,000

The cost of river transportation for 1844 was estimated in the same document.

For 110 boats of more than 200 tons each, 180 running days at $140 per day....	$2,772,000
For 140 boats of 120 to 200 tons each, 240 running days at $90 per day........	3,024,000

For 200 boats of less than 120 tons each,
270 running days at $60 per day.....   3,240,000

TOTAL EXPENSE FOR YEAR............ $9,036,000

This expense is divided into its principal items:

Wages, 36% $3,252,960
Wood, 30%   2,710,800
Provisions, 18%   1,626,480
Contingencies, 16%   1,445,760

TOTAL $9,036,000

According to this document, additional expenses for the year 1844 are:

Insurance, 15% on $7,200,000........... $1,080,000
Louisville and Portland canal tolls........   250,000
Interest on $7,200,000 at 6%...........   432,000
Depreciation of boats, 20%..............   1,440,000
For flatboats   1,380,000

TOTAL COST OF TRANSPORTATION FOR
1844 .... $13,618,000

The steamboat business was one of big risks and big profits. The average boat of the fifties and sixties cost from $20,000 to $40,000, and its life was about five years. From 1849 to 1862 the shipyards along the Ohio could not keep up with their orders. Sometimes extra gangs worked at night by torchlight for double pay. The foundries and machine shops shared in the rush of steamboat business.

This rush of business was not the result of speculation. The orders were given by experienced, practical rivermen who were out to make money by the operation of the boats. Frequently an owner who lost his boat by snag or fire ordered a new one within twenty-four hours after the accident. Time was money. The earnings of about twenty weeks would pay for a boat. Insurance premiums were high, and for this reason most owners carried their own risks.

An estimate of steamboat expenses and earnings on the upper Mississippi in 1857 has been made by Merrick, whose experience as a steamboat clerk qualifies him as an authority. He takes as an example a good stern-wheel boat 200 feet long, 30 feet in the beam, and with 5 feet depth of hold. Such a boat would measure about 200 tons, but would carry 300 tons of freight. Her passenger capacity would be about 200 in the cabin and 100 on deck, and her cost would be from $25,000 to $30,000.

Freight rates were higher up-stream than downstream, and varied with the distance.

Freight rates per ton, up-stream:

For 30 miles or less .... 6¢ per mile
    (No charge less than 25¢)
30 to 60 miles..................... 5¢ per mile
Over 60 miles..................... 4¢ per mile

Freight rates per ton, down-stream:

For 30 miles or less.................. 5¢ per mile
    (No charge less than 25¢)
30 to 60 miles...................... 4¢ per mile
Over 60 miles...................... 3¢ per mile

There were three principal points of departure for the upper Mississippi country: Rock Island, Dunleith or Galena, and Prairie du Chien. Sometimes the boats left Dunleith so crowded with passengers that men agreed to sleep on the cabin floor so that the women might have the rooms, and tickets to St. Paul brought a premium of four dollars over the usual price. Deck passage usually cost a little more than half the cabin fare:

Passenger rates, up-stream:

Dunleith or Galena to	*Miles*	*Cabin Fare*	*Deck Fare*
Cassville	30	$2.00	$1.25
Prairie du Chien............	66	3.50	2.00
La Crosse..................	150	6.00	3.25
Red Wing ....:............	256	10.00	5.00
St. Paul and Stillwater.......	321	12.00	6.00
Prairie du Chien to St. Paul...	255	10.00	5.00
La Crosse to St. Paul........	175	7.00	4.00

Passenger rates, down-stream:

St. Paul or Stillwater to	*Miles*	*Cabin Fare*	*Deck Fare*
Hastings	32	$1.50	$1.00
Red Wing..................	65	2.50	2.00
Winona	146	4.50	2.50

St. Paul or Stillwater to	Miles	Cabin Fare	Deck Fare
La Crosse	175	$5.00	$3.00
Prairie du Chien	255	7.00	3.50
Dunleith or Galena	321	8.00	4.00

Receipts from the average up trip are estimated at $4,450, about two-thirds of which is derived from freight:

Up trip receipts:
150 passengers from Dunleith or Galena at an average of $8 .... $1,200
50 deck passengers at an average of $5 250
300 tons freight at average of 50¢ cwt. 3,000

TOTAL $4,450

On the down trip the only important cargo was wheat, shipped in two-bushel sacks weighing 120 pounds each, at the rate of 12¢ a sack:

Down trip receipts:
80 passengers at an average of $8 .... $640
5,000 sacks wheat at 12¢ 600

TOTAL $1,240

Thus the boat took in $5,690 on every round trip. During the season of navigation she made four round trips a month, taking in $22,760. Merrick's estimate of the boat's monthly cost of operation leaves a large margin for depreciation and profit:

Salaries and wages:

Captain	$300
Chief clerk	200
Second clerk	100
Chief mate	200
Second mate	100
Two pilots at $500	1,000
Chief engineer	200
Second engineer	150
8 firemen at $50	400
Steward	200
Carpenter	150
Watchman	50
40 deck hands at $50	2,000
Cabin crew	800

Supplies:

Food supplies, 30 days at $75 per day......	2,250
Wood, 25 cords per day at $2.50 per cord, 30 days, about	2,000
Sundries	1,400
TOTAL	$11,500

Difference between monthly income and expense leaves $11,260 as monthly profit and fund to pay for the boat or buy the next one. During the running season of five months the boat would make $56,300, a sum sufficient to allow her owner to build a second boat and live well in the meantime.

Many boats were fully as profitable as this example. On the upper Mississippi in 1857 the boat owners had seen the advantages of organization.

The Minnesota Packet Company, at first only an association of owners, acquired a virtual monopoly of the Galena and Dubuque jobbing house freight. This company also made arrangements with the railroads at Dunleith and Prairie du Chien whereby freight and passengers from the railroads were transferred to the company's boats. This monopoly proved very profitable.

Furnishing wood to steamboats was a common industry along the rivers. It was estimated that an acre of good woodland would yield 100 cords. The price of the land varied according to its location and quality, ranging from $1.25 to $100.00 per acre. Upland wood was considered better than that cut in the bottoms. Frequently it was run through chutes down the bluffs, then cut and piled on the river bank. The cost of getting out a cord of wood was estimated at a dollar; fifty cents for cutting, twenty-five for hauling, and twenty-five for other labor. At a selling price of two dollars and a half a cord, the profit was a dollar and a half, less whatever had been paid for the land.

The wood was piled in four-foot lengths, eight feet high, in ranks eighty-four feet long; twenty cords to the rank. It was supposed to be evenly piled, fairly uniform, and fairly free from crooked sticks. The ends were cross-piled, and only one of the ends was included in the measurement. The mud-clerk (second clerk) of a boat generally did the measuring with an eight-foot stick. On their up trips the faster boats had their wood piled on flatboats which they took in tow and unloaded as they went up-stream. A half-hour was usually required to trans-fer a load of twenty to forty cords from the flat to the steamboat. The larger boats, requiring the larger loads, carried crews in proportion. After the flat was unloaded it was cast off, with a crew of two or three men who came with it, and drifted back to the wood-yard. No such arrangement could be made on the down-stream trips, as there was no way of returning the flats to the wood-yards against the current.

On the Missouri in 1866 salaries of most steam-boatmen were not quite as high as on the upper Mississippi. A captain drew $200 per month, a chief clerk $150, a mate or engineer $125. It was the pilot's pay that boosted the salary expense; some-times pilots drew as high as $1,200 a month each.

Freight rates from St. Louis to Fort Benton were 12¢ per pound. Insurance was 6½% on side-wheel boats and 8% on stern-wheelers. Cabin passengers paid a fare of $300 for the St. Louis-Fort Benton run.

Reported profits of some of the boats for the sea-son of 1866 were very high. The "St. John" made $17,000, the "Tacony" $16,000, the "W. T. Lewis" $40,000, and the "Peter Balen" $65,000. In 1867 the "Octavia" of Captain LaBarge cleared $40,000. Surely a business profitable and perilous enough to satisfy the most adventurous steamboatman of those adventurous days.

Most of the river towns followed a short-sighted

policy in the matter of wharfage dues. They were in many cases unreasonably high, and graded in such ways that a steamboat could not afford to land a small consignment of freight, or less than a party of passengers. The rates compelled a few large consignments rather than the many small consignments which would have been far more beneficial, both to the towns and to the steamboat business.

The sale of liquor on steamboats seldom was handled by the management of the boat. The bar was rented as a concession to the barkeeper, who furnished his own goods and took his own profits. Frequently a man who knew the business rented the bars of several boats and placed in them barkeepers of his own choosing, paying them salaries or percentages. Billy Henderson, of St. Louis, was one of the barkeepers who expanded his business. He ran between St. Louis and St. Paul on the "Excelsior." Later he leased the bar on the "Metropolitan," and when the Northern Line was organized he bought the bar lease on all its boats. He put trustworthy men in charge, and took returns from each based on the number of passengers carried, without regard to age or sex. This arrangement proved very satisfactory, and paid well both the contractor and the barkeepers.

The barkeeper must dress well, be a good fellow and a good mixer, both socially and in the matter of fancy drinks. Southerners required their mint-julips, and easterners their whiskey cocktails. No skill as a mixer was necessary to please the westerners. They took their whiskey straight, four fingers deep, and thought any one who took a chaser must have a weakness somewhere.

The barkeepers knew and practiced many tricks, some of which suggest these modern days since America has become, more or less, a nation of teetotalers. It was a common practice of many steamboat barkeepers to make French brandy by mixing burnt peach stones, cod liver oil, and nitric acid with new Kentucky whiskey. This drink was popular with the inexperienced, but, even as to-day, it was shunned by judicious drinkers.

In the days when steamboats carried the travel of the west, the bars were very profitable. Some times a barkeeper with good liquor and a good line of talk cleared two thousand dollars on a trip. Everybody drank, and the cabin passengers required the best in drinkables. In the later days the railroads took the best of the travel, and the bars were compelled to cater to a cheaper trade. Firemen and deck hands wanted their drinks, but they wanted them big and cheap, without much regard to quality. From being a perennial gold mine, a bar lease became a hand-to-mouth business or a poorly-paid job. Finally a large number of the boats discontinued their bars. The business of the bars waxed and waned with the business of the boats themselves. Small and uncertain at the beginning, they rose to the height of luxurious elegance, and then traveled the downward road as changing conditions took their patronage away.

CHAPTER IX

THE PILOT AND THE ENGINEER

"There was runnin' and cursin', but Jim yelled out
Over all the infernal roar,
'I'll hold her nozzle agin the bank
Till the last galoot's ashore.'"

WILD, uncontrollable and strong, the Mississippi and its tributaries meander back and forth through miles of lowland, sometimes slowly, sometimes swiftly as a gallop, cutting away forests and fields in one place, piling up new land in another; full of tricks and vagaries and savagely practical jokes. And their beds are as changeable and rapacious as the ochre water that flows over them.

The Mississippi boatmen went down a channel in fair weather and foul where sandbars built up in one part of the river bed only to crawl treacherously to another soon after they were discovered, where trees, torn from caving banks by floods, lay underneath the surface with their jagged limbs pointed downstream. These are the snags that have ripped out the hulls of so many steamboats, letting the boat submerge with its crew and passengers.

Of these snags there were many kinds: the sawyer, that sways up and down as the current sweeps past it; the planters, a group of trees grown fast to the bottom with their spikes thrust upward; and the wooden islands, formed by great masses of driftwood lying just beneath the face of the water. None of these obstacles remains in a fixed place. For the current brings them, and the current moves them on.

At low water, western river pilots seldom went downstream at night. It was too dangerous. Their boat was hard to steer at the low speed which they were forced to keep and the urge of the current always was behind it, pushing it down upon the scarcely perceptible perils ahead. But going upstream was a little different, a trifle safer. For they could go at a crawl against the current, and when the snags and bars threatened the river itself helped the engine and wheel snatch the craft away from the menacing obstacle.

But even so, the risk was great and the sharpest precaution was taken that nothing might interfere with the pilot's vision. Any light on the boat that was visible to him blinded him to the dim sight of the river flowing down through the darkness. Canvas curtains were fitted over the forward part of the boiler deck, and the forecastle was covered to hide the light from the furnace doors. Skylights were draped, while on the hurricane deck not even the light of a cigar was permitted.

The pilot made use of what few things could be seen at night and of everything that could be heard. A story is told of a Missouri river pilot who always was aware of approaching a certain dangerous crossing at night by the barking of a dog. The sound, coming time after time from the same place, was a reliable guide through the darkness. But one night the dog barked from a different point, and shortly the boat rammed the sandbar and was wrecked. A grotesque tale, but it illustrates the scantiness of the material on hand for the pilot to guide his ship and passengers in the thick, enveloping night.

Not so much things heard and seen as things *sensed* enabled the pilot to make his journeys safely. As a cub, of course, he had learned the name and location of every town, point, bend, island, sandbar, snag and wreck—of which there was a countless number—on the river. And in his mind was a map of the shape and appearance, always changing, of every part of this great river, in calm and in storm, at high water and at low. The depth of the channel at every point, at all stages of the river, the amount of water on the bars, the habits of the river in tearing down banks and building up bars, the changing depth of the water between one trip and the next— all these things he had to know; also the marks, the trees, houses, points, bars, posts, hollows,—anything by which to lay his course through every mile of the river. And as the river changed he had to know the new marks, new channels, new bars, new islands; sometimes a whole horseshoe bend would be turned into a lake by a cutoff, and any towns along it left out in the woods; and he must learn the new stretch of river that ran between fresh raw banks across the neck.

Night piloting was comparatively easy above Baton Rouge, for there the trees grew along the bank, somewhat marking the channel even when the river had sprawled far out of its bed; but in the lower river there were no such reliable markers. Timber was cut off clear to the farthest edge of the sugar plantations, and the planters, to make matters worse, piled up the cane stalks after they had been ground and set fire to them. These heaps burned slowly and smoked heavily, throwing a smudge across the already black river. A pilot coming down at night might as well have been blindfolded. Not infrequently, river, levee and smoke all looking alike, he was unexpectedly shaken, and the boat as well, by bringing his craft hard up against a levee.

From his unobstructed view where he stood at the wheel in his little compartment on top of the vessel the pilot had to read and interpret every line and dimple on that flowing yellow surface. A line on the water, unseen by most people, meant to the pilot that there was a reef below, not a rock reef, but one of mud and sand that would wreck the boat just as surely as if it had been made of granite. Sometimes the wind made a mark on the water, just like the mark of a reef; but the canny pilot knew the difference. When the cub pilot, Mark Twain, asked the veteran Horace Bixby how he told the reef mark from the wind mark Bixby replied, "I can't tell you. By and by you will just naturally know one from the other, but you will never be able to explain how or why you know them apart."

To the pilot a spot ahead of the boat that looked like a boiling cauldron meant that a reef was being washed away, to form elsewhere; a peculiar combination of lines and circles showed that a spot was becoming shoal; a dimple in the surface gave warning of a rock; a wrecked boat, or some other solid obstruction; a streak like a wake meant that a snag, just under the surface, was waiting to stab a hole through the planks of the boat and sink it.

And thus it was throughout the most gala days of steamboating. For it was much later that anything of consequence was done towards marking and lighting the channels. Pilots of the biggest packets had no outside aid to navigation; it was all in themselves.

High water brought the pilots an extra combination of problems. Speed being always imperative, they took every possible short cut in running upstream, going in back of islands where at low water there was hardly room to float a skiff; navigating bottom lands that men had planted with grain before the water had risen; meeting hosts of rafts and trading boats that at every high tide came awkwardly down with the rushing current. The law required the rafts and small boats, just as the steamboats, to carry lights at night, but these were seldom burning; when the lights did burn it was down in the cabin where the card game or dance was in progress. Thus collisions between rafts or flatboats and packets were often imminent, and when they came so close to one another that only the quickest handling averted disaster the night grew lurid with rivermen's curses and sometimes bullets flew through the darkness from one deck to another.

Low water added more difficulties. When the water went down in the heat of the summer months, the banks on either side baking dry and the leaves from the bordering trees hanging lifeless from the limbs, the pilot who was not on watch took the cub he was training and got aboard the yawl to locate the best places to cross the reefs and mark the points where the shallowest water had to be worked through. The marking was done with a buoy, a board with a piece sticking up at one end to keep the current from pulling it beneath the water. This was fastened to a rope which had a stone at the end for an anchor. And at night a paper lantern was fastened on top of the bobbing board, its light capable of being seen for a mile or more.

Setting out ahead of the steamboat the pilot not on watch and his cub, whom he was training for a pilot's job, rowed the yawl to the place where the buoy had to be dropped, then signalled the big boat and stood by, resting on their oars. The big boat came slowly down until she reached the shallowest point, where she jerked ahead under tremendous steam pressure to clear the mud caught at the bottom of the hull, then slid over. It was a feat that required great expertness, such as Horace Bixby, in "Life on the Mississippi," possessed. Bixby made his famous run through the crossing at Hat Island. Delayed by grounding, the boat was steaming towards Hat Island just at nightfall, half an hour too late for a less daring pilot to make the crossing. But not for Bixby; he knew his river, and instead of landing the boat for the night he rang for the leadsmen. Their calls floated up to him from below while critical but admiring pilots stood behind him and watched.

As the water shoaled, Bixby rang the engines down to half speed. Accurately he brought the boat down through the intricate channel to the head of the island. Here he stopped both wheels and let her drift into the one place where she could get through. Nearer and nearer she drew to the island, shoal and more shoal was the water under her. She touched bottom, and as she touched Bixby gave her all the steam in the boilers. She ground through the sand, hung a moment, and slid over into safety. The pent-up anxiety of the visiting pilots burst out in a yell of approbation, and the echoes of it went up and down the rivers among the boatmen, to whom such a piece of navigation was a supreme exploit.

But even Horace Bixby might have been embarrassed in taking a boat down to Cairo from St. Louis when the water was at its lowest. When this happened the pilot, while his own vessel lay at St. Louis, took another steamboat whose pilot had just been through the river, and went for a fresh and careful scrutiny, then returned to St. Louis on another boat and piloted his own craft down. Pilots who were looking at the river for this purpose were always guests of the boats on which they traveled. Many a pilot out of a berth and out of luck has bridged a lean month by getting aboard a boat—almost any boat—and carefully watching the river and thinking of the food he was going to get.

For pilots were treated with a great deal of respect by every one aboard a steamboat: captains, waiters, deck hands, clerks, engineers, firemen and passengers. Ashore they were envied for the pay they drew. Quite naturally they developed a grand air of authority, a heavy swagger. They never asked any one for anything: on all occasions they gave orders. They were, in fact, the accepted aristocrats of the steamboat business. While the pilot was on duty, his authority was almost absolute. Though the captain was in charge while the boat was landing or backing out from a levee, and though he could order the boat to land for repairs if he thought they were needed, he gave way the rest of the time to the pilot. And while the vessel lay loading or unloading the pilot had no duties; he could go into his cabin, put on his high-heeled, shiny boots with tassels, twist the ends of his mustache into swordpoints, grease his hair until it glistened and lay flat and then set out for town where the doors were wide open to him and his pocket chock-full of greenbacks.

But the pilots, respected and well paid, went a little too far in making their work easy. Almost every pilot kept a cub in training to do his steering for him, and as these young fellows acquired pilot's licenses the ranks of the aristocracy of steamboating became a little too full. Salaries began to fall. A few of the pilots organized the Pilots' Benevolent Association, with unemployment benefits to members, and fixed wages at two hundred and fifty dollars a month, the figure customary before the cub crop began to undermine the pay. The organizers promptly lost their jobs, and the association was looked upon by captains as something of a joke.

But the organizers knew what they were doing. Unemployment benefits drew into the organization the younger pilots who could not depend on employment in the dull season, and pensions for the widows of pilots, and the payment of funeral expenses for members who died in good standing, brought in the older ones. Soon the association had a large membership, practically all out of work, and the non-member pilots were reaping the benefit of the rise in pay caused by the unemployment of member pilots. The association was the biggest joke the rivermen had ever seen. But when the rush season came, captains began to solicit the services of association pilots, and to receive shocks that made them think the association was no joke after all. For the members would not ship on any boat where the other pilot was a non-member. The result was that the captains had to yield. The association men got most of the work, and the outsiders were left idle. Many of them joined the association—paying greatly augmented initiation fees.

Captains thought this dictation of wages and terms by the association could not last after the busy season was over. But the member pilots had developed a system of furnishing to each other information about the rivers that gave them a marked advantage over non-members. They wrote up and deposited in locked boxes at every wharf-boat detailed accounts of conditions on the stretches of river they had just passed. Thus a member pilot—and no others could unlock the boxes—kept himself in possession of river information that seldom was more than a day old. Boats carrying non-member pilots began to have all the accidents. The victory of the association was complete when the underwriters ordered the employment of member pilots only.

The association removed the danger of an oversupply of pilots by refusing to take any more for training for a period of five years. After that, a limited number would be taken. There were no outsiders left, therefore nobody to train cubs except under these rules.

From an old Carrier & Ives print in the collection of Karl Schmidt, Esq.

ON THE MISSISSIPPI

When the association put pilots' pay up to five hundred dollars a month, the captains and owners did not fight it. Instead they took advantage of it by raising freight rates enough to cover the added expense and leave a profit for themselves; a trick older than steamboating, but apparently workable anywhere at any time.

For a little while the pilots sat on top of the world. Then the Civil War brought the steamboat industry almost to a stop, and when it revived again the railroads were taking the best of the business. A little later barges were introduced for carrying the cargoes of several steamboats in a single tow, and the supremacy of the pilot ceased through lessening demand for his services.

Mark Twain's story of his life on the Mississippi is a perfect picture of steamboating as seen from the pilot house. Mark Twain was there, and he knew how to tell what he saw. But as a picture of life on the rivers it is hardly complete. "According to Clemens," say old steamboatmen—and they always think of him as Sam Clemens, the pilot, rather than as Mark Twain, the writer—"the pilot is the only man aboard."

It is not strange that a man should write in terms of his own profession. The pilot knew piloting, and while he practiced it he found little time and little need to learn the other business of the boat. Possibly much of his lack of general steamboat knowledge was voluntary. An old steamboat captain remarked, "The pilot is generally the most ignorant man aboard. If he breaks a rudder or a paddle-wheel, he doesn't know the first thing about repairing it. He sits and smokes and drinks his coffee while the engineers do the work."

Quite a natural remark for a captain to make, for the captain must be everywhere and know everything. But for the pilot, surely coffee and a cigar in the texas is nicer than a sweaty job on the guards.

The pilot, with his wheel and his engine-room bell-pulls before him, held the working of the boat in his hands. He was the visible head of the whole human and mechanical organism that was the boat. But, when she drifted down to a shoal, and at just the right instant the pilot rang full steam ahead, it was the engineer on watch below who must know that his engines were ready, who must apply the power that carried her across. It was seldom that engineers made themselves conspicuous among the passengers. Let the captain play host and the pilot play lord. The engineer knew his job was as important as any aboard even if he did do his work in grease and sweat and was usually laboring in obscurity while the captain and the pilot were going through the pomp and show of landing and departing.

In the early days engineers' jobs were filled by firemen who had worked into them. For there was relatively little that had to be learned. The engine makers themselves set the cams that worked the engine valves, and marked the arms of the safety valves. So if an engineer could properly line his shafts, keep water in the boiler, replace worn-out packings and take care of a few minor repairs, that was all that was asked. But as steamboating developed more knowledge and training was required for an engineer and young men who were handy with tools and liked the smell of hot oil and steam were taken on and trained by the veterans.

Boats of the experimental days carried both paddle wheels on the same shaft. There were only two ways to run them: ahead and astern, one engine serving for both wheels. Later, the wheels still turned by a single engine, were carried on stub shafts, enabling one wheel to be disconnected by throwing out a clutch so that the boat could be turned rapidly by the use of the other wheel alone. Then came the two engines, one to each wheel and each wheel independent of the other, so that the boat could be whipped from right to left or left to right without any forward or backward movement. This pliancy never was possessed by the stern-wheeler. Even after it carried two engines, connected directly to the wheel, and had the multiple balanced rudders, which were attached so that there was an even pressure of water on each side, the stern-wheeler was hard to handle in close places.

As boat-building improved there were needed two strikers in the engine room besides the first and second engineer. The engineer always handled the engine to starboard, while the one on the larboard side—the portside remained the larboard side throughout river days—was manned by the cub on the regular engineer's shift. Thus in supplying the power, the responsibility of the cub, or striker, was as great as that of the engineer. And many a cub went to the throttle, trembling in fear that he would center his engine and so make a lot of work for men who would have to turn the wheel past this center point with levers.

Steamboat engineers of the swift and gaudy days couldn't reverse their engines so easily as they can to-day. The engineer had to move the cam rods by hand from the forward to the reverse position. And at first he could fill his boilers only when the engines were in motion to work the pumps, but later all the boats carried steam-feed pumps, which the engineers called "the doctor." As the boats improved more and more boilers were added, sometimes as many as eight on one boat, connected up in three places: at the sides, through the steam drum at the top and through the mud drum at the bottom. It was from the mud drum that the thick, slimy sediment of the river had to be taken five or six times a day by the engineer's crew.

Weak boilers, as in the case of the first swift steamboat, Captain Shreve's "Washington" which blew up, often caused the wrecking of a boat; in the long, impressive casualty list of steamboats there are hundreds which went down with an exploded boiler. It was so bad that as early as 1834 Louisiana passed a steamboat inspection law, creating the office of State Engineer, and provided for the inspection of all boilers every three months. Under this law boilers were tested with hydrostatic pressure to three times the steam pressure they were supposed to carry, and in case of accident to a boat they had not been inspected the captain would be fined $2000 and imprisoned from three months to a year. He also faced manslaughter charges if any lives were lost. These same penalties were in effect against overloading, racing, carrying steam pressure higher than was permitted by the boat's certificate, or for any accident that happened while the captain, pilot or engineer was gambling or watching others who were gambling. The captains seldom gambled, but what's a law compared to the thrill of a race and a greater cargo in the event the race is won!

The engineers received their signals from the pilot by means of gongs and "jinglers," small tinkling bells that were jerked by the pilot. In addition there was a speaking tube that ran from the pilot house to the engine room, terminating in a trumpet above the engineer's head. Side-wheelers had a separate set of bells for each engine. But when the signalers needed more expression than was afforded by the bells— the bells being unable to curse, no matter how furiously jingled—the speaking tube was used to good purpose.

Here again the engineer was unfortunate. For though his vocabulary was as flaming as the pilot's,

the big end of the speaking tube was in his room
and the smaller end went up to the pilot. And he
couldn't even take out his anger on the fireman by
adorning *his* orders with picturesque oaths; for, when
he wanted the doors open to ease the steam pressure,
he too had to jingle a bell.

From the days of his cub-hood the engineer's life
was an exacting one. As a beginner he would usually
be set to cleaning the copious mud from the boilers,
dragging a chain around the flues to remove the
scale; and while he crawled about in the thick ooze
he could reflect upon the gay time the rest of the
crew were having ashore. Later on he had to know
blacksmithing so that he could make almost any piece
of ironwork that could be forged on an anvil. But
sometimes he could turn that anvil to other purposes.
Billy Hamilton, for example, known as a hot engineer, had a line run from the safety valve arm to a
pulley and, whenever his boat was racing, which was
often, he hung the anvil on the end of the line and
kept the safety valve down while steam mounted
terrifically and dangerously and the boat shot ahead
of its rival.

When the cub engineer received his license he still
got the worst of it. Always he had to keep every part
of the boat's machinery in the best of order, and
through fire, storm or collision he had to stay at his
post beside the pulsing cylinders. When the pilot
rang the signals the engine had to respond, and if
an engineer wasn't of the first class the pilot's sharp
eyes and finesse in maneuvering were wasted.

CHAPTER X

STEAMBOAT RACING

"Shoo, fly, don't bodder me,
Shoo, fly, don't bodder me,
Shoo, fly, don't bodder me,
I'se workin' on de Lee."

GETTING THERE FIRST TO GET THE BUSINESS—THE OLD LADY AND
THE LARD—CARRYING THE MESSAGE TO ST. PAUL—RACING
AT ITS FINEST—SPEED RECORDS AND TROPHIES—THE RISKS
OF RACING—THE "LEE-NATCHEZ" RACE—DECLINE OF RACING.

AWAY back in the early days, a small low-sided
steamboat makes her way down the Mississippi on
the Natchez-New Orleans run. She is a high-pressure boat, a new thing at that time. Her boiler in
its brickwork stands on deck, protected only by ranks
of cordwood. Smoke and sparks fly briskly from her
single stack, and with each stroke of her engine a
white jet of steam shoots from her escape-pipe. Her
flat, blunt-pointed hull has only narrow guards along
the sides; her cabin and engine room take up almost
the full width of the boat, leaving only footways to
port and starboard. Forward and aft she is loaded
with cotton. The cabin passengers are lounging in
shady spots. The deck passengers, in among the
cotton, have started a dance, the deck-planks ring
with the stamp of heavy boots. Rollicking notes of
a fiddle float out over the water, with the sing-song
cry of the caller and the loud laughter of the dancers.
Forward, a fireman throws open the furnace door,

199

cleans his fire, and pitches in a few sticks of wood. Another throws down more wood from the top of a pile.

In the little room that serves as an office, the captain is at work on his papers. His is an independent boat, he pays no royalty for the use of Fulton patents, and he runs in competition with the pioneer Fulton line. His accounts please him; a few more good trips like this and his boat will be paid for. If it weren't for the competing Fulton boat—the boat that sometimes noses in to the landing ahead of him and takes the freight he has a right to expect! And where is that boat now? He has heard she will be delayed by a trip up a bayou—a trip he himself will make next time there is freight there, or blow a cylinder head trying—and he expects to reach New Orleans first and get all the freight he can carry. The boat is almost opposite that bayou now. The captain stuffs his papers into a drawer and goes on deck to look for his rival's smoke.

There is the opening of the bayou, almost hidden in the tall cane, and—the captain turns loose a flatboatman's long and lurid oath—there comes the stack of the rival boat!

Captain, crew and passengers watch by the port rail while the long round-bellied hull of the rival slides out of the bayou and straightens down the river, almost abreast. Suddenly a cloud of smoke is belched from her tall stack. She has come through the bayou at half speed, now they are firing up. On the independent boat, the captain snaps a word to the firemen, who already have their doors open and are working with bar and hoe. A big black man heaves; a rank of wood crashes down before the furnace, is snatched up and thrown on the fire, and, as the door slams shut, the draft rushes through and up the chimney with a crackling roar. The paddles beat the water with more violence. The safety-valve sizzles.

But faster and faster works the gallows-frame beam of the Fulton boat. A little plume of steam rises above her engine room, expands, and shoots upward in a trailing cloud. Almost at the same moment the safety-valve of the independent boat lifts and the excess steam hisses away. The captain wheels and rushes into the engine room, where the engineer and assistant are busy with oil cans. Through the clank and groan of the machinery the captain shouts, frowning, "That Fulton boat is holding right abeam of us, and popping off too. We're wasting steam! Can't you make her hold a little more pressure?"

"The safety-valve weight's in the last notch now," answers the engineer, as he wipes his hands on his legs. "But," he spits judiciously, "she might hold a little more, the boiler's nearly new."

"Well then!" yells the captain. "Rig a line to the valve arm and tie it down. I'm going to beat that boat or blow up! Are you with me?"

The engineer grins and turns to the assistant.

"Rig that line," he says. "I'll keep her bearings cool."

The noise of escaping steam stops as the captain emerges on deck where he sees the rival boat still abeam; and as he looks, her plume of steam is suddenly cut off, floats and disappears in the air while the long low boat goes on, throwing yellow foam from her bow. The captain mutters, low but sincerely. It is a matter of firemen now, firemen—or boilers. He calls the mate and gives an order. In a few moments the mate appears on the forecastle and sets down a bucket of whiskey with a tin cup floating in it. "Any firemen," he says, "that'll let a damned tub like that pass 'em ain't fit to rake out ashes. Drink hearty, boys, and keep her hot—keep her hot! Where the hell's your resin? Make a fire, there! Keep her hot!"

This is not all the mate says, but it illustrates the general trend of his remarks.

Side by side, both seeking the strongest current, the two boats plow on down the river. The high-pressure boat is normally the faster, but she carries the heavier load, and her square-built frame strains with the unwonted urge of her machinery, while the rival boat is built like a ship and engined with the finest machine of its type to be bought in America. If the race were up-stream, it would be different, the Fulton boat would be held hopelessly back by the grip of the current on her deep round hull.

(Stanton's "American Steam Vessels")

The "Robert E. Lee"—the fastest and most famous steamboat of the Mississippi

Down-stream, neither boat can make more than a small momentary gain.

As the boats run side by side, the crews yell at each other in challenge and derision. Their voices are hardly heard above the noise of the machinery. An emigrant, standing on a pile of cotton, shouts and holds up a ten-dollar bill. A planter, on the upper deck, cups his hands and offers to bet any one a thousand dollars that his boat will pass the Red Church in the lead, and another thousand that she will be first at the levee.

On the independent boat, the captain stands beside the pilot at the wheel. "How about the old cut-off behind that island?" he asks. "The Fulton boat can't make it; she draws too much water. Let's see; current in her favor, distance saved in ours; it would put us a mile or two in the lead. Do you reckon there's water enough for us?"

"I reckon," says the pilot. "Put a leadsman on the bow and I'll try it."

At the head of the island, the boat swerves to take the short and shallow course. A yell of delight goes up from both contestants; on the independent boat they imagine themselves running safely through the shallows while the deep-draught Fulton boat takes the long course and drops behind. And on the Fulton boat they imagine their rival stuck fast in shoal water, laboriously working off, wasting the time that might have given her the victory.

Aboard the boat in the shallows, beset with sandbars and snags, the race is no longer a matter of firemen and boiler. Race, boat and cargo, the lives of the passengers—all are in the hands of the pilot. Everything staked on the skill and nerve of one man, backed by engineer and leadsman, the strength of the boat's hull-timbers the only hope in case the one man makes a single mistake. The boat misses snags by inches. Her flat hull grates and drags over bars, her wheels churn up yellow mud, and the decaying smell of the river-bottom mingles with the smell of burning wood and pitch and sizzling-hot oil. There are no more yells. The firemen drink their whiskey and feed their furnace in silence. Passengers anxiously watch the water. Overhead, the pilot stands at his wheel, nerves tense, hands steady. Above the clank of the machinery and the swash of the paddles rises the leadsman's call.

The boat slides over the last bar, into the open river again. All hands look astern, and as she clears the island they see behind them the rival, hopelessly out-distanced. Then the yells break loose, long loud yells of triumph. The people on the Fulton boat are too far away to hear them, but they sense them when they see the victor so far ahead. As the winners watch their beaten rival, they see a jet of steam rise from her. She has released her safety-valve, acknowledging defeat. The victorious captain orders the line taken from his own valve-arm. He thinks, perhaps, of what might have happened if his boiler had not been strong enough to stand the pressure, but it is only a passing thought. He has beaten his rival, he will get the business at New Orleans! Everybody is happy, and everybody takes a drink.

Thus, in the very beginning of Mississippi steamboating, racing became an institution. Primarily the race was not a sporting event, it was a race for business. And the great races of later years, the building of faster and faster boats that culminated in the "J. M. White," the "Robert E. Lee," and the "Natchez," the steamboatman's fever for speed and more speed, all of these were primarily for the purpose of getting business. Just the ordinary motive that makes the majority of us work, the force which, tempered by a few others, has made the world what it is.

But the contest of two steamboats for supremacy in speed appealed irresistibly to the sporting instinct of the American people. To the captain who regarded his boat with love and fierce pride, the pilot who felt her answer his touch on the big wheel, the engineer who grinned and hoped as he tied down his safety-valve, the firemen who labored and sweated and doused their scorched bodies with water outside and whiskey inside, the stewards, the cooks, the roustabouts; to all these men, white and black, the race was Life; the sweet cup that must be snatched recklessly or never tasted.

Primarily the race was for business; shippers and passengers preferred the fast boats. But it was far from cold-blooded business. The boat that the captain risked was worth more than the freight on any cargo. The life that every one on board risked was the only life he had. To almost every one connected with boats and shipping, racing was a lure. They knew it was dangerous, many disapproved of it strongly. But when the occasion came, they bet their money and gave the word, "Beat him or bust!"

And to those who merely looked on, a steamboat race was a spectacle without an equal. To the people of the lonely plantations on the reaches of the great river, the sight of a race was a fleeting glimpse of the intense life they might never live. To see a well-matched pair of crack steamboats tearing past, foam flying, flames spurting from the tops of blistered stacks, crews and passengers yelling—the man or woman or child of the backwoods who had seen this had a story to tell to grandchildren.

A dangerous, costly sport, but young people will have their sport, and most Americans of all ages were boys then—except those who were girls.

On the levee before a Kentucky town, a gray-haired woman stood with a group of friends. She was wearing her Sunday best hoop-skirt, and looked worried. Held tightly in her black-mitted hand was a steamboat ticket to New Orleans where she was going to visit relatives. By her were several barrels of lard from the woman's plantation; she was taking these to market in the Big Town Down the River. She looked with some trepidation at the big white steamboat that was approaching. She never had set foot on one of them, and her friends had told her quite freely of the dangers of steamboat travel. Snags, collision, fire, the perils of racing with its risk of bursting boilers; all these had been dwelt upon with solicitous kindness. Really, the prospective first-time passenger was in something of a fret.

The boat circled in over the pale water and made fast to the levee. The old lady walked carefully aboard, and, after making sure her lard followed her, sought the captain.

"Captain," she said, "I know anybody takes a chance when they ride on a steamboat, and I can take mine with the rest, but I want you to promise me, Captain, before we start, that you won't run any races."

"Madam," answered the captain, briskly, "I never race; that is, hardly ever, and I assure you I never do anything at all dangerous." The captain crooked a finger, and a steward disappeared.

"But, Captain," continued the lady, "you have no right to risk lives, just to beat some other boat, and maybe blow up a boiler or something, and I want you to promise—"

"Ah, Madam," broke in the captain, "here is the stewardess who will conduct you to your stateroom. I promise you to do nothing dangerous, and I assure you everything will be done to make your voyage pleasant."

"Thank you, Captain," breathed the old lady in

relief, "thank you, so much! I feel much safer now. Are you sure my lard is all right? And you'll take care of my trunk? That's good, now I'll go to my room."

Down the river steamed the boat, safely, sanely, and serenely, until one day a rival boat nosed alongside, and the firemen began to shake themselves, and the roustabouts to yell. The Kentucky lady asked of another passenger, "Goodness me! What does this mean? Is it a race?"

"Yes," was the answer, "and if our captain don't look out we'll be beaten. Look how that boat is gaining on us!"

The Kentucky lady walked the cabin deck, twisting her fingers, watching the rival with bright eyes that made her face look younger as she watched. Suddenly she darted up the stairs to the hurricane deck. "Captain," she called, "Captain, you can take back your promise. Don't let that boat beat us! I come from where they race horses, I do, and I won't be beat!"

A smile crossed the captain's tense face. "Madam," he cried, "we're doing the best we can."

"What!" cried the old lady, "and that boat getting ahead?"

"Yes," was the answer, "she's putting oil on her wood—see the black smoke—and we haven't any oil. We can't beat her on wood alone; can't get the boilers hot enough."

Just then the stewardess ran up the stairs, a flat

iron in each hand. "Cap'n, suh," she shouted, "if de engineeah want my ahns he can have 'em. Ah swo' las' time when dey got all rusty 'at Ah neve' lend 'em again, but Ah'll sand 'em 'nothah time befor' Ah let dat pack o' stovewood an' scrap-ahn beat me."

"Thank you, Lucy," answered the captain, "but he won't need the irons. He's got a sledge-hammer and two kegs of nails on the safety-valve now."

"Oh, Lawd!" wailed Lucy as she vanished down the stairs, waving her irons, "what kin Ah do?"

The old Kentucky woman faced the captain and stamped her foot. "Captain," she demanded, "where is my lard? I saw your boys put it down a hole in the floor."

The captain stared. "Your lard? Why, it's in the hold. It's perfectly safe."

"Safe!" shrilled the lady. "Safe! Oh—oh—oh, hell! Captain, make your niggers bring up that lard this minute, and put it on the wood, and get your old boilers hot! If we lose this race I swear I'll never travel with you again! What are you standing there for looking at me? Make your boys jump, or I will!"

The captain called an order, up came the barrels to the forecastle. The fires leaped, faster turned the wheels. The boat quivered, strained, drew even —forged ahead. And up on the hurricane deck the old woman with glittering eyes stood abaft the roaring chimneys and laughed and wept and shook her fists at the rival boat, and waved her good-bye.

Most of the great races were run on southern rivers by southern-owned boats. Much more than the Southerners, the Yankees refused to let sport interfere with their business and a race that resulted in a blown-up boiler was a very serious interference. Races on the upper Mississippi generally were hardly more than spurts to the next landing. In most cases the effort was made for the freight to be carried, sometimes it was for the fun of getting there first. There was, however, one long race that occasioned a good deal of excitement, although some declare it was no race, claiming that the captain of one of the boats did not know he was racing until the last few miles were being run. However this may be, he was making good speed.

This was the race between the "Itasca," Captain David Whitten, and the "Gray Eagle," Captain D. Smith Harris, to be first at St. Paul with copies of the first telegraphic message sent under the Atlantic. It was in 1856 that the first cable message was sent by Queen Victoria to President Buchanan, and telegraphed across the country to Dunleith and Prairie du Chien. There was no telegraph line running to St. Paul. Captain Whitten started from Prairie du Chien and Captain Harris from Dunleith at six o'clock of the same evening. Harris' run was the longer by sixty-one miles, but his boat was the fastest on the river and he handled her for speed and nothing else that trip. He stopped only at landings where mail must be delivered, and then only long enough to throw it off the gangway. As he was running ahead of schedule, there was no mail ready for him to take aboard. He took on no freight, and what he had aboard for intermediate points he carried to St. Paul and delivered on the way back. For fuel he had the best soft coal, and to keep it burning well the firemen fed the furnaces with pitch. Captain Whitten made all scheduled stops, and handled freight as usual, possibly feeling secure in the knowledge that the "Gray Eagle" had started sixty-one miles behind him.

The "Gray Eagle" overtook and passed the "Itasca" only a few miles from St. Paul. Captain Whitten strained every nerve to regain his lead, and he all but succeeded. As the speeding boats neared the levee the "Gray Eagle" was less than a length ahead. Captain Harris stood on the hurricane deck with the trans-oceanic message wrapped and tied around a lump of coal. As his boat drew in to the bank he threw the parcel ashore, and the message was taken up and read by the assembled crowd.

The "Gray Eagle" ran the 290 miles from Dunleith in eighteen hours. The "Itasca" made the 229 miles from Prairie du Chien in the same time. The average speed of the "Gray Eagle" was 16.1 miles per hour; of the "Itasca," 12.7 miles per hour. The "Itasca," of course, made more stops than her rival. The closeness of the final spurt shows that the boats were better matched in speed capabilities than their average speeds in this race would indicate.

In contrast with the short spurts and desultory

races of the northern rivers, there were the days in New Orleans when every afternoon at five o'clock big rival packets backed out from the crowded levee and headed north. Their business took them to various landings, with stops of varying length, but at the beginning of the run, with several boats starting abreast, there was almost always an exciting race.

These steamboats were the craft that seamen sometimes called derisively "a steam engine on a raft." Without doubt their low flat hulls and towering upperworks looked queer and unsubstantial to a sailor's eye. And to some of us moderns, the steamboat seems a relic of a crude and hap-hazard age, a thing that has not kept up with the times. But the steamboat at her finest was the product of a long line of mechanical evolution. She was developed to meet a set of conditions and needs, and disappeared only when the conditions changed and the needs were met by other means. The steamboat carried the freight and the passengers and she carried them fast. She was beautiful with the beauty of a thing that fulfills its purpose well. In their own way, her lines were as trim and clean as the lines of a racing yacht. And her speed would compare favorably with the speedy water transportation of to-day.

At the levee where the boats are moored, the crowd presses close to those that are ready to start. Friends of departing passengers have gone ashore and are shouting their last instructions and good-byes. Big wheels are turning slowly, beating the water with sluggish swashing strokes. Wet steam hisses from opened cylinder-cock and streams away over the brown river.

On the hurricane deck of a big boat with a pair of gilded antlers on her pilot house, the captain stands watching his crew on the forecastle below. The mate looks up and calls, "All ready, sir!" With a final glance that takes in crew, boats, levee and river, the captain rings the big bell. His hull is greased and its timbers are partially sawn through so that it will be more flexible to the uneven thrust of the wheels.

The mellow note is echoed by the bells of other boats about to start. The wheels are stopped, the black roustabouts take the mooring-lines aboard. Bells jangle in the engine-room; another, and another. Reversed wheels beat the water, exhaust steam hisses up through coroneted escape pipes, and the boats back into the current, belching clouds of black smoke from chimneys crowned with showy ornamental tops. Passengers are waving hats and handkerchiefs. The roustabouts are calling badinage to their friends or rivals, or, under the leadership of some negro with the gift of music, singing songs in praise of their boats. Wheels are stopped, and started ahead; the boats straighten their courses upstream, and the race is on.

Back on the crowded levee they are making bets. Sportsmen, gamblers, shippers, friends of passengers, officers of boats still tied up, hackmen, porters, newsboys, stevedores, pickpockets; all feel the fascination of the race. They make their wagers, a thousand dollars or a dime, watch their favorites disappear around the bend, and go about their business. But in the recesses of their minds where the emotions lie, there lingers the image of the smoking monsters battling for leadership.

Gradually the boats steaming up-river forge ahead or drop behind, according to their speed, their loads, and their business. No more sooty smoke is poured from their chimneys; the black cloud at starting is only a showy trick, done by throwing some powdery coal over the fires. Two of the boats drop their smoky streamers when they are hardly under way. These are the packet with the gilded antlers and another of about the same size and build. No ostentatious foolishness for them; by the time their pilots ring for full speed ahead, their fires are clean and white-hot. This is a race, and their people, from captains to scullery boys, are racers. They have been there before.

Leading all the rest, the two fast packets run side by side up the brown river between the low-lying levee banks. Supper is prepared and served. The meal is over and the passengers are coming out on deck as they reach the old Red Church, pass and leave it to starboard. Between nine and ten o'clock the gangways touch the Donaldson levee and the rush of loading and unloading begins. The mates stand on barrel or capstan, urging speed with profane exhortations. The roustabouts seem to like it. They want speed, too, and they enjoy being cursed by men they admire. In a few minutes the work is done. Bells clang, the boats round into the stream and are on their way again. The light from the furnace doors shines weirdly red on the glistening bodies of the firemen on the forecastle. High above the cabin lights, above the darkened pilot house, showers of sparks fly glaring from the stacks, swirl in the air, float and gleam and die. On the levee the people watch until the lights of the matched rivals are gone from sight.

It is after midnight when the racers stop for a few minutes at Baton Rouge. Most of the passengers have gone to their staterooms. A few men lounge about the bar. Among them a gambler and his capper are plying their trade. They have bet on the race, of course, but not everything; they can not let even a race interfere with the regular pursuit of business. When the boats resume their trip each craft takes a coal barge in tow, and as they labor up the river dragging these unwieldy boxes the roustabouts work like fiends in the light of flaring pine torches, transferring the fuel from the barges to the boats. They finish the work, and, panting, throw themselves down on the deck. In an instant the barges are loosed, to drift back with their crews to the town.

Through the night and the early morning the racers strive for advantage, now one, now the other gaining the lead. At sunrise the passengers are com-

From an old Currier & Ives print in the collection of Karl Schmidt, Esq.

MIDNIGHT RACE ON THE MISSISSIPPI

ing out on deck, looking for the rival boat and finding her close at hand, thinking first of the race, then
of breakfast. The morning advances, and still the
rival pilots jockey their craft with no decisive gains.

All at once there is a stir that every one on board
feels. Perhaps it is the almost unappreciable quick-
ening of the engines' beat, the higher note of the
threshing paddles, the louder hiss of the exhaust as
the big boats breathe like sprinters nearing the tape.
Perhaps it is the undertone of excitement in the
voices of the firemen.

Down on the main deck of each boat, something
has been hung on the arm of the safety-valve; something the makers of the valve never intended should
be hung there. And the weight hangs there, too, in
the last notch at the end. On the racers' forecastles
barrels of resin are opened, and as this fuel is thrown
in with the coal the fires leap hissing and roaring
through the flues. On the heated chimneys the paint
begins to blister. On each forecastle a keg of whiskey has been opened, and the firemen help themselves.

Now is the real test of speed, the proof of a boat's
lines and engines and boilers, of her officers' skill
in loading, of her pilot's fitness to be called a light-
ning pilot, of the nerve and endurance of all her
company. Slowly the boat with the gilded antlers
draws ahead. Triumphantly her roustabouts start
a song of victory. She holds her lead, gradually in-
creases it, and now the low buildings and the levees

of Natchez come in sight. Down on the forecastle of the antlered boat a big black roustabout stands on the guards, yelling, waving the end of a cable, derisively offering a tow to the beaten rival.

The keen competition of river steamboats, in which business rivalry went hand in hand with the irrepressible spirit of sport, is a thing that would be impossible in these days of huge and highly organized transportation corporations. But remember that the Mississippi captain was usually the owner of his boat. Not only that, he designed and built her, from her keel to the lacy iron crowns on her chimney-tops. The lines of her hull, the size and type of her engines and boilers, the dimensions and placing of her wheels, her outside and inside finish, the general look of her as she stood in the water, all were the results of his own experience, shrewdness, and good taste. No newlywed, building his first bungalow, ever regarded the fruit of his labors with more affectionate pride than the builder-captain's pride in his boat. And to the men of the rivers, the game never palled. Built into the wood and iron of each new boat were the ideas her captain had gleaned from his experience with her predecessor. There was no going backward, no duplication of previous steamboats. Each boat must be bigger, better, faster.

From the very beginning of steamboating, the run from New Orleans to Louisville was regarded as the test of a boat's speed and navigating qualities. The "Enterprise" was the first boat to make this run, in the year 1817. Her time was twenty-five days, two hours, and four minutes. Her run was not regarded as a conclusive test of up-river navigation, because she came up on flood waters, cutting across bends and finding deep water where normally there was dry land. In the same year Captain Shreve's "Washington" made the run at mean river stages in twenty-five days. This run proved the practicability of steam navigation both ways and established the supremacy of the flat-hulled, high-pressure boat. In 1819 the "Shelby" made the run in twenty days, four hours, and twenty minutes, and in 1828 the "Paragon" lowered the record to eighteen days and ten hours.

The first really fast trip was made in 1834 by the "Tecumseh," in eight days and four hours. In 1837 the "Express" and the "Sultana" tied the record at six days and fifteen hours. In 1838 the "Diana" won a prize of five hundred dollars offered by the Post-office Department by making the run in less than six days. Her time was five days, twenty-three hours, and fifteen minutes. In the following years the crack packets clipped the record, hour by hour and minute by minute, until the days of the fast "Eclipse" and "A. L. Shotwell."

The roster of speed shows a continuous increase:

1842   "Edward Shippen" 5 days 14 hours
1849   "Sultana" 5 days 12 hours
1851   "Bostona" 5 days 8 hours
1852   "Belle Key" 4 days 20 hours

1853 "Reindeer" 4 days 19 hours 45 minutes
1853 "Eclipse" 4 days 9 hours 31 minutes
1853 "A. L. Shotwell" 4 days 9 hours 19 minutes

The run from New Orleans to Cairo was closely contested by the fastest boats of the days when a record run was the chief pride of captain, pilot, crew and patrons. In 1844 the "J. M. White" set the record at three days, six hours, and forty-four minutes. This record stood for nine years, and many rivermen say that it never was beaten. Before the time was lowered, the river had shortened itself by cut-offs, so that while the elapsed time was less the distance traveled was less also.

In the years during which the "White" held the record, the nearest approach to it was made by the "Reindeer," in 1852, with a time of three days, twelve hours, and forty-five minutes. In 1853 the "Eclipse" lowered the time to three days, four hours, and four minutes, and the "A. L. Shotwell" clipped it down to three days, three hours, and forty minutes. This record stood until 1870, when the racer "Robert E. Lee," on the run that sent her name over the wires to all the world, set it at three days, one hour, and one minute.

There was keen rivalry on the run from Helena to Memphis. The record of the "Peytona," six hours and thirty-six minutes, stood for some time. In 1853 the "Eclipse" lowered it to six hours and seventeen minutes. Later the river shortened itself fifteen miles by cut-offs, and in 1882 and 1883 fast boats raced sharply for first place, lowering the record by minutes only:

"Belle Memphis" 5 hours 53 minutes
"City of Cairo" 5 hours 52 minutes
"City of Providence" 5 hours 49½ minutes
"Kate Adams" 5 hours 18½ minutes
"James Lee" 5 hours 14 minutes

The run from New Orleans to Natchez, the first run regularly made by a steamboat on western rivers, was a favorite course for short races that were tests of speed rather than endurance. Speeding was begun by the old "Comet" and the high mark was set by the "Lee" and the "Natchez" in their historic race. For a long time there hung on the wharf-boat at Natchez a pair of antlers with a shield between them bearing the name of the record-holder and the inscription, "Come and take them." The records of speed over this run, from 1814 to 1870, illustrate well the progress of steamboating in a little over a half-century:

1814 "Comet" 5 days 10 hours
1815 "Enterprise" 4 days 11 hours 20 minutes
1817 "Shelby" 3 days 20 hours
1819 "Paragon" 3 days 8 hours
1828 "Tecumseh" 3 days 1 hour 20 minutes
1834 "Tuscarora" 1 day 21 hours
1838 "Natchez" 1 day 17 hours
1840 "Edward Shippen" 1 day 8 hours
1844 "Sultana" 19 hours 45 minutes
1853 "Natchez" (new) 17 hours 30 minutes

1856 "Princess" 17 hours 30 minutes
1870 "Natchez" (racer) 17 hours 11 minutes
1870 "Robert E. Lee" 17 hours 11 minutes

The steamboat "Ruth" had a pair of gilded horns for her record run from Natchez to New Orleans, made in 1867, in fifteen hours and four minutes. This record stood until 1909, when the battleship "Mississippi" made the run in fourteen hours. The battleship, however, landed in New Orleans about two miles above the landing made by the steamboat. The "Ruth" had another pair of horns for the run from New Orleans to Donaldsonville, seventy-eight miles, in four hours and twenty-seven minutes. The "Ruth" never lost her trophies to a rival, but she did not carry them long. In 1868, when twelve miles above Vicksburg, she caught fire and burned. Of all the boat, the antlers were the only things saved.

The strain of driving a boat's machinery at its utmost capacity inevitably caused accidents. Fires were forced, boilers made to carry pressures beyond the danger point, engines driven with only one thing in view, speed. The most apparent risk was boiler explosion, but strangely enough instances of boilers bursting while a boat was running at racing speed are rare. Probably this is because engines, boilers and furnaces were so well proportioned with regard to each other that the engines could use up any amount of steam the hottest fires could generate. The greatest risk of all was fire, the terror of the sea and equally of the rivers.

On April 9, 1832, the "Brandywine" and the "Hudson" were racing, thirty miles above Memphis. A strong wind was blowing. The "Brandywine" had been compelled to stop for repairs, and now, feeding her fires with resin, was overtaking her rival. Suddenly fire flared up on her boiler deck. Sparks had come up her chimney casings and ignited some crates of carriage wheels wrapped in straw. The crew threw the blazing crates overboard, but it was too late; the boat's woodwork had caught fire, and in five minutes she was ablaze from stem to stern. The pilot turned and ran her for the bank, but she struck a bar a quarter of a mile from land and stuck fast. The boat's yawl, manned by a crew untrained for such emergencies and overloaded by panic-stricken people, was swamped and lost. The boat burned to the water's edge, with the loss by burning or drowning of more than a hundred lives.

Five years later, May 8, 1837, the "Ben Sherrod" was lost in a similar way. She was running second in a race with the "Prairie" and was straining for the lead. It was past midnight. The lights of the "Prairie" were in sight ahead, and the firemen of the "Sherrod" were forcing their fires with resin spread over the fuel, keeping up their strength and spirits with whiskey from a barrel that stood open on the forecastle. As the boats were racing up the river fourteen miles above Fort Adams, the heat of the "Sherrod's" furnaces set fire to sixty cords of wood piled on her decks. The fire spread with amazing swiftness. The pilot, Davis, steered for the bank, but before he could make it the tiller ropes burned and the flaming boat became unmanageable. Davis died at his wheel. He had said as he was leaving New Orleans on that trip that if his boat ever burned and he failed to save the passengers it would be because he was killed or the tiller ropes burned.

The excited crew swamped the yawl, cutting off the only means of escape. Crew and passengers jumped overboard, supporting themselves as best they could on anything that floated. In half an hour the "Columbus" came to the scene of the disaster and was picking up the survivors when the "Alton" came up and, her captain failing to hear the cries of the people in the water, steamed right among them, the wash of the wheels drowning many whose strength was failing. The "Prairie" did not turn back to give assistance. Her captain reported the fire at Natchez and Vicksburg.

The burning of the "Sherrod" was made more terrible by three explosions. First, a number of barrels of liquor exploded, flooding the deck with burning liquid. Then the boilers burst, and finally forty barrels of gunpowder in the hold let go, tearing the wreck to fragments. About two hundred lives were lost.

Boiler explosions sometimes are queer and paradoxical things. All are caused by over-pressure, but what is it that raises the pressure to the bursting-point at the particular moment of explosion? Sometimes an over-strained boiler lets go just as the accumulated pressure is released. It was in this way that the boilers of the "Moselle" blew up, on April 25, 1838.

Captain Perrin of the "Moselle" was a fast driver, proud of his boat's speed. The boat was considered the finest on the rivers, and her captain claimed she was the fastest in America. On her last trip she made the seven hundred and fifty miles from St. Louis to Cincinnati in two days and sixteen hours. Captain Perrin determined to establish his boat's supremacy by beating the opposition boat on the return trip to St. Louis.

A few minutes after leaving Cincinnati, the "Moselle" stopped at a landing on the Ohio side to take aboard some German emigrants. During the stop the firemen did not cease feeding their furnaces. The steam pressure rose so high that one passenger, reading the gauge, protested against the foolish risk and went ashore. His remonstrance went unheeded. As the boat rounded into the stream with opened throttle, all four of her boilers exploded with terrific force.

The deck and upperworks were blown to splinters. Fragments of timbers and boilers and human bodies were thrown as far as the Kentucky shore, a quarter of a mile away. One body fell through the roof of a house. The racing captain, standing on his boiler deck, was blown high in the air and killed. The blast resulted in eighty-one known dead and fifty-five missing. As some of the passengers had not yet registered, there may have been more casualties than these.

On June 12, 1850, a race ended tragically through the weakness of a boiler-head. The "St. Joseph" was racing with the "South America," and as they were passing the mouth of the Arkansas River the after head of one of the "St. Joseph's" boilers blew out, instantly killing the second engineer and a helper. At once the boat took fire from scattered coals. Most of the deck passengers jumped overboard, and about ten of them drowned. The "South America" picked up the rest and took the crew and cabin passengers from the burning boat.

Captain Baker of the "St. Joseph" took three thousand dollars from his safe and passed it to the clerk of the "South America" for safe-keeping. Next day he asked for his money to pay off his crew. The clerk, showing that good sportsmanship was not universal, handed Baker three hundred dollars, claiming the balance for salvage. Captain Baker stopped at Memphis and had the "South America" attached by the sheriff and detained for twenty-four hours. The people of the city learned of the case and made things uncomfortable for Captain Greenlee and the clerk of the "South America." These officers, fearing the popular indignation, returned Baker's money.

In December of the same year the "South America" burned nine miles above New Orleans with the loss of forty lives.

The dangers within the boat itself were not the only ones that beset the racers. On March 9, 1854, the "John L. Avery" raced the "Sultana" off Black Hawk Point, forty miles below Natchez, and left her a mile astern. The exultant crew and passengers were congratulating each other on the victory when the boat struck a submerged tree, washed into the channel by a recent freshet. The torn boat heeled, lifting her wound above water, but before her pilot could beach her she righted again, the racked upperworks tore loose from the hull, and the hull sank in deep water. As the cabin settled in the stream the water forced the floor up against the roof. Some of the passengers were taken out through the skylight. A mother saved one of her children in this way, but another was drowned by the rising water. The deck passengers, mostly Irish emigrants, were walled in by hogsheads of sugar and nearly all were drowned. In all, about ninety lives were lost. The "Sultana" picked up practically all who were saved.

The loss of life and property incident to steamboat racing could not deter the racers. We Americans were a reckless lot in the days of our youth. And those that didn't want to race could always take the "Jacob Strader" which made a bid for the conservatives by painting "Low Pressure" in large letters on the paddle-boxes.

Steamboat racing culminated, in 1870, in the great race of the "Robert E. Lee" and the "Natchez," from New Orleans to St. Louis. For a long time before the race little else was talked about in shipping circles, and that included everybody on the rivers. Betting ran high. The "Natchez" was generally considered the faster boat, but she was a little top-heavy and therefore slow in landing and getting under way. Partizans of both boats were confident of victory.

On June 20 the rival boats lay at New Orleans ready for the race, watched by milling crowds of steamboat enthusiasts. Captain Leathers of the "Natchez" had his boat in her usual spick-and-span condition. He had taken aboard a limited amount of freight. Captain Cannon of the "Lee" had stripped his craft until she was a racing machine and nothing more. Every unnecessary pound was taken off, anchors and chains, cabin furniture, beds and bedding, all were left ashore. Even the doors and shutters were taken off their hinges to lessen the wind resistance of the boat's upperworks. There was no freight aboard the "Lee," her deck and hold were filled with dry pine knots and other choice fuel. There was even some fat side-meat to force the fires in a pinch. Captain Leathers, confident of his boat's superiority, was preparing for the race on the basis of amateur sport. Captain Cannon was making a professional event of it.

At five o'clock in the afternoon the racers backed out from the crowded levee and began their historic run. Almost at the beginning of the race, an unexpected maneuver by Captain Cannon practically decided the outcome. Captain Cannon had chartered a fast boat, the "Frank Paragoud," and sent her up the river above Baton Rouge, loaded with the finest fuel. When the "Lee" reached this point she did not stop her engines, but only slackened her speed while the "Paragoud," under full steam, lay alongside, and her load of fuel was transferred to the deck of the "Lee." Captain Leathers, with no such arrangement, had to land the "Natchez" and take a coal barge in tow, losing precious time that he never could make up. In addition to the initial advantage given him by fueling while under way, Captain Cannon had the advantage of a stripped craft. The winds whistled through the opened cabins of the "Lee," while the "Natchez," with her windows and doors in place, caught them all.

As the racers passed Memphis, Vicksburg, and Cairo, their time was telegraphed to all parts of the country and cabled to Europe. At Cairo the race was practically over, the "Natchez" was so far behind that she had no chance of regaining the lost mile. The "Lee's" time to Cairo was three days, one hour, and one minute. She finished at St. Louis, setting a record of three days, eighteen hours, and fourteen minutes for the run of twelve hundred and seventy-eight miles, an average speed of fourteen and one-sixth miles per hour, including stops.

The race occasioned some controversy among the men who had bet their money on it. Some of those who had backed the "Natchez" contended that it was no race, because the "Lee" had received assistance from the power of the "Paragoud." It was the beginning of the end of steamboat racing on a large scale. It showed the possibilities of professionalism, and in a sport such as steamboat racing the expense of professionalism was too high. Only a few years, and the competition of railroads reduced steamboating to a business of close margins and careful calculations. The most spectacular sport this country has ever seen was gone forever.

CHAPTER XI

THE PEOPLE OF THE BOATS

"Oh, I wouldn't be a fireman,
He works amid the coal;
I'd rather be the gamblin' man
That wears the ring of gold."

FRONTIERSMEN—FLATBOATMEN AND KEEL-BOATMEN BECOME
STEAMBOATMEN—SUPERSTITIONS—RED MOUTHS AND GER-
MANS—NEGROES ON THE STEAMBOATS—SLAVE TRAVEL—THIR-
TEEN KINDS OF DESSERT—STEAMBOAT GAMBLERS—NATCHEZ-
UNDER-THE-HILL—NEGRO BOAT SONGS.

THE inland rivers, like mirrors of extraordinary
power, constantly reflected the progress of the
country. There were until 1780 only the quiet
Indians and adventurous traders going with their
pirogues and canoes over the lonely stretches where
the tall, unshorn forests made the rivers green
canyons with yellow beds. Then, that scene changed
with the push of the frontier farther west, over the
Alleghenies; and there appeared along the Monongahela and upper Ohio the flatboatman and the keel-
boatman, poling their cumbrous craft from the tiny
settlements through the wilderness and the Indian
country, far down for week after week towards the
fabled New Orleans. And now these hardy men,
making a regular path over the hundreds of miles of
water, take the frontier farther westward, bringing
the emigrant with his stock, rude implements and

231

scanty household goods to the banks of Kentucky, Ohio and Indiana. Thus trading posts were born and Marietta, Cincinnati, Louisville, St. Louis come into being as small settlements dropped down in the great forest, separated by great intervals.

And the emigrants, clearing off the land along the river, penetrating the smaller streams and creeks that feed the bigger water where they make their farms, raise abundant crops which have to be shipped and exchanged for goods that will enable them to live and grow more crops. And meanwhile more emigrants are waiting in the eastern country to come to the new land. And so conditions have been wrought that hasten the arrival of the Fulton boat. For the great country, the length between Pittsburgh and New Orleans, between New Orleans and the Falls of St. Anthony, cannot be physically shortened; distances must be bridged by speed.

The Fulton boat with its round deep hull comes steaming down, holding a fourteen year's monopoly on swift craft building. But the keel-boatmen, the rivermen, see the faults in the new boat and build better ones themselves, so that they too may further their occupations and be of benefit to the waiting emigrants, the farming frontiersmen who are already on the ground, the fur traders with their important freight and the planters of the lower Mississippi region who are growing more cane and cotton year by year.

At last the flatboatmen and keel-boatmen were on

the steamboats, using their knowledge of the river and pioneer affairs as captains, pilots, engineers or deck hands, carrying over into their new profession the characteristics of the old. Going downstream at night, they thought their boat went swifter than in the daytime. After an accident they were always apprehensive until two more had occurred; believing that all bad luck came in triplets, they could not breathe easily until the misfortune had wholly spent itself. A white horse on board was cause for anxiety, an ill omen of almost unparalleled force. And a worn sock, tied about a sick man's neck, cured all fevers. Horseshoes brought good fortune, and corpses brought neither bad nor good; they were simply disregarded as omens, and sometimes white roustabouts and engineers used the lid of a coffin as a table for their game of cards. Ghosts, however, were another matter, and as the history of steamboating with its frequent tales of wrecks by snag and boiler explosion grew the river became haunted from one end to the other. A story is told of a pilot aboard the "St. Louis" who, having to share his place with a corpse which had been put there to keep cool, kept up his nerve by drinks every half hour which were brought him from the bar-room. As he stood there in the impenetrable gloom by the wheel, steering by the dimly seen marks along the shadowy banks, glancing now and then at the forbidding square of black by the window, he looked over his shoulder and saw a human figure in spectral white. He did not wait for another look, but went over the wheel in one jump, clear to the hurricane deck twenty feet below. As he painfully got to his feet for another leap he saw over the wheel which he had just left the head and arm of the specter. "Hey," it yelled, "where the hell are you goin'? Here's the key to the bar. Come and get it before I take my death of cold. I forgot about it till after I was in bed, and I tell you it's chilly up here with nothing but my underclothes on."

Flatboatmen and keel-boatmen also carried over to the steamboat the songs they had sung before. One of them sung in early days on the Ohio shows its origin:

> The boatman is a lucky man,
> No one can do as the boatman can,
> The boatmen dance and the boatmen sing,
> The boatman is up to everything.

> #### CHORUS
> Hi-O, away we go,
> Floating down the river on the O-hi-o.

> When the boatman goes on shore,
> Look, old man, your sheep is gone,
> He steals your sheep and steals your shote,
> He puts 'em in a bag and totes 'em to the boat.

> #### CHORUS
> When the boatman goes on shore
> He spends his money and works for more,
> I never saw a girl in all my life,
> But what she would be a boatman's wife.

> #### CHORUS

Certainly a song to delight Mike Fink's crew, even if transplanted to the forecastle of a steamboat that goes up the river as well as down.

Steamboat crews and officers at the beginning were all Americans; that is, they were all foreigners who spoke English intelligibly, with the burr of the Scot, the twang of the New Englander, and the flatness of the Kentuckian most marked among them. Then for a time the deck was supplied with Irish, called Micks and Red Mouths, and the Germans, who had come to the rivers penniless. Steamboatmen had grievances against the Irish. They said they would willingly, nay gladly, sign up for a trip and then not turn a hand until the mate raised the club he carried and released some crimson oaths. Old steamboatmen trace much of the reputed toughness of the mates to the needs of these hands for strong urging and an occasional blow. Billy Wilson, a mate on the upper Mississippi, had a pork barrel stave with holes bored through it so that, to cure mere laziness, he could use the flat of it with stinging effect, and in a mutiny he could use the edge.

But gradually the negroes replaced all others as deck hands. They began as servants in kitchen and cabin and the more brawny found jobs as firemen. Even before the war there were enough negroes working on the river boats to make the whites in less important positions fear for their jobs. As waiters their grins and native flattery were more pleasing to the officers and passengers than the grim condescending attendance of the whites; as cooks they were more satisfactory, and as firemen they would put up with more heat and abuse. They supplanted the white stewardess, that strange victim of her times and surroundings who, having to earn her own living, which was considered queer and unfortunate in those days, fell into the habits of the male members of the crew, there being no other women with whom to associate. Traveling women might have been surprised to see their stewardess when off watch sitting at the kitchen table with the cook, drinking from his flask and either chewing natural leaf tobacco or puffing contentedly at a black cigar.

It was not long until the happy, unworldly negroes made up more than half the crew of the steamboats. They cooked and served the meals, made the bunks, stoked the fires and rolled the freight up and down the gangplank, working as stevedores in the hey-day of high wages for no more than fifty dollars a month. But they were free, and perhaps better off than the slaves who were always to be seen traveling on the main deck, having been bought by a slave dealer who was taking them to sell somewhere else. Of this period a woman traveler wrote, "We have taken on board two small droves of Negroes, bought in Richmond for a plantation in Vicksburg. They cost the owner, all expenses included, $1050 a head. I asked the best looking girl of the lot her name. She said it was Cinderella and that her master had bought her for his own use. I asked her what that meant, and she said to work on his plantation, and not to sell again. They all seemed satisfied with their emigration to Louisiana. Another lot of 21 were taken on board lower down the river, and were on their way to the New Orleans market to be sold, all except one, a mulatto girl, who seemed to be the traveling companion of the owner and would return with him. One fellow became obstreperous and had to be put in irons." Another traveler noted that the slaves, accustomed to hard work, but free of all responsibility, sang and frolicked and made a holiday of the trip and seemed much happier and more carefree than their masters.

The slaves were quartered on the main deck along with the whites who traveled cheaply. Bunks were furnished for sleeping and a stove for cooking, but deck passengers brought aboard their own food, generally sausage, dried herring, crackers and cheese, with whiskey to wash the dry meal down. They brought their own bedding or went without. Among these passengers were easterners who had left their rocky farms and were looking for better and cheaper land in the west; emigrants direct from Europe seeking work, and a constant stream of the restless folk to whom distant fields looked always greenest, ever moving with their reluctant wives and their brood of children, helping the crew carry wood aboard at every chance so that they would be given a rebate on their fare.

But up in the cabins steamboat travel was more

pleasant. There was a steward to look out for all of the first-class travelers' needs, and his department was of great importance to the success of the boat. Under the direction of the steward the meals were prepared and served and kitchen supplies bought at the landings: fruit and vegetables, lambs, pigs and chickens. The animals were killed and dressed on board. The chickens lived until the menu called for a chicken dinner, whereupon three or four negroes in the starboard galley where the meats were prepared gathered around a barrel of hot water which had been filled from the boilers, broke the necks of the fowls over the edge of the barrel, scalded, picked and cut them—sometimes as many as a hundred and fifty in an hour. In the larboard galley were made the breads, cakes, pastries and desserts; stewards kept it for a show place of cleanliness, but always found some excuse for not taking sight-seeing passengers to inspect the starboard galley.

Boats competed with one another to be known as serving the cabin passengers the most elaborate meals. On one of the packets thirteen desserts were served, six of custard, jelly and cream in tall glasses, and seven of pies, puddings and ice cream,—one each trip. Some of the northern line boats served a meal at the beginning of each run that was so heavy that it was called the foundering meal and left the passengers with digestions that made them squeamish towards food for the remainder of the journey.

To the cabin passengers went this food, to men

with money enough to afford the most agreeable comforts that kind of travel offered: the cotton planter
from the south and southwest, officers in government
service, manufacturers, men of business, sight-seeing
easterners, growers from the middle west who had
come to market their produce and were returning
with large rolls of banknotes. Let the roustabouts
below eat the left-overs, which the cabin passengers
after every meal saw put on the deck in pans, the
meats in one, the bread and cake in another and
jellies and custards in a third, followed by the cry
of "Grub-pile." To see the roustabouts rush for the
broken food, grab for it and sit down on the deck
to munch what they had managed to get their hands
on! That was a spectacle to aid the digestion of the
cabin passengers! To put them in a good humor!
"Fine weather we're havin' for this trip, sir!" "Yes,
and good for the crops!" "Altogether a very satisfactory and prosperous year," they would say to one
another as they sat in the shade after their meal, looking out over the broad lands that ran back from the
banks of the river, and look until they were bored
with looking.

And among them would be a very pleasant and
amiable man, a fellow with a drooping mustache that
curved a little more attractively, that shone a little
more brilliantly than the mustaches of any of the
others. And he would have eyes with the flash of
fire in them, provocative, daring eyes. Carefree with
his money and with plenty of money to be carefree

with, he seemed, judging from the rich texture of his broadcloth, the frills on his shirt front and the not too ostentatious jewelry about his person. A man who might place a bet,—and laugh lightly if he lost.

And somehow this agreeable, amiable, well-dressed man was always drawn into a little game to while away the slow hours, just a game for a few gentlemen, you understand, a game to pass a friendly hour or so; —and somehow this man would always have his pockets sagging with the other players' money by the time the game was ended.

For the steamboat, a little world in itself, well isolated, but not remote enough to make escape impossible, was the professional gambler's paradise. There was plenty of money aboard; time was heavy; a holiday spirit pervaded the whole cabin, and there were few restrictions on the gambler's activities. Passengers came and went; it was not often that a gambler encountered any of his previous victims or became known for what he was to the boat's patrons. The officers, of course, knew him, but he was thoughtful not to win officers' money, and few captains felt it their duty to protect passengers from their own foolishness.

These professional gamblers followed the old maxim: "Make the sucker think he is going to fleece you, and know that you are going to fleece him." So they had their stage set before anybody else aboard thought of gambling or betting, except on the prospective race between their boat and a rival. They had become well acquainted with the barkeeper, so well that he had permitted them to mark all of the cards that they had for sale and to prepare for them a bottle of colored water which they could drink while the other players thought it was whiskey. Thus with their stripped deck, which was accomplished by putting all the face cards and tens between slightly concave metal plates and trimming them with a razor, they were ready. Or perhaps they had a partner aboard who, at the proper time, would lure some gullible person to believe that he and the partner were going to get the best of the gambler.

For the honest gambler is met mostly in fiction. No man ever made a decent livelihood by fairly playing a gamble in which his opponent has an equal chance. Many have tried; all have been beaten eventually by better players or crooked players. Like all others the professional steamboat gambler took no chance of losing; the only thing he left to fate was the behavior of the sucker from whom he had taken money; and usually he backed that up with a brace of clean, hair-trigger pistols.

One of the many interesting gamblers of the river boats was George Devol, a hard-headed business man in more ways than one. A story about him will show somewhat how gamblers arranged matters and how their profession was tolerated and also how widespread it was. One day while Devol was waiting for a boat at Donaldsonville a stranger suggested a game of cards. Devol said that he didn't mind, and after the first hand, which he lost, saw that the stranger's cards were marked in a way thoroughly familiar to him. And in a short time he had won everything the stranger possessed, except his clothes, and returned from the saloon to the wharf to wait for the boat. But while he was standing there the stranger reappeared with a police officer and Devol was taken to the justice of the peace where the stranger complained that he had been cheated.

"No, sir," said Devol. "The man tried to cheat me, and I'll prove it, if he'll give me the cards." The cards were brought forth and Devol took them and began to read them from the backs. About halfway through the deck he called out "Ten of hearts," and turned the card face up on the justice's desk.

"Whoa," said the justice and leaned eagerly forward. Seizing the card he examined it carefully, then glared at the stranger who, apparently, was no stranger to him. Turning to Devol he said, "Sah, I owe you the drinks. That scoundrel has been skinnin' me with these marked cards for over a week. I recognized that ten of hearts because it fell in the spittoon last night and the tobacco juice is still on it. The defendant is released. The plaintiff is under arrest and is fined one hundred dollars for gambling. The court will now adjourn to the nearest bar."

Devol always managed to escape the wrath of his victims, though at times he came perilously close to being shot. A passenger on the "Robert E. Lee" after losing $800—all he had—to Devol grew desperate and drew his pistol to demand his money back. Devol smiled at him ingenuously and whispered, "I'm not goin' to keep your money. I'll give it back to you, but not in this crowd. If I did all the others would want theirs back. I tell you how we'll do: you bet your pistol on the next turn. I'll bet the $800 against it and lose. Then we'll both be all right."

The pistol was put up, and as Devol turned the winning card he picked up the pistol. "You've acted the wet dog about losing a little money, and you get nothing. I'm going to give this pistol to my friend, the mate. If he'll sell it to you, and if you can raise the money, you can get it from him, but don't pull it on me or you'll get hurt. Now get out of here!"

When Devol could think of no tricks to get him away from a gulled customer he either brought out his pistols or else used his head for a battering ram— it was, he proudly said, harder than a negro's—and started a rough and tumble.

Natchez-under-the-Hill was one of the best known hangouts for steamboat gamblers, thugs and prostitutes in the country. Here the gamblers would get into games among themselves and there would be no limit to the stakes for which they played. One night they were surprised to see no less a person walk into their rendezvous than a gentleman of God, a real preacher. He had come ashore from a boat commanded by Captain John Russell, but for what reason nobody knew, unless it was to gather firsthand material for hot sermons about sin to his congregation. But during his visit he entered a game of chance, or what purported to be a game of chance, and lost every penny he had. Then he returned to Captain Russell for sympathy.

"Now if that ain't a shame," Captain Russell commiserated with him. "Them confounded gamblers! Don't have respect for anybody, not even the Cloth!" It angered him to think that a minister of the Gospel had been treated in this scurvy way; it showed him how terribly the morals of the gamblers had degenerated. And calling the mate he ordered him to arm the crew and be ready at the gangplank in five minutes. "We'll see about this," said Captain Russell as he waited.

The crew came, and with some passengers that liked excitement, went where the red lights gleamed so sinfully but enticingly. Leading his crew, he went to every gambling house in the district and demanded that the preacher's money be given back. But all he got was a laugh.

"H'm," said Captain Russell. And he sent back to the boat for a heavy spar. The spar was brought and husky shoulders behind it broke down every door that led to a dive. But no money was discovered.

"If that money's not brought out here I'll dump this whole shebang in the river," said the outraged captain. At that the laugh was louder than before.

But Captain Russell was not bluffing. He went back to the boat and unmoored her, had a cable made fast to one of the houses, snubbed it around the capstan and rang the engines full speed astern. The house shook, caved and came down from its foundations. If one of the inmates hadn't cut the cable just then the house would have gone into the river.

Undaunted, Captain Russell went back to his task. He substituted a chain for the cable and the armed crew proceeded to fasten it to the building. As it slid down towards the bank the gamblers saw they were beaten by the determination of Russell and gave back the money.

Soon after this the citizens of Natchez drove out the worst of the underworld characters, and they established themselves at Vicksburg. But at Vicksburg they did not remain unmolested either. In the popular excitement that followed John A. Murrell's attempted negro rebellion a gambler named Cabler was driven out of town, but came back to kill the people who had attacked him. But he was caught, disarmed and taken to a wood where he was tarred and feathered. And after this the spirits of the citizenry rose so high that they gathered in front of the courthouse and passed resolutions giving all gamblers twenty-four hours to get out of town. Most of the gamblers heeded the warning, but a number of them remained. Two days later the town militiamen and virtuous Vicksburgers started through the gambling district, taking out all tables and wheels for a big bonfire. They came to a house operated by a man named North and found it barricaded. Nothing else to do, they broke down the door; it fell as the gamblers fired, killing one of the mob outside. Then the attacking party rushed in and great was the slaughter. Some of the gamblers who were hanged were North, Hullams, Dutch Bill, Smith and McCall.

But there were other places for the gamblers to go. Covington, Nebraska, just across the river from Sioux City, Iowa, became headquarters for some of the most vicious characters in the country. It was so bad that Covington and Suez were called the two toughest places in the world. With Natchez-under-the-Hill and the Swamp of New Orleans, Covington is only a memory. Even the name is gone. Where bright lights blazed and painted women chucked old men's chins while the gamblers went through their pockets and murderers consigned their victims' bodies to the swift brown river, to-day stands a quiet, stolid suburb known as South Sioux City.

But the gamblers had no greater picturesqueness than the negro in the days of steamboating. For from these dark throats came the only music and accentuated rhythm that the river travelers knew. Black men at times might not feel happy or tuneful, but there was always at least one in the crew that did, and when he started to sing it was in the nature of the others to sing with him. And soon they all would be patting Juby (jubilee), clapping their hands and slapping their knees, making sounds like the popping of a cork by striking the palm of their hands against their big mouths for accompaniment.

As their boat approached landing where the crowd waited the leader of the singers stood on the capstan, waving a flag in the brave sunlight, or at night, in the glare of the pine torches, iron baskets hung over the water at the bow, filled with burning pine and powdered resin, scenting the air with pungent smoke, dripping burning drops that floated away in a trail of fiery flakes.

When a boat leaves her landing for a long trip, the friends and sweethearts of the crew gather to see them start; and from deck and levee come songs of farewell.

> Farewell, brothers, if you's gwine fo' to go,
> We'll weep fo' to see you' face once mo'.

and all join in the refrain,

> On de levee by de river side.
> I've left my girl in New Orleans
> Fo' she is young, jes' in her teens.
> On de levee by de river side.

A sportive roustabout breaks in with a rollicking tune,

> Ducks play cards and chickens drink wine,
> And de monkey grow on de grape vine.
> Corn starch pudding and tapioca pie,
> Oh! de gray cat pick out de black cat's eye!

Another changes the song, and everybody joins:

> Walk that, Loo, O Miss Loo,
> Ah! Ah! Ah! Here we go!
> Fo' we're gwine fo' to leave you,
> Good-bye, good-bye,
> Fo' we're gwine fo' to leave you,
> Good-bye, good-bye.

Some one starts another fanciful song:

> Monkey dress in soldier clo'es
> All cross ober to Jordan!
> Went out in de woods fo' to drill de crowd;
> O! Je-ru-sa-lem!
> Jay bird sat on ol' hickory limb,
> All cross ober to Jordan!
> I up wid a rock an' hit him on de chin,
> O! Je-ru-sa-lem!

And all join in the chorus:

> Shine on! Shine on!
> All cross ober to Jordan!
> Shine on! Shine on!
> O! Je-ru-sa-lem!

The song starts the religious feelings of the negroes. They sing with fervid enthusiasm:

> Oh, I long fo' to reach dat heavenly sho'
> To meet ol' Peter standin' at de do';
> He say to me, "Oh, how you do?
> Come sit right yonde' in de golden pew."
> Fo' de good colo'ed people do go clea' through
> To dip in de golden sea!

Den dip me! bave me!
Sisters, you an' me!
Come git in de boat
Fo' we all gwine to float
Fo' to dip in de golden sea!

Good Mistah Jesus a-sitting in de prow,
Come, all you niggahs, make you' bow!
Oh! I look down on de world below
An' I watch dem white trash shovelin' snow,
While angel fishes dey nip my toe
While I dip in de golden sea!

Another biblical expounder takes the lead with a song supposed to be a lesson to the ladies:

Oh! Adam, he was fust built man,
Dat's just what de Good Book say;
An' Eve come next!   Den sin began,
Dat's just what de Good Book say.
Eve bit de apple right in two,
A wicked thing fo' Eve to do;
Yes, dat's what de Good Book say.

But the ladies as well as the men on boat and levee join in the chorus:

Dat's just what de Good Book say, it am,
Yes, dat's just what de Good Book say;
I's read it through, you'll find it true,
Fo' dat's what de Good Book say.

Some one else starts another verse:

> Dere was a man, his name was Lot,
> Dat's just what de Good Book say,
> An he hab a wife an' daughter got,
> Dat's just what de Good Book say.
> His wife she balk an' make a halt,
> An' de Lord he turn her into salt;
> Oh! dat's what de Good Book say!

As the boat draws away from the land, the voices of the singers on board are raised in one of the songs of their race:

I's gwine from de cotton fields, I's gwine from de cane,
I's gwine from de ol' log hut dat stan's down in de lane;
De boat am in de river, dat comes to take me off,
An' I's gwine to join de exodus, an' strike out fo' de no'f.

"The Roustabout's Refrain," written on the deck of the "J. M. White" by R. A. Wilkinson for the New Orleans *Times-Democrat,* carries the spirit of the forecastle singers:

> Oh, roll, Nancy gal, roll, gal,
> I'll meet you by-and-by;
> We gwine to roll de cotton
> Way up ten tiers high.
>
> A-dancin' up de river,
> A-dancin' down again,
> With rousters all a-hustlin',
> Jes' look at "Tobin's Train";
> Her wheels is beatin' "Juba,"
> While b'ilers sing de tune,
> De whistle calls de figgers,
> De chimbleys scrape de moon.

Oh, all aroun' de capstan
Jes' clear de deck a while,
And wake de Mississippi
In good ol'-fashioned style.
De jackstaff is a-hummin',
De guys is clangin' loud,
De furnaces is roarin',
De mate's done lef' de crowd.

Oh, Cotton-hook Jim, come pat yo' time,
Oh, Sandbar Joe, come shake yo' heel,
Oh, Yallerback Bill, come shout yo' rhyme,
Ontwill we make her tremble to de keel!
Oh, shuffle an' cut an' walk aroun',
De "coon in de holler" an' de "corn in de groun',"
And "possum fat an' taters" an' "Betsy Brown,"
Twell eben de capstan j'ines de reel.

Backstep, front step, set 'em down ag'in,
Sachez to de left and swing to de right;
Polish up de planks like de debil beatin' sin,
Fo' you gwine ter roll cotton to-night;
Rattle up de middle, clatter down de side,
Jolly as a clam at de floodin' o' de tide,
Happy as a groom a-huggin' o' de bride,
Twell de fus' signal landin' is in sight.

You hear dat whistle shoutin',
You hear dat little bell;
Oh, swing around de derrick,
We's got ter work a spell;
And dar's de mate a-comin',
De captain's up on deck,
Oh, hurry up, you rousters,
You'll cotch it in de neck!

Dong! From de landin' backin',
Oh, look out for dat stage!
De safety-valve is hissin',
De greaser's at de gauge;
Oh, shovel up de furnace
Twell de smoke put out de stars,
We's gwine along de river
Like we's bound to beat de cars.

Oh, roll, Nancy gal, roll, gal,
I'll meet you by-and-by;
We gwine to roll de cotton
Way up ten tiers high.

In contrast to the light-hearted songs of the hard
working, hard playing roustabouts, there were the
plaintive melodies such as the old plantation song
that began,

De night is dark, de day is long,
And we are far from home.
Weep, my brudders, weep!

and ended with

De night is past, de long day done,
And we are going home.
Shout, my brudders, shout!

CHAPTER XII

THE GOLDEN DAYS OF STEAMBOATING

"Oh, I'm Captain Jenks of the Horse Marines,
I feed my horse on corn and beans."

STEAMBOATING AT ITS FINEST—THE NEW ORLEANS LEVEE—RIVER
TRADE OF MEMPHIS—THE BIG DAYS ON THE BIG MUDDY—
SOME OF THE FINE BOATS.

OLD rivermen of all shades and colors, of all sections of life, experience and temper, look back with pleasure and wistful regret to the days when they were boys aboard the proud, memorable packets that trailed swift streams of smoke up and down the Mississippi in the fifties. As an old negro said, "We sho' live' high in dem days. Twenty-five stewahds we'd tote, an' the table, it would look jus' lahk it was spread fo' a weddin'. The ladies would ma'ch in tu music and ma'ch out to music. Some er ouah boats toted lady bands, an' we'd serenade the big towns when we leave 'em. Yessah, Ah've seen some powe'ful fine livin'."

Those ten years before the Civil War, and a few years afterward, were the best for steamboating on the Mississippi and its tributaries: the Golden Age for the packets. The steamboat itself had come to its finest development, and was the most modern means of transportation of its time, a sort of floating hotel and warehouse that resounded with life and music and color. Crews walked with a swagger and jingled their plentiful silver; passengers on the broad, shaded decks sat and critically compared the luxuries of the various boats on which they had traveled. And the owners in their counting houses nodded satisfactorily at the large profits and knew that though their craft might snag, blow up, collide with another or catch fire, there was more than enough money to buy new boats, which the shipyards along the Ohio were busily making day and night.

To midwesterners of those days cabin passage on a packet was a luxurious orgy. More comfortable than their "settin' rooms," more ornate than their prim and uncomfortable parlors—which they entered only on ceremonial occasions—they saw the steamboat's cabin as a bewilderingly beautiful palace. The wooden filigrees that stretched down the long aisle in a tapering vista illuminated by the glistening cut-glass chandeliers; the soft oil paintings on every state-room door; the thick carpets that transformed walking into a royal march; the steaming foods piled high on the long linen cloth in the dining room, with attentive waiters standing at the traveler's elbow, waiting with more food, and gaily colored desserts in the offing—neither homes nor hotels of the fifties were ever like this.

There is a story of a trapper following his lines in the back-river swamps and finding a steamboat bill of fare. That night in his camp he read over and over the enticing names of the viands like a solemn litany. He made up his mind to travel on that boat, to sit in the cabin and have those fine dishes brought him by a waiter; for once in his life really to live! He carried this dream through the long cold season, then sold his pelts and traveled to New Orleans. Along the levee he searched for the boat, asking where she docked and when she sailed, but nobody could tell him. Finally an old negro heard him. "You ain't goin' to travel on 'at boat no mo'. Her bilers blowed up an' she buyned thutty yeahs ago, an' they an't been no boat o' that name since. Wheah y'all come fum, anyhow?"

Steamboat travelers of those gala years when they came to New Orleans saw the wharves all along from Canal to Julia Street piled high and deep with the white, square bales of cotton, while a short way farther on were the Girod Street landings where packets that steamed between New Orleans and Memphis, St. Louis, Louisville and Cincinnati lay, often moored two and three abreast: the elegant "J. M. White," the "Natchez," the "Great Republic," the "Queen City" and the famous "Robert E. Lee," speediest of them all. All the boats that are remembered as the finest on the rivers were there. And farther along, from Canal Street to St. Louis Street were clustered the boats that made short trips, bringing the trade of the Red River, the Black River, the Ouachita, the Atchafalaya, the Tensas, of Bayou Lafourche, Bayou Sara, Baton Rouge and Vicksburg, boats loaded with cane, cotton and tobacco, traveling all the year up and down the wide brown river and disappearing in the narrow, tropical streams where cargoes waited.

And farther up the river was Memphis, without the languorous-eyed creoles, the French cafés where strange food cooking gave out delectable odors and little glasses of liquor held the power to lull a man to pleasant dreams under the table, as in New Orleans —but a pleasant, attractive city at that. For Memphis had her friendly niggers, her bustling wharves, her stiff-backed white-mustached colonels and her share of southern belles as much as any city on the lower river, just as she had her thriving steamboat trade. At Memphis was the first steamboat organization in that part of the country, the Memphis and St. Louis Packet company, which ran the "Philadelphia," the "John B. Dickey," the "Platte Valley" and the "James H. Lucas." It was connected by steamboat with Cincinnati, Nashville, Vicksburg and New Orleans, and the shining decks of the "Charleston," the "Silver Moon," the "Glendale" from Cincinnati, the "James G. Kline" and the "Embassy" running to Nashville, the "Kentucky" and the "Victoria" to Vicksburg, and the "H. R. W. Hill," "Belfast," "John Simonds" and "Nebraska" to New Orleans were often to be seen at the Memphis wharves.

And everywhere along the lower river were the boats stacked high with cotton. Shipped in from the smaller rivers it stood at various points on the Mississippi waiting for the boats to come for it and take

PUBLIC LANDING, LOUISVILLE, KY.

Levee Scene Before the Civil War

it down to New Orleans. Sometimes these boats bound up-river for Memphis turned back before they got there, having loaded to capacity at some lower point, Helena or Napoleon. Napoleon, which is now no more than a memory, having been washed into oblivion by the changing river, was then one of the largest cotton ports on the Mississippi, sharing the glory of Memphis, Natchez, Lake Providence, Greenville, Skipworth, Milligan's Bend and Friar Point.

Like snouting pigs among a flock of fleecy sheep came the coal barges through the packet-traveled river, barges loaded full with fuel for the speedy steamboats that had found coal safer than wood, as it gave out fewer sparks, and requiring a much smaller space than wood for storage. Many, many barges came down in those years, were unloaded at Memphis, White River, Greenville, Vicksburg, Natchez, Bayou Sara, Baton Rouge and New Orleans and then broken up and thrown into the fires of the sugar-mill furnaces.

Steamboat trade was booming everywhere in the fifties, though on the Missouri the most favorable years were from 1855 to 1860. West from St. Louis went the side-wheelers, their full-length cabins well fitted up for passengers. Fifty-nine steamboats were on the lower Missouri in 1858 and during that year there were 308 arrivals at Leavenworth, Kansas, where the freight charges paid for the season amounted to $167,000. And the next year the advertisements in the St. Louis papers showed there were more steamboats leaving that city for the Missouri than for the upper and lower Mississippi combined. It might have been that there was a story in those figures for the reflective to read, but apparently nobody read it, or, if they did, put out their hands to avert the trouble that the story augured. In 1857 Sioux City, Iowa, in spite of its being a new village, welcomed 28 steamboat arrivals before the first of July. There were 23 regular boats on the upper portion of the river that year and their aggregate freight business was a million and a quarter dollars.

But cotton was king, and though the steamboat business extended over the Mississippi, the Missouri, the Ohio and practically all their navigable tributaries, it is the lower Mississippi that is remembered as the river of steamboats; the river where every boat had a nigger on the safety valve, a gambler on the hurricane deck and romance in the cabin. And it was for this trade that most of the finest boats were built.

One of them was the "Eclipse," called the outstanding boat of her time. And when, in 1853, the "Eclipse" made her extraordinary run from New Orleans to Louisville in four days, nine hours and thirty-one minutes, there were few if any sea-going vessels of her size and power. She was 363 feet long, 36 feet in the beam, with a hold that was nine feet deep. Her two engines had 36-inch cylinders that gave a 11 foot stroke; they were fed by eight boilers, each thirty-two and a half feet long and 42 inches in diameter. Her wheels were 41 feet in diameter and had buckets 14 feet long and 26 inches wide. She was built by Hippel and Evans of New Albany, Indiana, where so many of the good boats were made.

The "Eclipse" was meant to live up to her name. Her cabin glared with the gilt and paintings that adorned it. At the men's end of the long hall was a gilt statuette of General Jackson; and at the women's end a similar figure of Henry Clay, while in between were rows of richly colored canvas. There was a piano for the use of passengers, sleeping rooms for their servants, and the awe-inspiring number of 48 bridal chambers aboard! Her crew and officers numbered 121 and there was room aboard for 180 passengers.

But the "Eclipse" was not alone in her speed and finery. When she went down the river to New Orleans there were many along the wharves ready to challenge her. One of them was the "A. L. Shotwell," built in 1852, 53 feet shorter than the "Eclipse, with a 36 foot beam, an eight foot depth of hold and engines, measuring 30 inches by 10 feet, were fed by six boilers of 32 foot length and 42 inch diameter. Her wheels were five feet less in diameter but her buckets were one foot longer than those of the "Eclipse." Though smaller, the "A. L. Shotwell" proved herself the speedier boat of the two: in one of the most famous races of the rivers she outdistanced the "Eclipse," and at another time she made a trip from New Orleans to Louisville in four days, nine hours and 19 minutes, eleven minutes less than the best time of the "Eclipse."

Compared with these boats the "J. M. White," racer of 1844, was small, though a very large boat for her day. She was 250 feet long, 31 feet wide, with a hold a little over eight feet deep; her two engines were of 30-inch bore and 10-foot stroke, and steam was supplied by seven boilers 32 feet long and 42 inches in diameter. Her wheels were 32 feet in diameter and the buckets were 15 feet long. Nevertheless, there are many rivermen who say that the "J. M. White" was not only unbeaten but that she never could have been beaten by a steamboat of the rivers.

Perhaps the most famous racer of all, the "Robert E. Lee," was much larger than the "White." The "Lee" was built by Captain John W. Cannon to take the place of his "General Quitman" (260 feet long, 40 feet beam, eight and a half foot hold, 30-inch by ten feet engines, seven boilers of 30 feet by 40 inches), which served the Confederate states during the Civil War. The "Lee" had a 300 foot length, 44 foot beam, ten foot hold, two engines with a ten foot stroke and cylinders of 40 inch bore. She carried eight boilers 32 feet long by 42 inches and her side-wheels of 38 foot diameter had buckets 16 and a half feet long.

The "Lee" and the "Natchez," which ran the most widely known race on the rivers, were pretty well matched, the "Natchez" being 307 feet long, 43 feet in the beam, with a 10 foot hold. Her engines, though, were slightly smaller than those of her rival, having the same stroke, but only a 34 inch bore to the "Lee's" 40. The "Natchez" had eight boilers of 40-inch diameter and 34 foot length. Her wheels were of 42 feet diameter, with buckets 16 feet long. The "Frank Paragoud," which served as a fuel boat for the "Lee" in her famous race, was just about the size of the "J. M. White."

The names of those three swift boats, the "J. M. White," "Lee," and "Natchez" were later applied to the crafts of other builders. There was a 303-foot "Natchez" made in 1879, a 315-foot "Lee" in 1876, and another "J. M. White" in 1878, 321 feet long, 49 feet wide with a hold 11 feet deep.

But these boats never made the races that their predecessors ran.

In the palmy days of steamboating, the ten years before the Civil War, steamboatmen built boat after boat, each a little better than the last. Business was good; most boats paid for themselves and yielded good profits before they were lost or retired from service. There was virtually no competition except that between the boats themselves; railroads were in their early stages of development. Only a few people dreamed that in the future the little steam wagons that ran on rails would make the proud packets a thing of the past, and these people were not steamboatmen. Life on the rivers was at its best. The steamboatmen with their perfected craft were reaping the rewards of the long years of experiment and development that began with 1811 and the "New Orleans." When the talk of war became menacing, there were few who thought that the conflict, if it came at all, would be more than a short campaign ended by an easy victory. But in the midst of the rivermen's prosperity war was declared, and the peaceful pursuits of business gave way before military necessity.

CHAPTER XIII

THE CIVIL WAR ON THE RIVERS

"He seen de smoke way up de river
Where the Lincoln gunboats lay.
He took his hat and he left mighty sudden
And I spec' he's run away."

WAR changed the whole aspect of the rivers.
Boats that had carried passengers in luxury were
taken over by the military authorities, to be packed
with troops and supplies and sent about more imperative business, often to be fired upon from the banks,
to be captured and looted, or to be burned to prevent their falling into the enemy's hands. The white
packets that had plied regularly up and down the
rivers were replaced by armored gunboats with their
bare slanting sides pierced for cannon; light steamers
protected with sheet iron against rifle fire; side-
wheelers and stern-wheelers, big and little, barricaded
with timbers or cotton bales. And with these war-
craft of the rivers steamed boats with no protection
except an iron shield for the pilot house, carrying
men and munitions, depending for their safety on
the presence of the armed and armored steamers.

To the Confederacy, the Mississippi was the highway over which the sinews of war must be transported to the front. It was the gateway to the agricultural wealth of the South. From the land controlled by the river must come the corn, the meat, the horses and mules for the southern armies, and men for the armies as well.

The occupation of New Orleans by Federal forces was the entering wedge in the campaign to open the river for the Union cause; when, with the fall of Vicksburg, the river was finally opened, the outcome of the war was practically settled: For it robbed the South of its food supply.

When the Federal fleet steamed up the Mississippi below New Orleans, they hammered Forts Jackson and St. Philip into rubbish-piles. Then, with Porter's victorious squadron anchored across the river, the officers of the two forts came aboard his flagship to surrender. A huge Confederate ironclad, the "Louisiana," was moored above the forts, helpless because of disabled machinery. While these officers were in Porter's cabin, other Confederates set fire to the "Louisiana" and cut her loose to drift down on the Federal fleet. But the fire reached her magazine too soon to do any damage to Porter's fleet; she blew up a hundred yards above the nearest Federal ship. . . . At New Orleans two powerful steamers intended for ironclads, but not completed, were burned to prevent their falling into Federal hands. . . . Stores of cotton also went up in smoke.

From an old Currier & Ives print in the collection of Karl Schmidt, Esq.

"LOW WATER" ON THE MISSISSIPPI

General Butler took command of New Orleans, and was so strict with the citizens that whenever one of the patriotic women of the streets called a Union soldier an unprintable name he wanted to court-martial her. He maintained a secret police over whose activities he kept strict watch. But on one occasion, at least, his rigid supervision reacted against him. One day after court, Butler called the captain who held office of chief of police and declared that he, Butler, knew everything that happened in the city before the chief did, and, judging by his reports, the chief never found out anything at all. The chief replied that he did not wish to bother the General with the details of his work, but that he knew of everything that occurred in the town and was aware of everybody's movements.

"Bosh!" said Butler. "I don't believe it; you had better say you know my movements."

"But, sir," replied the captain, "you are the commander-in-chief, and we don't pretend to know what you do."

"It is your business," declared Butler, "to know every one's movements. You are a humbug, sir, and I don't believe in you."

"I am sorry," said the captain, "to have lost your confidence, but if it will afford you any satisfaction, I could tell every movement you have made in the last twenty-four hours."

"Where was I last night at ten o'clock?" inquired the general.

"At General Shepley's, eating a terrapin supper," answered the captain.

"At eleven o'clock?" continued Butler.

"Closeted with your brother at his quarters."

"At twelve o'clock?"

"Well, sir, you left your brother's at eleven-fifteen, went to Number 1220 Canal Street, knocked at the door, which was opened by—"

"Shut up, damn you," broke in the general. "You are too infernally inquisitive. I'm satisfied; that will be all."

With New Orleans in Union hands, the river was opened as far up as Vicksburg. But Vicksburg was strongly fortified; heavy rifled guns had been sent by rail from Richmond after the fall of New Orleans, and mounted on the heights 280 feet above the river, and Farragut could not reach them with the smooth-bore guns of his ships. Moreover, the defenders built a water battery a half-mile from the levee, mounting twelve powerful guns which the Union sailors knew as the Twelve Apostles; the largest, a ten-inch rifle, they named "St. Paul the Great X-pounder."

President Lincoln was fully aware of the importance of Vicksburg and the control of the Mississippi. Speaking of the river campaign, he said, "See what a lot of land these fellows hold, of which Vicksburg is the key. Here is Red River, which will supply the Confederates with cattle and corn to feed their armies. There are the Arkansas and White Rivers, which can supply cattle and hogs by the thousand. From Vicksburg these supplies can be distributed by rail all over the Confederacy. Then there is that great depot of supplies on the Yazoo. Let us get Vicksburg and all that country is ours. The war can never be brought to a close until that key is in our pocket. I am acquainted with that region and know what I am talking about, and, valuable as New Orleans will be to us, Vicksburg will be more so. We may take all the northern parts of the Confederacy, and they can still defy us from Vicksburg. It means hog and hominy without limit, fresh troops from all the states of the far South, and a cotton country where they can raise the staple without interference."

And so the Federal fleet under Farragut came up the river to Vicksburg and passed the batteries; his flotilla of mortar-boats bombed the earthworks of the town, but without result, and returned down the river, passing Natchez again.

After this failure a campaign against Vicksburg was begun from the north by Colonel Charles Ellet, Jr., a bridge builder and hydraulic engineer, who conceived the idea that a fleet of steamboats equipped for ramming could clear the rivers of Confederate craft. However, Confederate engineers had the same idea; and were building five rams of their own, the "Merrimac," re-named the "Virginia," at Norfolk, two at Mobile, and two at New Orleans.

Colonel Ellet got steamboats at Pittsburgh, Cincinnati, New Albany, and Madison, and converted them into rams for use against the Confederate river fleet. He prepared nine vessels; three large stern-wheel tow-boats, the "Lioness," "Sampson," and "Mingo"; three large side-wheel steamboats, the "Queen of the West," "Monarch," and "Switzer-land"; a small side-wheeler, the "Lancaster," and two small stern-wheel tow-boats, the "Fulton" and "Horner," as tender and dispatch-boat. In addition he took three large coal barges and equipped them with heavy timber sides, to be used as shelters in passing batteries. The rams are best described in Ellet's own words: "The preparation of these steam-boats for the purpose of converting them into rams, consists simply in running three heavy solid timber bulkheads, from 12 to 16 inches thick, fore and aft, from stem to stern, placing the central one directly over the keelson; in bracing these bulkheads one against the other, and the outer ones against the hull of the boat, and all against the deck and floor tim-bers, and staying the hull from side to side by iron rods and screw bolts. In fact making the whole weight of the boat add its momentum to that of the central bulkhead at the moment of collision. In ad-dition the boilers and machinery are held in iron stays in all directions; the pilot house protected against musketry, and the engines and boilers shielded by two feet thickness of oak timbers well bolted to-gether. . . . The boats are not large but are made very strong in one direction and are quite swift, and will assuredly make their way through the hull of any ordinary transport or gunboat they may chance to hit fairly."

Colonel Ellet recruited his crews among boatmen, who understood that they were to navigate the boats, and not to do any fighting. For defence he planned to carry detachments from the army. The status of the crews was somewhat indefinite. They were in the Federal service, but were neither soldiers nor sailors. However, there was more latitude allowed in such matters then than at present. There is a story of a steamboatman who enlisted in the infantry, but, hearing that one of Ellet's rams was being fitted out in his home town, decided that he preferred service in familiar steamboat surroundings to carrying a rifle and being compelled to walk when there was traveling to do. Therefore he deserted his outfit and signed for service on the ram.

He was missed at roll-call, and on investigation his officer found that he had announced his intention of going to the shipyard where the ram was in preparation. Accordingly a guard was sent to bring him back. The officer of the guard presented himself to the officer in charge of the ram. "I'm looking for a deserter," he said. "We got to take him back and shoot him. Here's his name and description. Have you seen a man like that around here?"

The officer of the ram needed no more than the name. "Sure," he said, "that man's here; he just signed on. But what do you want to shoot him for? He's a good steamboatman, and we need him."

"You say he signed on?" asked the infantry officer. "What do you mean by that?"

"What do I mean? Why, he signed up with us; took service on the ram we're building to lick the Rebs with. What more do you want?"

"Oh, you mean he enlisted with you," said the deserter-hunter. "Well, I'm willing; he was a damn poor infantryman, anyway. Can you spare a chew of that tobacco? Thanks; I'll be going."

Ellet, with part of his ram fleet, joined Davis' naval squadron above Fort Pillow a few days before Forts Pillow and Randolph were evacuated; then both floated to a point just above Memphis, where Ellet moored his rams above Davis' gunboats.

Early in the morning of June 6, 1862, Ellet with the side-wheel rams dropped down through the fog to where the gunboats lay with banked fires. His intention was to land, but just as his boats were drawing up to the bank the Confederate squadron, creeping up from below, loomed through the mist and opened fire. Davis' gunboats answered, but, with their anchors down and their fires banked, they could not move to attack.

Ellet, aboard the "Queen of the West," with steam up in his boilers, saw his chance to prove the worth of his rams, and, with the "Monarch," he steamed down past the anchored gunboats to the attack. Ellet, standing behind the pilot, gave orders to steer straight for the Confederate "Lovell." The pilot turned the wheel till the bow pointed directly at the

"Lovell" and unflinchingly kept it there while the water between the two boats seemed to disappear with a leap.

There was a terrible rending as the "Queen" stove the "Lovell" amidship. Right through the side she went—and stuck. And while her timbered prow was held by the shattered woodwork of the "Lovell" the "General Beauregard" bore down from the larboard side and crashed into the "Queen," carrying the wheel away. As the impact tore the boats from their death-grip the "Lovell" folded up like a broken umbrella and went down. And the pilot of the "Queen," wiping the sweat from his face, rang his bells furiously as he worked his half-disabled vessel to the safety of the Arkansas side.

Meanwhile the "Monarch" and the Confederate "General Price," lying outside the scrimmage, prepared for a ram. And the two boats drove at each other, bows on, and under full steam. But the blow was a glancing one; the prow of the "Monarch" stove in the bow of the "Price," and, scraping aft, carried away one of her wheels. But as the "Monarch" drew away unharmed, the Confederate "General Bragg" tilted towards her, its safety valve screaming, and a 32-pound Parrot gun on her bow aimed and loaded.

"Monarch" sharpshooters drove the gunners to cover, but the boat kept on; and as it neared to strike, Colonel Alfred W. Ellet, its commander, saw that the "General Beauregard" was steering to ram him from the other direction.

There was only one thing to do and Ellet did it. He shot his craft out of the way and as her stern cleared the path the "Beauregard" and the "Bragg" struck each other head-on and butted their timbers mortally. And the "Monarch," carrying along her spurt for freedom, rounded to and rammed the "Price" and put her out of the fight.

And now the gunboats were coming down, firing as they came. The Confederate "Little Rebel," disabled by the gunboat fire, was drifting down the river away from the gunboats. She got in the way of the "Monarch" and once more the "Monarch" struck, slamming her up on shore.

The rams' first fight was over. On the Arkansas shore lay the wrecked "Lovell," the disabled "Queen of the West," the stranded "Price" and "Little Rebel," and two other Confederates, "Sumter" and "Bragg," not badly hurt. Lower down was the Confederate magazine boat, the "Thompson," blazing and popping with the fire which within an hour was destined to blow her into the skies. The Confederate "Van Dirn" was fleeing down the river, the "Monarch" after her, but a little too short of wind.

Colonel Ellet, designer and commander of the rams, out of the fight for once and all, was lying in the cabin of the "Queen" with a knee that had been shattered by a Confederate bullet, saying, "It's nothing serious. I'll be all right in a little while," and raising himself to see Lieutenant Crandall of the "Lioness" raising the Federal flag over Memphis. Ten days later Ellet's condition had become so much worse that he was forced to transfer command of the ram fleet to his brother Alfred who had so ably commanded the "Monarch" in the fight, and in five more days, as the "Switzerland" steamed north with the wounded officer, Colonel Ellet died.

With Memphis in Union hands the expedition steamed on south and tied up in the bend above Vicksburg where they looked down on the only Confederate stronghold which remained to bar Federal navigation of the river. And there Farragut's fleet, which had been lying below the city, ran the ominous Confederate battery and joined Davis' gunboats and Ellet's rams.

On July 15 two gunboats accompanied by the repaired "Queen of the West" ran up the Yazoo, but were driven back by the powerful Confederate ram "Arkansas." Not content with driving them out of the Yazoo the "Arkansas" chased them through the whole Federal fleet, which was lying at anchor with low steam, and into the protection of the Vicksburg batteries. The "Lancaster" of the ram fleet sidled out and attacked her, but was put out by a shot through her steam drum. And while the "Lancaster" was being towed back to her anchorage by the "Champion," the "Arkansas" steamed into the protection of the Vicksburg batteries where pursuit was impossible.

And that night Farragut's squadron, fearing to be left aground in the falling river, again ran the Vicksburg batteries and rejoined the fleet in the Gulf below.

A little later the combined fleet made an attempt to destroy the "Arkansas" as she lay under the guns of Vicksburg. In preparation the naval vessels engaged the Confederate batteries, above and below. Then the gunboat "Essex" crept up on the "Arkansas" and ran aground within a few yards of her barricaded sides, and turned loose her guns. The shot went through the armor of the "Arkansas" but she would not sink. Then the "Queen of the West" sallied forth to give a death blow, but as the Confederate ram lay with her stern to the bank, the "Queen" struck only the strong bow and did no damage, though she delivered her blow with such force that one of the sharpshooters aboard was thrown overboard and had to swim under the Confederate batteries to the lower fleet before he was picked up.

The "Arkansas" still sat there, firm and warlike as a setting hen, while the "Essex" worked herself off the ground and returned to the lower fleet and the "Queen" went upstream through the fire of the batteries, from which she was so badly damaged that she was sent to St. Louis for repairs.

A short while afterwards malaria developed in the fleets and they retired to Helena, leaving Vicksburg for Grant to prove his mettle on.

In the fall of 1862 Admiral Porter took command of the Mississippi squadron, including the ram fleet and resumed the campaign against Vicksburg. The

"Queen of the West" ran the batteries, struck the Confederate transport "City of Vicksburg" as she had struck the "Arkansas," and attempted to fire her by throwing a burning turpentine ball aboard, but the attempt failed. The "Arkansas" was later blown up by the Confederates when her machinery failed and she was in danger of capture. The "Queen" went below the city to cut off supplies that were coming from the Red River. She captured and burned three supply boats and returned to her anchorage below Vicksburg for fuel. A coal barge was set adrift above the city, and picked up by the "Queen" below. The "Queen" then returned to the business of destroying supplies. With the ferry boat "De Soto" she went up the Red and the Black rivers, capturing on the way the small steamboat "Era." Three Confederate boats were reported at Gordon's Landing, and the "Queen" went after them. At the landing she was met by the fire of a strong battery. In turning to get away she ran ashore, a fair mark for the gunners, and her steam pipe was carried away by a shot. Her crew escaped to the "De Soto," and in the ferry boat ran down the river until she struck the bank and tore off her rudders. Then they set fire to the "De Soto," boarded the captured "Era," and made the best of their way back into the Mississippi. Here they were pursued by the Confederate steamboat "Webb," but the Federal ironclad "Indianola" appeared, chased the "Webb" away, and saved what was left of the unlucky expedition.

A little later the Confederates repaired the "Queen of the West," and with her, the "Webb," and two cotton-clad steamboats rammed and sank the "Indianola." With the "Queen" in Confederate hands, and the probability that the Confederates would raise the powerful "Indianola" and use her offensively, the outlook was none too bright for the Union forces on the river. It was at this point that Admiral Porter played a trick which he described as a sailor's prank, but which saved the situation and brought down on the Confederate naval and military authorities a howl of derision from the southern press.

Porter, above the city, prepared a log raft to simulate a large and heavily armed ironclad. The raft carried log casements, wooden guns, and two smoke-stacks made of hogsheads, with iron pots of burning tar and oakum to provide the smoke. It was surmounted by two sham pilot houses decorated with the legend, "Deluded rebels, cave in!" Two old boats hung at the davits; the United States flag flew aft, and the skull and bones forward. On a dark night the sham warship was pushed into the current above Vicksburg, and drifted slowly and majestically down before the city.

Signal lights flashed; cannon boomed from the fortifications on the hills, and in a few minutes all the artillery of the city's defences was firing on the huge and sinister craft that held steadily down the river, not even deigning to fire a shot in return.

An eddy below the city caught the terrible craft,

but some Union soldiers got it free and sent it drifting again just as the "Queen of the West," in Confederate hands, came to Warrenton for pumps to raise the "Indianola." In the half-light of the morning the crew of the "Queen" was as badly fooled as were the gunners in the fortifications. They cut their cable and let the "Queen" drift down-stream, away from the oncoming menace. Then, crowding their steam, they hurried down to the sunken "Indianola." Word of the supposed ironclad had preceded them, and the crew of the "Webb" was trying to take off the "Indianola's" guns. When the "Queen" came down with word that the ironclad was almost upon them, they blew up the sunken vessel and with the "Queen" ran down the river at their best speed. The dummy was destroyed by gunfire at Warrenton, but word of its real character came too late to prevent the destruction of the "Indianola," which was never raised. The "Webb," injured when she rammed the "Indianola," was obliged to go to Shreveport for repairs. The "Queen" was recaptured and eventually destroyed.

The *Richmond Examiner*, in commenting on the incident of the dummy ironclad, derided the authorities at Vicksburg for allowing themselves to be fooled by a "flatboat or mud scow, with a small house taken from the back garden of a plantation, put on top of it." Whatever the construction of the dummy may have been, it served the Union cause very effectively.

In the meantime, the officers of the ram fleet had been having difficulty with the indefinite status of their men. To overcome this trouble the Mississippi Marine Brigade was organized to operate the rams and to fight against guerrillas on both water and land. Alfred W. Ellet, made Brigadier General, was in command of the organization, which was under the orders of the Army but operated with the Navy.

Recruiting for the new outfit was slow, but picked up when Gen. Ellet was given authority to re-enlist convalescents from hospitals, with the promise that the work of the Marine Brigade was to be far less arduous than that of the regular Army. A recruiting letter began in this alluring style:

"MISSISSIPPI MARINE BRIGADE
SOLDIERING MADE EASY!
NO HARD MARCHING!
NO CARRYING KNAPSACKS!
$100.00 BOUNTY!!

A Marine Brigade, to act in concert with the invincible Ram Fleet, is to be raised immediately.—All under the command of Brig. Gen. A. W. Ellet. Large Steamboats are engaged to carry the troops down into the heart of Rebeldom, and open the Mississippi and her tributaries to the navigation of the Northwest. There will be but very little marching for any of the troops. They will be provided on the boats with good cooks and bedding."

A handbill held out further inducements to the war-weary:

"The proposed service is especially attractive to old soldiers. It has the following advantages:

1. There are no trenches to dig.
2. There are no Rebel houses to guard.
3. There is no picket duty to perform.
4. There is no danger of camps in the mud, but always a chance to sleep under cover.
5. There is no chance of short rations.
6. The command will always be kept together."

On November 19, 1862, at Mound City, Illinois, General Ellet took command of the Brigade, known as the "Ellet Scouts," consisting of one regiment of infantry, four companies of cavalry, and one battery of field artillery. Later the infantry was mounted, and the whole command came to be called "Ellet's Horse Marines." Their uniforms were the same as those of the army except that the caps were larger. The steamboats "Autocrat," "B. J. Adams," "Baltic," "Diana," and "John Raine" were bought and fitted for the use of the men besides the "Fairchild" which served as a commissary boat, and the "Woodford," a hospital boat. Double thicknesses of two-inch oak planks covered the boats from the main deck to the hurricane deck, and the boilers were barricaded by coal bunkers and timber. Loopholes were provided for firing, and swinging ports for ventilation. The pilot houses were protected with curved sheets of boiler iron. The after ends of the cabins were partitioned off for officers' quarters, and the forward parts used for the men's mess. Sleeping quarters for soldiers were on intermediate decks built in abaft the boilers. Each boat carried a railed gangway wide enough for two horses abreast; and water hose, fed from the boilers, was carried to repel boarders.

The command wintered and drilled at Benton Barracks through cold weather. There were not enough stoves, and when one of the companies asked for more, the captain told the men that he sympathized with them, but the quartermaster did not own a stove foundry. One of the men replied, "We can draw a stove if you let us."

"Go ahead," said the captain, "but don't come and tell me how you do it."

Next day the company had the stove. They had stolen it red hot, pipe, fire, and all, from another regiment. Which was all very well until a sharp-nosed officer from the other regiment retrieved it.

Discipline was hard to maintain in the Marine Brigade. Apparently the men took seriously the promises of the recruiting literature. When, in March of the next year, they anchored above Vicksburg, there was dissatisfaction with the food which went so far that on one boat the men broke down the partition between their mess room and the officers' quarters and punched the nose of the officer of the day.

To aid Farragut in his blockade of the lower river, the "Lancaster" and "Switzerland" were ordered to run the batteries of Vicksburg on the night of March

BOMBARDMENT OF ISLAND NO. 10

24. The crews spent the night in loading coal and stores, and when they started it was nearly dawn. As they drifted down, with engines stopped to avoid all sound, they were seen by Confederate lookouts. Lights flashed from battery to battery, followed by the flash and roar of the guns. On the "Lancaster" a shot tore through the steam drum; the engines, which had been started at the first shot, stopped as their steam blew away through the broken drum. The crew, scalded and smothered by the steam, rushed for the air outside the barricades. The boat's wheel was shot away, as were the stairs leading down to the forecastle. Just then a shot crashed into her stern, raked through her entire length, and plunged through the bottom at her bow. She settled by the head, turning on her side as she plunged, and as her bow sank and her stern rose the machinery tore loose from its bed-bolts and dropped into the river.

The crew of the "Lancaster" escaped by swimming to the "Switzerland," which was drifting down, her boilers pierced by cannon-shot. None of the shot went through her bottom; she drifted past the batteries without suffering many casualties, and was taken in tow and landed by Farragut's "Albatross," while the "Hartford" engaged the batteries of Warrenton. Only enough men were aboard the rams to work them; most of the crews had been sent down overland.

Farragut and Porter had no very high opinion of the rams and their crews; to these naval men the boats appeared unseaworthy and the men unseaman-like. In their opinion the "Lancaster" was old, rot-ten, unfit for service away from a machine shop, and would have shut up like a spy-glass if she had at-tempted to ram anything. The dashing but inex-perienced officers of the Marine Brigade caused the seasoned naval commanders some uneasiness. Por-ter wrote to Farragut, "In relation to the 'Switzer-land' keep her with you, but please make the com-mander understand that she is under your command, or he will go off on a cruise somewhere before you know it, and then get the ship in trouble."

The boats of the Brigade were no match for iron-clads; they carried no heavy guns, and their plank barricades gave scant protection against artillery fire. Success of the rams in action depended more on au-dacity than strength, and their escape from heavy cas-ualties when engaged with Confederate boats was because of the accurate work of the sharpshooters they carried; the riflemen drove enemy gunners from their cannon that might have sunk a boat with a single well placed shot.

Brigade officers were not experienced in military or naval procedure and discipline was generally loose and sometimes uncertain. The crews, made up of steamboat captains, pilots, engineers, and mates, were not used to the punctilious conduct required in the armed services. Admiral Porter, however, has a good word to say for the pilots and engineers, both of the Marine Brigade and of the naval boats. He writes, "One can hardly realize the danger to which the pilots and engineers of the squadron were exposed. I have seen a pilot receive a ball in his brain just as his hand touched the wheel. The pilots were targets for the enemy to shoot at, and he who could boast that he had killed one was a popular man.

"The pilots were mostly Western men by birth, but passing their lives on the Mississippi brought them into intimate relations with the Southern people, who looked upon all who were loyal to the Union as traitors to the Southern cause.

"I never knew one of these men to quail in the presence of danger, and when I have beheld them passing a battery with balls flying all about them, I have been struck with the coolness they displayed.

"I think there is a magnetism in a ship's wheel in time of action which is communicated to the helmsman. He feels that the lives of all are in his hands, and I never knew a pilot faithless to his trust."

The principal functions of the Marine Brigade were the suppression of guerrillas along the rivers and the destruction of enemy supplies. It was quite natural that, in addition to burning boats and stores, the men should help themselves to the contents of smoke houses and cellars. When coal ran low, they took the nearest fence rails. At one time the crew of the "Switzerland" relieved a meat shortage by firing cannon loaded with canister into flocks of wild geese.

The men, half-boatmen and half-cavalrymen, had

some experiences that amply justified the name of Horse Marines. Two officers went ashore to trade coffee for butter and eggs with two young women. After the deal one of the gallants brought the horses which the girls had been riding, and led one of them to a stump for the fair rider to mount. The girl hesitated, then burst out in a laugh which was echoed loudly from the boat. The officer stared—then realized that he had placed the horse on the wrong side of the stump. "Oh, hell!" he said, and ran precipitately for the yawl.

Of an expedition through a swampy region, Captain De Coster, of the Marine cavalry, writes quite seriously: "We had proceeded about three miles, when we found the water up to our horses' bellies all the time. Coming to a stream, no one dared to cross, but I tried it. My horse plunged in all over, but I stuck to him, and he swam to the opposite shore. No one would follow me, so I moved along the bank with the water to my horse's back, but could find no crossing place, and the company went off and left me. I then thought I would go back, and coming to a log across the stream, I got a pole to measure the water, but could find no bottom. But I concluded to try it anyway. I walked the log and led my horse. In he went over head and ears, and came near pulling me in with him. Reaching the other side, he could not get up the bank. The water was just running over his back. I got into the water, took off the saddle, and in about an hour succeeded in getting him out, and following on after the command found them waiting for me."

While the Marine Brigade steamed from place to place on its errands of guerrilla fighting, capture of supplies, and convoy of unarmed steamboats, the campaign against Vicksburg continued. During flood water an attempt was made to leave Vicksburg out in the woods by diverting the river across a peninsula on the opposite side. A ditch was dug in the hope that the river would cut through and enlarge it until it carried the entire flow, but the current ran well out from land at the entrance of the ditch, and little water entered it. The river did not break through until after the war was over. General Grant did not have much faith in this project, or in the attempts that were made to run boats over the flooded country and attack the city from the rear. These things, however, gave the besieging forces something to do while they waited for the flood waters to subside.

A naval expedition attempted to get behind Vicksburg by way of Yazoo Pass, about seventy miles above the city, and the Yallabusha and Sunflower rivers. A ditch was dug through the levee into the old unused Yazoo Pass, and the water, cutting away the levee, flooded the plantations and woods. The ironclads, with three or four lightly armed boats, including the "Lioness" and "Fulton" of the Marine Brigade, and transports carrying four thousand troops, steamed through the broken levee into the flooded forest. Floating logs and trailing vines hindered the boats. Branches of trees wrecked the upper works of the vessels, often forcing them to stop until the obstructions could be cut away. After a tedious time of navigating war vessels through the natural habitat of birds and squirrels, the expedition found an open stream and steered thankfully into it. But their relief was short-lived; at a bend in the stream they almost ran over a battery of artillery which the Confederates had just put in place to stop them. The gunners had not yet loaded their pieces; if they had been ready to fire, they might have destroyed at least the transports and the unarmored boats. There was no way to run past them before they could load as steamboats had been sunk to block the stream. The boats of the expedition could not turn in the narrow stream; they backed behind the point and engaged the battery in an artillery duel, without decisive result. But the chance of surprising Vicksburg from the rear was gone, and the boats returned through the woods to the river.

Another expedition, under Porter, tried to get behind Vicksburg by way of Steele Bayou. Porter commanded five ironclads, four tugs, and two mortar boats. An army contingent under Sherman accompanied the boats, first in transports and later marching alongside the bayous through which the boats passed. Every precaution was taken to keep the expedition secret, but as the boats churned and rammed their way through flooded forests little secrecy was possible. The pilots, trained to the river and not the woods, were uncertain of their way. Often it was necessary to drive a boat under full power against a big tree to clear the course. Chimneys were knocked down and upperworks wrecked. Porter expected any moment to see a Confederate ironclad make her way through the bushes and open fire. "If one had suddenly slid down a tree and attacked us," he says, "I should not have been much surprised."

Porter had little fear of the rams reported under construction at Yazoo City. Of these craft a negro had told him, "Dey has no bottom in, no sides to 'em, an' no top on 'em, sah, an' deir injines is in Richmon'."

After a long and laborious passage through the twilight of the flooded woods, Porter was advised by Sherman to steer into Cypress Bayou, leading into the Sunflower. Porter found the bayou only four feet wider than his boat, with levees so high that his guns could not be fired over them. But it was open water, and the boats, unimpeded by trees, got ahead of Sherman's men. At the approach of the boats the people along the bayou drove away their stock and poultry and set fire to the cotton bales that were piled on the levees. With their crews at fire quarters, the boats ran between the fires. Once they rammed a bridge hidden in the smoke and knocked it to pieces.

The cultivated land ended, and the bayou, flanked by a road, took its winding course through the woods. Sometimes each boat of the squadron was pointing a different way. The boats were obliged to stop frequently while sunken logs were taken from the bottom of the bayou. Often overhanging trees caught and held the leading boat, and the line stopped while the trees were cut down. As the boats ground against the trees, they knocked off dead limbs which in falling broke the small boats at the davits and showered the decks with rotten wood and bark and small animals and insects of the woods.

That night after the squadron tied up, they heard wood-chopping ahead. One of the boats went to investigate, and drove away a gang of negroes that, under Confederate officers from Vicksburg, were felling trees across the bayou to stop the boats. Next morning when the squadron proceeded, they sent a tug ahead to stop the tree cutting. Sailors with brooms stood on deck, sweeping off as they fell the rats, mice, cockroaches, snakes, and lizards that the boats in passing shook down from the trees. Once a coon was shaken from his arboreal perch and fell on deck.

Next day, when they approached Rolling Fork, the sailors occupied an Indian mound and placed four boat's guns on it. At the entrance to Rolling Fork the bayou was filled by a patch of innocent-looking willows; they appeared hardly more formidable than pond scum. The leading tug drove confidently

into them, slowed down, and stopped. Then she reversed to pull out and make another drive, and found
that she was stuck fast. Porter went in with his
boat to push the tug through, but the willows stopped
and held him before he even reached the tug.

While the tug and the ironclad were in this em-
barrassing position, a Confederate steamboat came
up Rolling Fork and landed four miles below. In
a short time two batteries of field artillery opened on
the Indian mound which the sailors had occupied.
The sailors scampered back to their boats, but not
in panic; they remembered to bring their guns with
them. The Confederate gunners then opened with
shrapnel on the boats; Porter answered their fire with
nine-inch mortars and silenced them. Another Confederate steamer, full of troops, landed where the first
one was tied up. The Confederate batteries began
firing again, forcing Porter's men to stay between
decks.

Things began to look serious; Sherman had not
appeared. Porter sent a message back to him by a
negro who claimed to be the best "telegram-wire"
in the country, urging haste. Also he sent a tug back
with the same message, but the tug returned and reported the bayou blocked by felled trees. Scouts
came in with word that two thousand Confederate
troops were about to attack.

The fire of Porter's mortars again silenced the
Confederate batteries at about four o'clock in the
afternoon, and in the respite from falling shrapnel

the Federal sailors connected all their boats together by lines. All backed at once, and managed to pull the leading tug and ironclad free of the willows. The boats drifted back with the current, their rudders unshipped to save them from being smashed as the boats bumped the banks. The Confederates fired on them from the Indian mound, and again the mortars answered them. That night the Federal boats tied up, sparred out four feet from the bank, with their sides greased to prevent their being boarded. Scouts and parties with boat's guns were sent ashore.

The Confederates did not attack that night; neither did Sherman appear. Before morning scouts captured two Confederate officers and two sergeants who told Porter that he would be attacked and captured at daylight. To confuse the enemy, Porter ran three miles up the bayou. When he started back the leading vessel struck and sunk a coal barge, and the flotilla had to wait two hours while the coal was spread on the bottom of the bayou. Confederate artillery attacked the boats while they were held up by the coal, and after they were free the attack was renewed by sharpshooters. Porter kept them off with mortars, and by elevating his main guns and throwing shells over the levees with light charges of powder. The boats' next difficulty was with trees that had been felled across the bayou and pinned down. Four hours were spent in removing them. The boats were hardly under way again when a large body of Confederate infantry appeared and moved to attack.

They never reached the boats. Sherman's men arrived at the crucial moment, and the attack turned into a retreat from overwhelming numbers. The prisoners in Porter's cabin heard the noise, and said, "We told you; our boys have got you now."

But in a few minutes they found how matters stood. "Oh, hell," said one of the officers, "if that's the case we might as well take a rest." And they promptly went to sleep.

The danger of attack by the Confederates was past, but the boats were by no means out of danger. It would be no hard matter for the enemy to shovel a little dirt in among the willows at the Rolling Fork entrance of the bayou, and by stopping the flow leave the expedition stuck in the mud. They went on down the bayou, the banks for miles lit up by the fence-rail camp-fires of Sherman's army. The camp equipment of the army was meager; although a rain had set in, the headquarters of Sherman himself consisted of only a tent-fly stretched over a tripod of rails. But if it be true that an army travels on its stomach, this army surely knew how to travel. It was said of one regiment of Sherman's corps that the men could catch, scrape, and cut up a hog without breaking ranks.

When Porter's boats tied up in the bayou near Sherman's improvised tent, a canoe with a tarpaulin over its load tried to squeeze by. Porter demanded to know what the canoe carried. "General Sherman's baggage, sir," answered one of the soldiers in the canoe; "just brought from the transport."

"How long has it been," asked Porter, "since General Sherman took to carrying baggage? Let me see what you have there."

"Only baggage," answered the soldier, "except some turkeys we picked up for you on the road up here." Lifting the tarpaulin, he exposed a pile of picked turkeys, geese, and chickens, and neatly-scraped sucking pigs.

"Where's the baggage?" asked Porter.

"Why, sir," answered the soldier, as he handed up an appetizing assortment of pork and poultry, "there was so much of it, sir, it's coming up on a tug—a large carpetbag of it, sir."

Watching his steward receive the delicacies, Porter said, "Pass General Sherman's baggage."

The Steele Bayou expedition ended as the Yazoo Pass venture ended. No attempt to get at Vicksburg from the rear could succeed unless it could be a surprise. Confined in narrow bayous, gunboats were far less effective than infantry and artillery. Without army support, they would fall easy victims to the Confederate forces. And as for surprising the defenders of Vicksburg, such a thing was practically impossible.

Another expedition in which the naval craft of the river, with a part of the Marine Brigade, co-operated with the army was the Red River expedition. The gunboat fleet, with the "Switzerland" and some other boats, steamed up the Red River, encountered shoal water, and ran back until they stuck in the shallows above Alexandria. Only Porter's light-draft "Cricket" was able to reach the town, a hundred and fifty miles from the mouth of the river. By that time the army was out of supplies and evacuating the region; the boats must be either floated or blown up. Wing dams were built on the rapids, a work of tremendous difficulty in which time was of greatest importance. The attempt succeeded; the water rose in the constricted channel and shot the boats through. Below Alexandria the river was hardly high enough for navigation, but luck was with the boats; a rise in the Mississippi backed into the lower reaches of the Red and carried them to safety.

Porter says that the principal object of the Red River expedition was to allow northern speculators to take out cotton under the protection of the army. The cotton, marked C.S.A., was hauled through the streets of Alexandria in wagons marked U.S.A. Porter saw one load drawn by mules with U.S.N. in red paint on their sides, and promptly stopped the use of the Navy's name in the business.

In Alexandria there was a near-riot over the use of a stable for a storehouse. The naval authorities had occupied it, and finally kept it, although it was demanded by the quartermaster in charge of army stores. The soldiers of General A. J. Smith took the part of Porter and the Navy. Porter and Smith had been friends since the capture by the Navy of Fort Hindman, formerly called Arkansas Post. The Marines were on guard, taking the prisoners aboard the gunboats, when Smith's army appeared. An adjutant rode up and ordered the fort cleared. Porter told him that the Navy had captured the fort and would keep it. The adjutant conferred with General Smith as he rode up. "Will he, b'God?" cried the general. "Let me see him. Bring the fellow here."

Porter stepped forward and said, "Here I am, sir, the admiral commanding this squadron."

The general reached for his pistol holster and opened the flap. "B'God, Admiral," he said, "I'm glad to see you." And, as he drew a bottle from the holster, "Let's take a drink!"

While ascending the Red River, Porter was cautioned about a Confederate ram reported to be under construction somewhere on the river. He asked a seedy-looking man on the bank if there was a ram anywhere near. "Yes," was the answer, "they's a ram about eight miles up here."

"Is it powerful?" asked Porter.

"Sure powerful; could knock the bows off all yo' gunboats."

"How large is it?"

"Biggest thing I ever see."

"Tell me about it."

"It's on Whitler's place, an' it sure is powerful;

butted a bull so hard it broke his horns off and knocked his tail out by the roots."

"I mean an ironclad Confederate vessel," said Porter.

"Don't know nothing about no Confederate vessel, but this ram could knock holes in your turtles, an' he must be Confederate, because he was borned in these parts."

Porter found later that the joker was a Confederate officer in disguise.

The numerous military and naval side-expeditions had little to do with the fall of Vicksburg. There were no surprises, no brilliant tactics. The city was reduced by the same old wearing-down process that wins most major campaigns. Isolated, bombarded, and starved, the city held out until all hope of defending it was gone. On July 4, 1863, General Pemberton surrendered to the army under Grant, General McPherson receiving the formal surrender. Both the Navy and the Marine Brigade were on hand to receive their share of the honors, and the "Autocrat," of the Marine Brigade, was the second boat to touch at the city wharf after it fell to the Union.

The men of the rivers, north and south, acquitted themselves well in the war between the states. The Marine Brigade, one of the most unconventional and picturesque fighting outfits in our history, was discontinued as an organization on August 3, 1864. The men finally were mustered out during December of that year and January of the next.

CHAPTER XIV

STEAMBOAT DISASTERS

"When the boatman goes on shore
He spends his money and works for more;
I never saw a girl in all my life
But what she would be a boatman's wife."

THROUGHOUT all history of steamboating there is one phrase that constantly recurs: Sunk by exploding boiler. In those four words are packed the fate of so many steamboats that the list becomes a solemn, fearful litany, including the first high pressure boat that churned the waters as well as the last fleet packet that lost its challenge to the swifter locomotive.

Of the several disasters faced by the steamboats the most sudden and terrible were those caused by the bursting of the boilers. For in that moment, for which there had been no preparation, the scalding steam enveloped the boat even as the sound of the explosion was heard; and woodwork and human-

296

ity were blown out by the terrific blast. Sometimes the people aboard, particularly the engineers, were scalded to death; sometimes the big explosion brought minor ones, more fire and desolation.

These boiler explosions came about in many ways. A boat might be racing, trying to force her steam to pass the other boat; and the engineer, helping his utmost, would be holding down the safety valve with a rope or with extra weights, an anvil, a pair of pressing irons, anything that came to hand; then of a sudden as the boat spurted ahead, the steam pressure would be too great for the boilers; and the boat would come to a stop, shiver as if to take a plunge, and then be hidden under the cloud of hissing steam that rolled about her. Or again, the water might boil too low in the boilers and a flue, above the reduced water level, would become red-hot, weaken; and out would roar the steam, rending the casing. For in the early boilers there were no fusible plugs to melt out and quench the fires with steam when the water was almost gone. Another peril against which the boatmen could not prepare were defects in the boilers. Being subjected to the motions of the boat they were hardly safe unless they were much more strongly built than similar boilers for stationary work. And then there was always the chance that the vessel might tip, causing the flow of water to one side of the bank of boilers as the boat heeled in turning, or while loading cargo, leaving one or two on the high side nearly empty for a moment—long enough for the remaining water to be flashed into steam at pressure no boiler could hold.

There was also a danger of too much water in the boilers, or from impurities that caused the water to foam and be carried into the cylinders. This, called priming by the engineers, was likely to result in accident to boiler or engine in the following way: The water is carried into the cylinders with the steam; the piston reaches the end of its power stroke, the exhaust valve opens, and the piston starts back. But the water in the cylinder cannot escape quickly enough, and back comes the piston with the push of steam and the momentum of wheel and rods behind it, bearing the tremendous leverage of the crank approaching its center. The confined water, unyielding as the face of a hammer, strikes the cylinder head; and the iron cracks, the stud bolts part like rotten straws and the splintered head goes tearing through the boat like a volley of jagged cannon shot.

The first high pressure boat of the western rivers, Captain Shreve's "Washington," fell a victim to boiler explosion. On June 9, 1816, Captain Shreve was leaving Point Harmar, on the Ohio near Marietta, with the "Washington." There was some difficulty in getting the boat on her course and to make the matter easier the kedge anchor was dropped at the stern. It was while Captain Shreve called the crew aft to haul on the kedge that the head of a cylinder blew off. The steam puffed out, sweeping the men overboard and scalding them. Shreve was

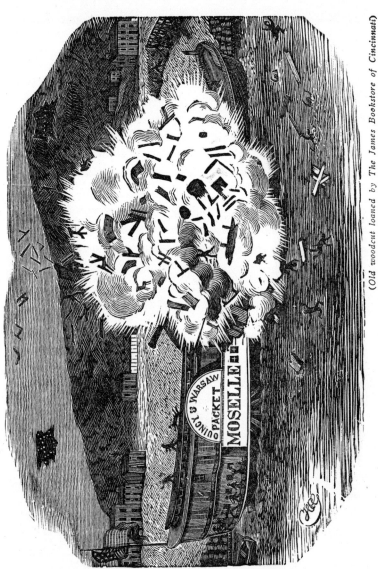

(Old woodcut loaned by The James Bookstore of Cincinnati)

Explosion of the "Moselle"

badly burned, but recovered. Many of the crew were killed. Afterwards it was discovered that the weight on the safety valve had slipped to the extreme end of the arm, causing the over pressure that blew off the cylinder head.

The case of the "Washington" was the first of exploding boilers on the rivers. But one of the most memorable of those catastrophes took place on the "Lucy Walker," twenty-three years later. On October 25, 1844, the "Lucy Walker," commanded by Captain Vann, was going down the middle of the Ohio. When she passed New Albany, Indiana, the engineer reported something had gone wrong and the captain ordered the engines stopped for repairs.

There were a number of passengers aboard in cabin and on deck, but there was nothing to alarm them in the fact that the engines had been shut down. On went the boat, drifting downstream towards the snag-boat "Gophar." At either side of the broad river lay a peaceful scene. On the Kentucky shore, to the left, were the fields of tobacco, and beyond a cluster of negro shacks there rose the white columns of the owner's mansion. On the Indiana side were the smaller farms with their solid, frame houses under wide-branched sycamores.

But down in the engine room the water in the boilers had got low. Before they could be replenished three of them, simultaneously, blew up and above the white cloud of sizzling steam flew hunks of iron and woodwork. And within the steam was the crackle of fire as the main deck began to burn from the coals which had been flung out of the furnace.

One man lay unconscious on the forecastle where he had been thrown from the boiler deck. And when he opened his eyes he found he could not get up. Lying there helpless, he saw his seven-year-old son standing on the deck in the path of the devouring flames. Another passenger was standing by the rail with his wife and his small daughter. Others were crowding the rail, some blinded by the steam, jumping over into the water.

From the "Gophar" a yawl was lowered and rowed swiftly to the blazing boat. It reached the forward part, which was not yet ablaze, and the crazed passengers tumbled in. The man standing with his wife and daughter, helped his wife into the yawl and then waited for the approaching flames. Beside him a child, unable to swim, slid into the river, grasping at the burning wreck.

The yawl was a long way off with its safe load of passengers. The man who had put his wife aboard and stayed on deck with his daughter waited until aid was no longer possible. Then, lifting the child, he flung her into the water and dove. The man who could not move saw, from the forecastle, his son jump into the water and clutch out at the débris that floated on the surface.

Dunham, captain of the "Gophar," came back with his yawl, and though a great many were saved by ropes and grappling hooks about sixty passengers died. But the little girl who had slipped into the water and clung to the burning wreck was not among them: Dunham found her splashing water on her face when he took her aboard; and the man who had thrown his child overboard managed to reach shore with her.

Boiler explosions meant almost sudden death to the engineers; but it was the snags that the pilots feared. Not even the best pilot who ever lived could always tell as he steered upstream through a foggy night when a snag lay ahead of him, its inclined branches ready to tear their way up through the hull, sometimes clear through the boiler deck with consequent danger to the steam. It was a hidden stump that took the life of the "New Orleans," first steamboat on the inland rivers, and it was snags that brought an end to many of the boats that followed. And very seldom did all of the crew and passengers get ashore. Heeling and straining, the boat lies pinned down by the snag that struck her as the water flows into the hull and makes it settle; meanwhile under the boilers the fires cool, and as the steam goes down the whistle-valve opens and emits a low and husky alarm, which is prolonged and enters into the moan of the dying steam that rises and falls and wavers as the wind whips about the whistle bell; its last note is lost in the pervading whisper of the water that flows on past this scene of tragedy, just as it was flowing a thousand years before the first paddle-wheel drove a boat through its many dangers.

When the "Tennessee" was snagged near Natchez sixty lives were lost. It was on the night of February 8, 1823, and there was a violent snowstorm that kept the windows of the pilot house white and made it almost impossible to steer. There was nothing to warn the pilot that a great snag had moved into a new place in the channel; and look as he might he had no way of knowing that it lay due ahead of him.

But the snag was there, and it caught the hull of the boat and tore a hole through it as large as a door. The "Tennessee" shuddered as if she had rammed the bank. The pilot toppled forward. Below crowded the passengers on deck from the cabins, crying out questions, growing more excited at the answers. Somebody in a voice of authority was saying, "Lower the yawl," and holding back people who tried to jump into the boat as it struck the water. "One at a time, one at a time," went on the danger-steeled voice, while from the yawl one of the crew shouted up, "What'll we do? We've only got one oar!" and ashore it went with its only load of passengers at the captain's order.

"Only one oar?" "Did you hear that?" "Then how'll they get back!" and passengers and crew alike jumped overboard as they felt the hull going down beneath them. One young woman whose husband was about to jump into the frigid water grasped his arm and held him back. "Wait," she commanded, and lifting off the shutters from the window in front of which they were standing, she threw them into the water for life rafts, then followed them.

Up in his berth lay a man who was moaning, who refused to move when people told him the boat was sinking. "My God, I can't go. I'm too sick," groaned the man and turned his face to the wall.

"But your poor old father's on board and not able to help himself!" some one reminded the sick man. At once he got well, shaken out of his self-absorption, and managed to save his father, himself and some others as well.

Another man went overboard with his teeth fastened into a bag containing $3000 in gold. He struck a floating stick of wood and, throwing his arm over it, held the gold as a weight to keep him from slipping off.

People crowded the chilly water, some fortunate enough to find wreckage that would hold them until the skiffs that set out from shore could reach them; but others got underneath the masses of floating firewood and were drowned.

Towards dawn the half-submerged "Tennessee" drifted loose and floated down stream, lodging in some willows that grew alongside the bank.

It was a snag that nearly brought an untimely end to General LaFayette while he was on his American tour; floating down the Cumberland from Nashville on May 6, 1825, the General's chartered boat was snagged near the mouth of Deer Creek, 125 miles below Louisville, and in attempting to get into the yawl which had been put out for him he stumbled, fell overboard and had to be fished out by a deck hand.

Fire aboard steamboats was more common than explosions, was nearly as destructive, and almost as sudden. Sparks from the tall chimneys were a constant danger, especially when wood was used as fuel. For the boats, made entirely of lumber, burned like tinder when a fire started. And a small blaze in loose packing material, or a smoldering spot on a bale of cotton, might in a few minutes become a roaring tornado of fire enveloping the boat from stem to stern.

An unusual combination of accidents occurred when the "Clarksville" was burned on May 27, 1848. She caught fire near Ozark Island where at once the pilot ran her up on the beach. But as the prow of the boat struck the bank the flames burst into the cabin, one of the boilers exploded and at the same time three barrels of gunpowder ignited and flashed out their black smoke, hiding the white, escaping steam.

Captain Holmes jumped overboard with his wife and was the first man ashore. Leaving his wife in safety he swam back to the burning boat and superintended the escape of the passengers. "Pick up chairs, everybody," he yelled to the cabin passengers. "Jump overboard. But take the chairs. They'll give you something to hold you up," Holmes went up and down the deck counseling the people aboard. The smoke was growing blacker all the time and the fire crept closer. Finally the last man was off the boat and Holmes, almost suffocated by the smoke, made a jump from the cabin deck. His body struck the lower guards, fell back into the blazing wreck and was burned.

Curiously enough, in spite of the original fire, the boiler explosion coupled with the gun-powder, all of the cabin passengers were saved, though many were injured, including Governor Poindexter of Tennessee; and only 30 deck passengers were lost. These too might have been saved if they had run through the fire to the bow as the boat lay on the beach; but instead they waited until the whole forward part was covered and then jumped, but were unable to swim the distance to shore.

Collisions also took their toll of boats and lives. It was in one of those that the "Talisman" and more than 50 of her crew and passengers went down. On November 19, 1847, the "Talisman" was nearing Cape Girardeau when, by an unfortunate blunder, she was rammed by the "Tempest" just forward of her boilers and caved in. The "Tempest" came back from the shock only slightly damaged, reversed her engines and worked around to a position of assistance.

Down in the engine room of the "Talisman" was engineer Butler. He had been knocked down by the force of the crash, but had got up again and was at his post, ready to answer the furious jangling of the bells from the pilot house. The "Talisman" was sinking and there was but one thing for the pilot to do. He tried to steer his craft for the bank.

Without the engines to turn her wheels the "Talisman" would sink. But engineer Butler had made up his mind that those wheels would be kept turning. And so, with the water up to his knees, he stayed by the throttle.

One by one the crew of the engine room went up above. But Butler remained at his post. He could see the shore; it wasn't getting much nearer. The water went up to his waist, and it was cold enough to make his teeth chatter.

An order came from above for Butler to abandon his engine. Butler shouted, "No." And in a few moments the water was over his head and the "Talisman" kept going down and down until finally she settled on the bottom.

It all happened in less than ten minutes. And though the "Tempest" rounded to and gave all assistance possible the damage was done and more than 50 lives were lost; and Butler was buried along with the machinery.

Fire, snags, exploding boilers and collisions caused the biggest mishaps in the open rivers, and the stories of the "Tennessee," the "Talisman," the "Lucy Walker" and the "Clarksville" are but chance examples of the fate of so many of the boats of steamboat days. And while there was such a number to fare badly on their trips there were others, tied up at some wharf, that suffered calamities equally terrible.

St. Louis saw her share of steamboat disasters. There was the "Shepherdess" which struck a snag in Cohokia Bend, three miles from the center of the city, at eleven o'clock on the night of January 3, 1844. Most of the passengers were in their berths; a few men, too cold to sleep, were sitting around the stove. When the boat snagged she tore a hole in the forward part of her hull; in two minutes the water was washing over the forecastle. The captain aroused the passengers, assured the ladies that there was no danger, and hurried forward. In another three minutes the water rose to the boiler deck. The cabin passengers, barred from the forward stairs by the rising flood of icy water, ran to the stern and scrambled up to the hurricane deck. The yawl was launched and loaded, but the oars were not to be found. The craft was paddled ashore with a broom.

The "Shepherdess" drifted as she sank, and struck a second snag. The shock threw her almost on her side, washing some of her people off into the freezing river. Again she lurched as she tore loose from the snag. Just above the old shot-tower she struck the bluff bank, and more people were drawn into the walls. Here the hull separated from the cabin and lodged on a bar above Carondelet; the cabin floated some distance below and grounded.

The "Henry Bry" was lying at the shot-tower, but with no steam up. Her captain went with a yawl's crew to the rescue of the survivors, but his small boat could take only a few at a time. He worked until he was covered with ice and benumbed with the cold. At three in the morning the ferryboat "Icelander" came down from St. Louis and took the last of the survivors from the grounded cabin.

While the "Shepherdess" was drifting, a man named Robert Bullock went through the staterooms, helping women and children to the hurricane deck, and with several others had the distinction of rescuing the "Ohio Fat Girl," a show woman weighing 440 pounds. Later Bullock was thrown into the water and swam to the Illinois shore, where, bent on rescuing, he shook back to consciousness two women who were almost frozen to death.

Among the passengers was an English family of ten. Five of them escaped to the Illinois side, four to the Missouri, and one was taken off by the ferry. Each party sought the others, thinking they surely were lost; but on the ferry at Cohokia they found each other.

Captain A. Howell, of Covington, Kentucky, had just bought the "Shepherdess" and was making his first trip with her. He was ringing the bell when the impact of the boat on the second snag threw down the boilers, engines, and chimneys. The captain, tangled in the wreckage, was carried overboard and drowned.

The mayor of St. Louis took charge of relief work, sending the chilled and half-naked survivors to the

Virginia Hotel. Estimates of the loss of life in this disaster run from 40 to 70. Among the dead were two children who died of cold after they reached land.

On the night of May 17, 1849, fire ravaged the shipping district of St. Louis and destroyed 23 steamboats, 3 barges, and some smaller craft. The fire started at 10 o'clock, at the corner of Locust Street and the levee. It crossed Locust Street and burned three blocks to Chestnut, went on up Chestnut, crossed to the next block south at Commercial Alley, burned from the Alley to Main Street, and down Main to Market. At Main and Market it crossed diagonally to the Market Street House, then followed both sides of Market up to Second Street. Across Main it swept from Locust to Market, burning everything in its path except a row of fireproof warehouses just below Locust, and continued up Pine, Chestnut, and Market. Checked by dynamiting houses at the corner of Market and Second streets, in which blast several people were killed, the fire made another start at the foot of Elm Street and spread again to Main and Spruce. It crossed Main and spread almost to Third, consuming everything as it went.

A large fleet of steamboats was moored at the levee. Between Washington and Cherry streets lay the "White Cloud," with the "Eudora" above her and the "Edward Bates," "Belle Isle," and "Julia" below. Shortly after the fire started on land it spread to the "White Cloud." A strong northwest wind was blowing, and in a few moments the "Eudora" and "Bates'" were burning. Either some one set the "Bates" adrift in the hope of saving other boats, or her hawsers burned. She drifted out from the levee, but the wind bore her inshore and she went scraping down along the line of boats, firing everything she touched. A few ahead of her were set adrift, but the flaming "Bates" ignited them too. As the fire along the levee ate through the mooring lines, the burning boats drifted out into the current and went crackling and blazing down past the city, to bring up on bank or snag or sandbar and lie until the fires burned down and smoldered and died.

After the fire, the city took measures to prevent another such conflagration of steamboats. Iron rings were set in the levee, and an ordinance passed requiring that all boats moor to these rings with wire cables. A burning boat so moored could not break loose, or be cut loose, and like the "Bates," spread the fire to everything below.

The value of boats and cargoes destroyed by the St. Louis fire was about half covered by insurance, but not all of the losses were paid, as several of the insurance companies were wiped out by the disaster.

Three years later, on April 3, 1852, the St. Louis levee was shaken by a terrific boiler explosion. The "Glencoe," from New Orleans, had just made fast when three of her boilers burst. Hotel runners, hackmen, and newsboys who had hurried aboard were killed, with the passengers who were looking after their baggage. All the boat's upperworks forward of the pilot house were blown away. The force of the blast threw the boat out into the river, where the tangled wreckage of her after cabins caught fire. All of the passengers and crew who were able jumped from the burning wreck and were picked up by the skiffs and small boats that hurried to the rescue.

On the "Cataract," lying next the "Glencoe," a woman was killed in her stateroom by the explosion. On the same boat were found five bodies blown from the wrecked steamboat. The body of John Denny, chief clerk of the "Glencoe," was found on the hurricane deck of another steamboat, the "Western World." A human leg picked up in Commercial Street was identified by the boot as part of the body of William Brennan, one of the "Glencoe's" engineers. Captain Lee of the "Glencoe" had left the boat with his wife and one child a few moments before the blast. His little son who stayed on board was killed.

A. R. Jones, a merchant of St. Louis, saved many lives by running close to the blazing boat with a yawl. The steamboatmen of the city gave him an inscribed silver cup in recognition of this service.

New Orleans, starting point of races, did not escape disasters along her levee. At five o'clock on the afternoon of July 1, 1845, the packets were backing away and starting north. On the "Marquitte" the last bell had rung and the deck hands were loosening the lines when it was discovered that the cook was not aboard. The boat waited, and after fifteen minutes the cook ran down the levee, jumped to the forecastle, and hurried aft to the galleys. The boat with her accumulated steam pressure backed out; her pilot stopped the wheels, set them ahead. They had hardly started when the boat's entire bank of boilers let go with a crash that was heard in every part of New Orleans.

Frederick Ostrander, the pilot at the wheel, was blown in the air and fell on the hurricane deck of the "Yazoo City" with a broken hip. The pilot house went high in the air, and in falling wrecked the forecastle of still another boat, the "James Pitcher." The wheel of the "Marquitte" never was found, nor was Powell, the other pilot, who had been sitting on the boiler deck reading a newspaper. Captain Turpin escaped with injuries.

The unfortunate cook was cut in two by a flying fragment of boiler iron. One part of his body was thrown forward near the jackstaff, and the other left lying by the engine.

The "Marquitte" drifted a short distance down the river and sank. All the women and children aboard were saved. None of them was injured except one girl who was scalded by steam.

Similar to the disaster of the "Marquitte" was the explosion of Captain Cannon's "Louisiana" on the afternoon of November 15, 1849. She lay at the foot of Gravier Street between the "Bostona" and the "Storm," which had just arrived from Cincinnati and had not yet discharged her passengers. The "Lousiana's" boilers burst just as she was backing from the levee; pieces were blown far out into the river and in over the levee. One cut a mule in two and, bounding, killed a drayman and his horse. Another tore through a pile of cotton and knocked down three iron pillars before a coffee house at Canal and Front streets. The upperworks of the "Bostona" and "Storm" were wrecked, their chimneys carried away and their cabins splintered, and the "Storm" blown fifty yards from the levee. On this boat about fifteen people were killed, including the wife of the clerk, as she was standing on the guards by the ladies' cabin. The captain of the "Storm" came out on deck with blood running down his face and gave orders for returning to the wharf. Human bodies from the "Louisiana" were blown two hundred feet high in the air. One went completely through the pilot house of the "Bostona," making a hole like a cannon-ball. People on shore were killed and wounded as far as two hundred yards away.

The "Louisiana" drifted only ten minutes before she sank. Probably some people who had gone on board after the blast to help were drowned. In all, about 150 people lost their lives.

The "Anglo-Norman," a fine new boat, exploded all her boilers while making her trial trip in New Orleans harbor. Apparently the accident was due to low water in the boilers, and foaming or priming. After the blast no piece of the boilers could be found as large as a man's hand. The boat had on board a pleasure party of 210 people, about half of whom were killed or wounded. H. A. Kidd, editor of the *New Orleans Crescent*, reported among the dead, was picked up by the steamboat "Naniopa," and wrote an account of his escape which he called "The Experience of a Blown-up Man." His story is well worth repetition:

"Mr. Bigny, one of the editors of the *Delta*, and myself, took the only two chairs remaining unoccupied on the deck; his chair having its back toward the pilot house, and mine with its back to the chimney. It will be seen at once that we had seated ourselves immediately over the monster boilers of the boat.

"We had been engaged in conversation but a very few moments, when a jet of hot water, accompanied by steam, was forced out of the main pipe just aft the chimney, and fell near us in a considerable shower. I had never noticed anything of the kind before, and thought the occurrence very extraordinary. Just as I was about remarking this to Mr. Bigny, I was suddenly lifted high in the air, how high it is impossible for me to say. I have a distinct recollection of passing rather irregularly through the air, enveloped, as it seemed to me, in a dense cloud, through which no object was discernible. There was a sufficient lapse of time for me to have a distinct impression on my mind that I must inevitably be lost. In what position I went into the water, and to what depth I went, I have not the slightest idea. When I arose to the surface, I wiped the water from my face, and attempted to obtain a view of things around me, but this I was prevented from doing by the vapor of steam, which enveloped everything as a cloud. This obscuration, however, lasted but for a short time, and when it had passed away, I had a clear conception of my situation. I found myself in possession of my senses, and my limbs in good working order. I looked around in every direction, and discovered that I was not far from the centre of the river, and in the neighborhood of some twenty or thirty people, who seemed to have been thrown into the water somewhat in a heap. They were sustaining themselves on the surface as best they could, many of them endeavoring to get possession of floating pieces of the wreck. I could see nothing of the exploded boat, and was fully satisfied in my mind that she was blown all to pieces, and that my fellow passengers were lost, except those who, like myself, were struggling in the water. I will do myself the simple justice to say that, from the time at which I had risen to the surface, I had no apprehensions of drowning, though to a more disinterested spectator the chances might have appeared to be against me. I never felt more buoyant, nor swam with greater ease. Still I thought it well enough to appropriate whatever aid was within my reach; so, like others, I began a race, which proved to be a tedious one, after a shattered piece of plank. I finally reached it, and putting my hands rather rudely upon it, I got a sousing for my pains. The piece was too small to render me any material service. I abandoned it, and turned in the direction of a steamboat, which I perceived advancing, and which I afterwards discovered to be the "Naniopa." To keep my face towards the approaching steamer, I found that I had to oppose the strong current of the river. This, together with the coldness of the water, so exhausted my physical energies, that, for a brief space I felt that I should not be able to keep afloat until the boat should reach me. As the steamer came near there was a cry from my unfortunate neighbors in the water, 'Stop the boat! Stop the boat!'

"There was, indeed, great danger of our being run over by it. I however had no fears on this point, and made no effort to get out of its way. Fortunately for myself, I was one of the first which the boat approached. A sailor threw out to me a large rope, which I succeeded in grasping at the first effort. I was drawn to the boat's guards, which were several feet above the water. While drawing me up, the kind-hearted sailor cried, 'Hold on, partner! hold on!' But I could not, my strength being exhausted; the rope was slipping through my hands, and I should certainly have fallen back into the water, and been irrevocably lost under the boat's guards, had not another sailor quickly reached down and seized hold of my arms. I was drawn on board as nearly lifeless as any one could be without being actually dead. Two stout men assisted me to reach the cabin. My chest, as I discovered from its soreness and my spitting blood, had been somewhat bruised, but a little bathing with whiskey soon gave me relief. My friend Bigny was one of the first I met on board."

One of the most sudden of all steamboat fires, and one involving relatively small loss of life, was followed by more legal complications than resulted from a dozen fires far more disastrous. The "Martha Washington," Captain Cummins, was on her way from Cincinnati to New Orleans when she caught fire near Island 65 in the Mississippi, at one-thirty in the morning of January 14, 1852. In three minutes the boat was ablaze from stem to stern and, deserted by passengers and crew, drifted down the river and sank. Very few of the passengers were lost; of the crew, all escaped except the carpenter.

Sidney C. Burton, of Cleveland, brought a charge of barratry against William Kissane, L. L. Filley, Lyman Cole, the Chapin brothers, Alfred Nicholson, clerk of the boat, and some others. Burton alleged that these men had loaded the boat with a heavily insured fraudulent cargo of old bricks, stones, and rubbish packed as merchandise, and purposely set her on fire. He stated that he had shipped fifteen hundred dollars' worth of leather on the boat and could not collect his insurance, as the officials of the insurance companies suspected fraud in the loss of

From an old Currier & Ives print in the collection of Karl Schmidt, Esq.

A HOME ON THE MISSISSIPPI

the "Martha." It is said that Filley, just before he died in the summer of 1852, confessed to the fraudulent cargo. Since lives had been lost in the fire, the charge of barratry carried with it the charge of murder.

Kissane was tried and convicted at Lebanon, Ohio, but secured a new trial and was acquitted along with all others included in the charge. But Burton was not satisfied. He secured from the governor of Arkansas a requisition for all the men involved, arrested them at the Walnut Street House in Cincinnati, and conveyed them in irons to Jeffersonville, Indiana, and thence to Helena, Arkansas, where they were confined for three months in a miserable jail. At the end of that time they were tried for murder, arson, and other crimes included in the barratry charge. Again they were acquitted.

Burton, however, continued to use every means to embarrass the supposed conspirators. To defray the expenses of his defence, Kissane committed a forgery on the Chemical Bank of New York, in the summer of 1854. He was arrested, but escaped from his guard through the wash-room of a railroad coach. Retaken, tried and convicted, he was sentenced to Sing Sing for two and a half years, but in December, 1855, he was pardoned by Governor Clark of New York. In the same month the Grand Jury of Hamilton County, Ohio, found a true bill against Burton and a man named Coons for perjury, Coons admitting that Burton had paid him for false testimony against those charged with the "Martha Washington" fire.

Burton died on December 11, 1855, the circumstances of his death leading to the suspicion that he had been poisoned. It was thought that there had been other attempts to poison him. The mysteries of the boat's destruction and Burton's death never were solved with certainty.

Probably the most memorable of all steamboat disasters was the explosion and burning of the "Sultana," on April 27, 1865. The boat, built at Cincinnati in 1863, had been commandeered by the Federal authorities. She left New Orleans on April 21, 1865, and arrived at Vicksburg three days later. Here she took on board 1965 Union soldiers and 35 Federal officers from the Confederate prisons at Andersonville, Macon, and Cahaba. In addition she carried two companies of infantry, bringing her passenger load up to 2200 or more. Most of these soldiers were from Tennessee and Kentucky; some were from Indiana, Michigan, Ohio, Wisconsin, Illinois, Nebraska, Kansas, and West Virginia. The boat was greatly overcrowded.

On April 26 she lay at Memphis, unloading sugar. The next day, as she was passing a small group of islands called Paddy's Hen and Chickens, one of her four boilers burst and she caught fire. There was no way for the soldiers to save themselves except by swimming. Some swam long distances down the river but failed to make land. Many were saved by floating wreckage. A few were picked up by men who rowed out in skiffs, but some of these men were more bent on loot than on life-saving. The loss in killed, drowned, and wounded was very heavy. The burning wreck drifted down the river and finally sank.

Many years later Alex Thompson, a negro who had been cabin-boy on the "Sultana," told a newspaper reporter of his experience. "I remember as if it were yesterday," he said, "when the 'Sultana' blew up. There were 2300 soldiers on board. The boat had been seized by the Government and the soldiers were being taken to Mound City to be mustered out. It was four o'clock in the afternoon. The decks were crowded. Some were playing cards, others were playing checkers. I was in the pilot house. It was my duty as cabin-boy to take a cup of coffee to the pilot twice a day. I was in the pilot house with his afternoon cup of coffee. The pilot's name was Caton, and he asked me to hold the wheel while he drank his coffee. 'Hold it tight,' he said, for the channel wasn't wide. Suddenly there was a shock, and both the chimneys of the boat rose up in the air. The next thing I knew I was in the water, and then I was pulled into a skiff and taken ashore. They claimed the engineers blew up the 'Sultana.' There were rebel engineers in those days. They didn't like to carry the Union soldiers. The engineers weren't on the boat when she blew up. They were found in a skiff down the river. I've heard they were shot."

While many northern people shared the old colored man's suspicions of the engineers, there was little ground for it. Before the boat started they had reported her boilers in bad condition, and had been told to patch them up as best they could. The fact that only one boiler burst indicates that the explosion was due to weakness and not to design. There is nothing to prove that the engineers left the boat before the blast, and there is no record of their execution. Many steamboatmen sympathized strongly with the Confederate cause, but when they fought for it they fought openly, as did those who believed in the Union.

Some of the survivors of the "Sultana" for many years held an annual gathering on April 27 at a small town near Knoxville to commemorate the disaster.

In 1844 the steamboat "Belle Air" figured in a series of mishaps more comic than tragic. In that year the whole valley of the Mississippi was flooded. Some of the river towns were under ten feet of water. The "Belle Air," coming confidently down-stream, free to choose her course from the whole river and most of the adjacent country, found herself churning through the streets of Chester, Illinois. But the street was not her element; she bumped, bows-on, into a three-story building, and tumbled the top story down into the water. Then she struck a stone mill and demolished it very completely. After this test of strength she made for the open river. On her way she pushed over several brick buildings, and butted her way through the county jail with no regard whatever for the dignity of the law. After these exploits the boat proceeded to New Orleans with hardly a scratch on her. In New Orleans harbor she collided with a ferry-boat and came very near sinking before she could be brought to the levee.

In a review of accidents to river steamboats of the old days, three facts stand out: the boats, because of their build, were easy prey to fire or snags or explosions; they were as a rule inadequately equipped with life-saving apparatus, and their crews were untrained or poorly trained to act in case of accident; and the passengers, many of whom were drowned within a few yards of land, were prone to lose their heads and were lamentably deficient in the common art of swimming.

On the upper Mississippi, with 360 boats listed, there were 73 losses by accidents between 1823 and 1863. Thirty-two boats were snagged, 16 were burned, 10 were sunk by ice, 5 by rocks, 3 by striking bridges, 3 by the fire of Confederate batteries, 2 by boiler explosions, 1 by striking a sunken wreck, and 1 by a tornado. The record covers only that part of the river between St. Louis and St. Paul. Some boats were lost in the extreme headwaters of the Mississippi by the hazards of shallow water.

While the steamboats carried the best traffic of

the country, boats were destroyed only to be re-placed; passengers were lost, but there were always more passengers. The hazards of business and of life were great, but they were accepted; the rewards also were great. The long succession of white-painted packets went on, up-river and down, in spite of snags and fires and explosions. The end of the steamboat era began when Sumter fell. The Civil War was the first of the two great disasters that swept the steamboats from the rivers. The second came creeping, slowly and laboriously, from the east; the construction trains, moving intermittently forward on the steel rails that sweating men spiked down ahead of them.

CHAPTER XV

THE PASSING OF THE PACKETS; STEAM-BOATING TO-DAY AND IN THE FUTURE

Juba in and juba out,
Juba, juba, all about;
Dinah, stir de possum fat;
Can't you hear de juba pat?
Juba!

RAILROADS INVADE THE MISSOURI RIVER COUNTRY—MODERN STEAMBOATS OF THE OLD TYPE—SHOW BOATS—BARGES AND TUGS SUPPLANT THE PACKETS—POSSIBILITIES OF THE WATERWAYS—CONCLUSION.

RAILROAD building, originating in the east and working westward into the territory served by steamboats, aided the business of these craft so long as the last leg of the western journey of passengers and freight was over water, but when, in 1859, the Hannibal and St. Joseph railroad was completed to St. Joseph much of the river traffic was carried overland on the swifter, more convenient and less expensive railway trains.

When this line was completed St. Joseph, on the upper bend of the Missouri, directly west of Hannibal, became an important transshipment point between river and railroad; packets made trips north from there to Sioux City and north from there to Kansas City. But in 1867 the Chicago and Northwestern reached Council Bluffs; five years later the Union Pacific bridge was opened across the river to

Omaha, and St. Joseph, lying south, between Omaha and Kansas City, lost its purpose. Omaha got the St. Joseph trade and still further restricted the use of steamboats from St. Louis.

Step by step the railroads cut off the steamboat traffic on the Missouri. The same year the Chicago and Northwestern reached Council Bluffs the Sioux City and Pacific entered Sioux City from Missouri Valley, and in 1870 the Illinois Central came in from the east. And Sioux City, thus connected by rail with Omaha and Chicago, became a more important river port than either St. Joseph or Omaha.

And now the point at which westbound traffic met the Missouri was moved almost on a straight line directly west of Chicago, making the steamboats which had carried the freight and passengers from St. Louis to Kansas City and north to Council Bluffs and beyond powerless. Then, in 1872, the Northern Pacific reached Bismarck and took a few hundred more miles of river traffic away from the steamboats. It needed only the laying of the tracks of the Great Northern into Helena for steamboat traffic to be given the final blow. And that happened in 1887.

From then on steamboats were practically useless. They had done their appointed job of settling a continent, and had done it well. But the job was finished. Some die-hard captains still ran their boats, but every trip meant a loss; and many a good boat was left deserted on a snag or sandbar, with the underwriters to close the account.

So the years went by, the locomotives growing fatter and sleeker and more numerous, while the steamboats that had been the pride of the rivers became fewer and dirtier. Why strive for the best in passenger accommodations when nearly all the paying passengers traveled on the railroads! And so far as freight was concerned it was not only gobbled up by the railroads, but what little remained, it was discovered, could be hauled by barges, a long line of barges which needed only one steamboat to pull them. And so the day of the steamboat was over, beaten by the railroads on one hand and by the tug and barge on the other.

The sight of steamboats of the old type, out of use and rotting at their moorings, moved a young newspaper man, Clyde Fitch, to write the following commentary:

"The steamboat is an engine on a raft with eleven thousand dollars' worth of jigsaw work around it. Steamships are built of steel and are severely plain except on the inside where the millionaire tourist is confined. Steamboats are built of wood, tin, shingles, canvas, and twine, and look like a bride of Babylon. If a steamboat should go to sea, the ocean would take one playful slap at it and people would be picking up kindling on the beach for the next eleven years. However, the steamboat does not go to sea. Its home is on the river, which does not rise up and stand on end in a storm. It is necessary that the steamboat should be light and airy because if it were heavy it would stick into the bottom of the river several feet and become an island instead of a means of transportation. The steamboat is from 100 to 300 feet long and from 30 to 50 feet wide. It is from 40 to 70 feet high above water, but it does not extend more than three feet into the water. This is because that is all the water there is. A steamboat must be so built that when the river is low and the sandbars come out for air the first mate can tap a keg of beer and run the boat four miles on the suds. Steamboats were once the beasts of burden for the great Middle West, and a city which could not be reached at low water by a steamboat with two large hot stacks, twenty-five negro roustabouts on the bow end, and a gambler in the cabin, withered away and died in infancy. But the railroad, which runs in high water or low and does not stab itself in a vital spot with a snag, came along and cleared the steamboat out of business. There are only a few left now, which is a great pity, for the most decorative part of a great river is a tall white steamboat with a chime whistle and a flashing wheel in the far foreground. Steamboats would still prosper if steamboat men would go to school and learn how to solicit freight and how to load and deliver it without depending on the umbrageous and dilatory roustabout. A course in a good cooking school would also produce a grateful change in steamboat travel. The government has spent a hundred millions improving the rivers, but the steamboat hasn't improved in fifty years."

(*Stanton's "American Steam Vessels"*)

The "Iron Queen"—a type of sternwheeler that still plies the Ohio and Mississippi

He was not entirely correct; there have been some improvements. Steel hulks have come into use. Steam machinery has been made to handle cargo and gangways. Electric lights were adapted to steamboat use about 1882. The first were open arcs, used only for searchlights and cargo lights. The dynamo served only one light at a time; the current was turned to the place where it was most needed. Kerosene, which had supplanted the lard oil burned in the chandeliers of the early boats, was still used for lighting the cabins. There were no lamps in the staterooms; their only light came through the transoms over the doors. Incandescent electric lights came into use on steamboats about 1895.

Cotton, pipe staves, and hogs still come into New Orleans by steamboat from the Red, Black, and Ouachita rivers; sugar bound down the Mississippi from Baton Rouge and Bayou Sara, produce from the network of bayous and canals that cover the low country. Also excursion boats of the Streckfus Line follow the tourist trade, and the Louisville and Cincinnati Packet company furnishes a daily service on the Ohio, and each year they send boat-loads of tourists to New Orleans for the Mardi Gras, carrying manufactured goods south and coming back with their holds packed with sugar. In fact the Ohio is now navigated for its full length by various old packets that are being put in service as the Government's lock and dam system nears completion.

But the Old Red Church, since flatboat days the

beacon that marked the approaching end of the south-bound traveler's journey, has fallen into decay, and has been replaced by a new building of white stucco which few travelers ever look at. Now, to the motorists who pass between the churchyard and the levee on the Jefferson Highway where the old red steeple once stood, the place is just Destrehan, an oil-refinery town.

About all that is left of the old Mississippi River life is the show boat. These floating theaters, which first appeared soon after the Louisiana Purchase, still find profit in tying-up at the small towns for a one-night stand just as did the first show boat of which any record remains—the one built by N. M. Ludlow, an actor, at the headwaters of the Cumberland. Ludlow's boat was simply a keel-boat fitted for theatrical performances by a small company before the scanty audiences that the frontier afforded. He played to the settlements down the Cumberland, the Ohio and the Mississippi, and his success induced Sol Smith to fit out a competing boat.

Soon afterwards there were numbers of show boats, one of the early ones having been fitted out by William Chapman at Pittsburgh. Chapman and his family gave the entire entertainment. But the show boat life attracted a class of people who were shuddered at by the stern moralists of the day, and shortly before the Civil War their unpopularity was so great that they were driven from the river. Even the two circuses which traveled by boat, one operated by Spaulding and Rogers, the other by Dan Rice, and both called Floating Palaces, did not survive.

Twelve years after the war, Captain A. B. French and his wife launched "French's New Sensation" at Cincinnati, and ever since there has been a boat of that name on the rivers. When Captain French died in 1902, his wife, who had got master's and pilot's licenses, took charge, but gave the position of manager to Captain John McNair. One time while the "New Sensation" lay icebound at Uniontown, Kentucky, B. F. and J. W. Mencke appeared with a gas boat to try their luck on the rivers. McNair engaged the brothers as advance agents during the next season; and the next year, when Mrs. French sold out to Captain E. A. Price, the Menckes went out as advance men for his "Wonderland." A few years later B. F. Mencke and Brad Coleman got a boat of their own, the "Sunny South." In 1914 they operated the "Floating Hippodrome," and in 1917 two of the Mencke brothers bought the "New Sensation" from Captain Price. Their present boat is the "Golden Rod." It has a 40 by 24 foot stage, an auditorium 40 by 162, and at the opposite end from the stage the box office and lobby open on a short deck from which the gangway is run ashore. Staterooms for the women and married couples of the company are back stage or in the texas built over the roof; the bachelors have the joy of living in a tow boat which attends the floating theater. Most show boats of to-day are of about the same build as the "Golden Rod," but are smaller.

D. Otto Hitner's "Cotton Blossom," seating 1200 spectators, is next in size to the "Golden Rod." Others of note are the "Princess," Nicol and Reunold's "Majestic" and Captain Roy Hyatt's "Water Queen." In 1925 fourteen show boats were working up and down the Mississippi and its tributaries. On the Ohio littoral they travel the Monongahela, the Muskingum, Kanawha, the Kentucky, Green, the Tennessee. Up the Mississippi they tow as far as Hastings, Minnesota, where they turn about and drop the whole length of the river, finishing the season in the bayous and canals of Louisiana.

The way for the show boat is prepared by an advance man, and as the floating theater ties up at the town or at the nearby bank, the calliope announces its arrival. Night falls and as the electric lights go on the boat glows and sparkles alluringly through the dark at the river bank. Again the calliope plays and the audience gathers, some coming afoot, others in automobiles over distances which their forebears, in wagons or on horseback, had come years before.

Excepting the engineer and pilot almost all the boat's company take part in the business of the show. Those who can't act serve as stage hands, ushers, sellers of peanuts and candy for the one performance before the boat makes ready to leave the following morning for the next stand. For they start early, so as to avoid the strong winds which cause the greatest difficulty in navigating the high built, box-like theaters.

Show boats were among the first river craft to use towing regularly. For in the days of the packets, with their passengers, mail and freight, speed was essential. Coal came down the river in barges that floated with the current and very seldom needed to be towed. Lumber was sent down in rafts and some heavy freight was shipped in flatboats. But as the railroads took the passengers and the more profitable freight, the economy of towing became apparent. And even coal, that had formerly drifted, was towed down in huge fleets of barges. Steam power could handle units far larger than could be steered by hand and haul the freight at less expense per ton. Powerful tow-boats, such as the "Sprague" and the "J. B. Williams," which took 32 barges containing 600,000 bushels of coal from Pittsburgh to New Orleans, were built for this work. Shipping cost of the coal was $18,000; the cost by rail would have been ten times that amount, but the time required was much longer than it would have been by rail.

Of late years the Federal Government has been operating, as a demonstration of the practicability of towing, on the Mississippi and some other rivers steel barges of one or two thousand tons which are pushed by compact, steel-built, propeller driven tow-boats, powered with marine type steam or heavy oil engines. There are no accommodations for passengers; the business is for freight only. The old stern-wheel tow-boat, patterned after the packets, may become almost obsolete, for the lower Mississippi, but still seems best for smaller streams. Still another innovation that should greatly facilitate the handling of large tows is a screw propeller which has been designed to be placed at the front of the tow and operated by the electric power of the tow-boat.

It is one of the ironies of fate that the improvement of the river channels, which wrought so much havoc for the pilots of packets, and the placing of lights and other aids to navigation was not undertaken on any mentionable scale until river traffic of the old type had almost succumbed to railroad competition. To-day, with the rivers unused, the principal channels are in better condition than they ever were in the best days of the packets; lights and marks being maintained by the Government make river navigation easy and safe.

But the rivers are there to be used, and the shippers who neglected them so long are beginning to realize their possibilities. Business men in the river cities are growing aware that, with the handling methods and some of the business methods that made the railroads the nation's carriers, the rivers may again become arterial highways. They have no sentimental dreams, however, of bringing back the old packet days! Their purpose is to use the rivers for moving only the heavy freight to which river transport is excellently adapted.

The old packets, being the only carriers, were necessarily built to carry all kinds of traffic; passengers, mail, package freight, and heavy freight. And steamboatmen did not adapt their business to the new conditions created by the railroads. The heavy, relatively cheap freight that did not require speed in transit still rightly belonged to the rivers. The steamboatmen, however, tried to get a general business, and in the matter of getting it the railroads had the advantage; the terminals and the organization, while the steamboatmen, with only the open levees as terminals, competed among themselves. There was no surplus of freight, in those days, to strangle the railroads with car shortages. The railroad men wanted all the business, and they got it, by fair means if possible, and by any means if necessary. This was a short-sighted policy on the part of the railroads. Now, with a car shortage every time business is good, they are beginning to realize it. Business growth is limited by transportation facilities. With the waterways functioning as they should, carrying cheaply the heavy freight and leaving the railroads free to take the higher classes in which there is more profit, there need be no car shortages. Relieved of the burden of freight they carry at no profit or at a loss, railways might reduce rates and still pay dividends high enough to make rail securities attractive investments.

Eventually the railroads must co-operate with the waterways. Meanwhile the river routes need protection from uneconomic competition. But it is useless to try to force trade into them. Water transport will have to be cheaper than corresponding rail transport, and equal to it in convenience if not in speed, or the business will remain with the railroads. Development of waterways includes development of terminals. The old-time levee, with no warehouses or other conveniences for shippers, can not compete with railroad facilities. Nor can loading and unloading by man-power compete with machine handling of heavy freight. The terminal charge in water transport must be made small if the expense of the entire haul is to be small.

In the matter of placing terminals, the waterways have an advantage over the railroads. Water terminals need not be established on expensive ground in the heart of cities; they can be built anywhere on the river banks within convenient distances. This would relieve the business of the high terminal costs due to excessive valuation of centrally located land.

The time should come when seagoing ships may enter the Great Lakes, go down the Chicago and Illinois rivers to the Mississippi, and proceed southward to the Gulf, making every river town in the Middle West a seaport and opening a new trade outlet to the Pacific Coast through the Panama Canal. Theodore Roosevelt, seeing the possibilities of this development, said, "The Mississippi should be made a loop of the sea."

There must be a great deal of waterway improvement before this can be accomplished. But all this work is physically possible, and will be done when America is convinced that the investment will pay. When it is done, other rivers will be improved and used as feeders for the new traffic. A great cross of water transport will extend from Pittsburgh to Fort Benton and from the Twin Cities to New Orleans.

River traffic is coming back, coming slowly, cautiously, with none of the old recklessness of pioneer days. But it is coming back to stay. There will be no more races, few passengers; just a freight business that serves the country well and pays good dividends. For the picturesque old Mississippi steamboat has disappeared with the American frontier, never to return.

Those crowded colorful cabins, the cotton piled to the hurricane decks, the rivalries and the races, all are memories now. The white scroll-work and the coroneted chimneys have passed with the singing firemen, and the old-time gambler who leaped from the wrecked packet with the prayer, "Now, gallows, save your own."

No longer do the pilots con their vessels through the night by the loom of forests and the bark of dogs. Laboring tugs with their tows of prosaic barges crawl up and down charted channels, lighted and beaconed at every turn.

Our country is no longer new. We step into a Pullman car at New York and step out at New Orleans, San Francisco, or St. Paul. We drive our motor cars from coast to coast over roads that are mapped and marked. We see places that are new to us, but in all of them we find people like ourselves to whom the places are old. There is no longer any frontier, and the lure of the unknown has vanished.

But even now there are many of us who feel as the Kentucky boys felt when they paused in the building of their flatboats to watch the river flowing to the sea. To us the blue-peter is an invitation and a challenge, and the rumor of big rewards in unmapped regions is a command. And there are places left to call us.

In the mouths of the Congo and the Amazon and the Plata the steamboats lie. In the Magdalena they wait for us; roughneck cousins of the "Lee" and the "Natchez," they lie ready to take us through tropical jungle to the mountains of promise. The dusky deck-hands are at the mooring-lines; slowly the wheel turns; steam hisses from the cylinder-cocks, billows out from the open engine room, and streams away down the trade wind. Hoarsely the whistle booms, as the whistles boomed at New Orleans and St. Louis and Pittsburgh long ago.

Close by the steamboat lies the wide-winged metal monoplane that flies as far in an hour as the steamboat travels in a day. Her propeller turns; with a crackle and a roar, her engine takes the spark.

Count your cash and take your choice. Let's go!

BIBLIOGRAPHY

ACCOUNT OF THE EXPEDITION OF MAJOR STEPHEN H. LONG, Edwin James.

AMERICAN STEAM VESSELS, Samuel Ward Stanton.

AMERICAN INLAND WATERWAYS, Herbert Quick.

ASTORIA, Washington Irving.

BEYOND THE MISSISSIPPI, Albert D. Richardson.

CAPTAIN OF THE AMARYLLIS, THE, Stoughton Cooley.

CHRONOLOGICAL HISTORY OF STEAM NAVIGATION, A, G. H. Preble.

CONQUEST OF THE MISSOURI, THE, Joseph Mills Hanson.

DOWN THE GREAT RIVER, Willard Glazier.

EARLY WESTERN TRAVELS, Reuben Gold Thwaites.

ENGINEERS' REPORT TO THE NAVIGATION AND HYDRAULIC COMPANY OF THE MISSISSIPPI RAPIDS.

EARLY STEAMBOATING ON THE MINNESOTA AND RED RIVERS, Edwin Bell.

EARLY STEAMBOAT TRAVEL ON THE OHIO RIVER, Leslie S. Henshaw.

FIFTY YEARS ON THE MISSISSIPPI, Emerson W. Gould.

FORTY YEARS A GAMBLER ON THE MISSISSIPPI, George H. Devol.

FIRST STEAMBOAT ON THE OHIO, THE, Nelson Wiley Evans.

GENESIS OF STEAMBOATING ON WESTERN RIVERS, George Byron Merrick.

GREAT EVENTS OF OUR PAST CENTURY, THE, R M. Devens.

HISTORY OF AMERICAN STEAM NAVIGATION, John H. Morrison.

HISTORY OF TRAVEL IN AMERICA, A, Seymour Dunbar.

HISTORY OF EARLY STEAMBOAT NAVIGATION ON THE MISSOURI RIVER, Hiram Martin Chittenden.

HISTORY OF VIRGIL A. STEWART, H. R. Howard.

HISTORY OF THE RAM FLEET AND THE MISSISSIPPI MARINE CORPS, Warren D. Crandall.

INCIDENTS AND ANECDOTES OF THE CIVIL WAR, David D. Porter.

LIFE ON THE WESTERN RIVERS, John Habermehl.

LIFE ON THE MISSISSIPPI, Mark Twain.

LIFE AND ADVENTURES OF JOHN A. MURRELL, Editors of the *National Police Gazette*.

LLOYD'S STEAMBOAT DIRECTORY, James T. Lloyd.

MISSISSIPPI, THE, Francis Vinton Greene.

MISSISSIPPI VALLEY BEGINNINGS, Henry E. Chambers.

MEMORIAL OF THE CITIZENS OF CINCINNATI . . . TO CONGRESS.

NAVIGATOR, THE, Zadoc Cramer.

OLD TIMES ON THE UPPER MISSISSIPPI, George Byron Merrick.

OHIO RIVER, A COURSE OF EMPIRE, THE, Archer Butler Hulbert.

OUTLAWS OF CAVE-IN-ROCK, THE, Otto A. Rothert.

PATHS OF INLAND COMMERCE, THE, Archer Butler Hulbert.

PROGRESS OF NAVIGATION AND COMMERCE ON THE MISSISSIPPI AND GREAT LAKES, John W. Monnette.

STEAMBOAT DAYS, Fred Erving Dayton.

STEAMBOATING ON THE MISSOURI RIVER IN THE SIXTIES, Charles P. Deatherage.

TRAVELS IN LOUISIANA AND THE FLORIDAS IN 1802, Berquin Duvallon.

TRAVELS IN THE CENTRAL PORTION OF THE MISSISSIPPI VALLEY, Henry R. Schoolcraft.

TONIGHT AT THE RIVER LANDING (Article published in the *Saturday Evening Post*), Wesley W. Stout.

VIEW OF THE MISSISSIPPI VALLEY, Robert Baird.

WEST, THE, James Hall.

WESTERN PILOT, THE, Samuel Cumings.

WESTERN ADDRESS DIRECTORY, William G. Lyford.